File for Divorce in Texas

(+ CD-ROM)

Fifth Edition

Karen Ann Rolcik
Edward A. Haman

Attorneys at Law

SPHINX® PUBLISHING
AN IMPRINT OF SOURCEBOOKS, INC.®
NAPERVILLE, ILLINOIS
www.SphinxLegal.com

Fifth Edition: 2006

Published by: **Sphinx® Publishing, An Imprint of Sourcebooks, Inc.®**

Naperville Office
P.O. Box 4410
Naperville, Illinois 60567-4410
630-961-3900
Fax: 630-961-2168
www.sourcebooks.com
www.SphinxLegal.com

This publication is designed to provide accurate and authoritative information in regard to the subject matter covered. It is sold with the understanding that the publisher is not engaged in rendering legal, accounting, or other professional service. If legal advice or other expert assistance is required, the services of a competent professional person should be sought.

From a Declaration of Principles Jointly Adopted by a Committee of the American Bar Association and a Committee of Publishers and Associations

This product is not a substitute for legal advice.

Disclaimer required by Texas statutes.

Library of Congress Cataloging-in-Publication Data
Rolcik, Karen Ann.
  File for divorce in Texas : + CD-ROM / by Karen Ann Rolcik and Edward A. Haman. -- 5th ed.
      p. cm.
  Rev. ed. of: How to file for divorce in Texas. 4th ed. 2004.
  Includes index.
  ISBN-13: 978-1-57248-541-9 (pbk. : alk. paper)
  ISBN-10: 1-57248-541-8 (pbk. : alk. paper)
  1. Divorce suits--Texas--Popular works. 2. Divorce--Law and legislation--Texas--Popular works. I. Haman, Edward A. II. Rolcik, Karen Ann. How to file for divorce in Texas. III. Title. IV. Title: How to file for divorce in Texas.

KFT1300.Z9R65 2006
346.76401'66--dc22   2006010581

Printed and bound in the United States of America.
SB — 10 9 8 7 6 5 4

Contents

Pension Plans
Social Security Benefits
Paternity
Grandparents' Rights

How to Use the CD-ROM

Thank you for purchasing *File for Divorce in Texas*. To make this material even more useful, we have included every document in the book on the CD-ROM in the back of the book.

You can use these forms just as you would the forms in the book. Print them out, fill them in, and use them however you need. You can also fill in the forms directly on your computer. Just identify the form you need, open it, click on the space where the information should go, and input your information. Customize each form for your particular needs. Use them over and over again.

The CD-ROM is compatible with both PC and Mac operating systems. (While it should work with either operating system, we cannot guarantee that it will work with your particular system and we cannot provide technical assistance.) To use the forms on your computer, you will need to use Microsoft Word or another word processing program that can read Word files. The CD-ROM does not contain any such program.

Insert the CD-ROM into your computer. Double-click on the icon representing the disc on your desktop or go through your hard drive to identify the drive that contains the disc and click on it.

Once opened, you will see the files contained on the CD-ROM listed as "Form #: [Form Title]." Open the file you need. You may print the form to fill it out manually at this point, or you can click on the appropriate line to fill it in using your computer. Once all your information is filled in, you can print your filled-in form.

•   •   •   •   •

Purchasers of this book are granted a license to use the forms contained in it for their own personal use. By purchasing this book, you have also purchased a limited license to use all forms on the accompanying CD-ROM. The license limits you to personal use only and all other copyright laws must be adhered to. No claim of copyright is made in any government form reproduced in the book or on the CD-ROM. You are free to modify the forms and tailor them to your specific situation.

The author and publisher have attempted to provide the most current and up-to-date information available. However, the courts, Congress, and your state's legislatures review, modify, and change laws on an ongoing basis, as well as create new laws from time to time. Due to the very nature of the information and the continual changes in our legal system, to be sure that you have the current and best information for your situation, you should consult a local attorney or research the current laws yourself.

This publication is designed to provide accurate and authoritative information in regard to the subject matter covered. It is sold with the understanding that the publisher is not engaged in rendering legal, accounting, or other professional service. If legal advice or other expert assistance is required, the services of a competent professional person should be sought.

> —From a Declaration of Principles Jointly Adopted by a Committee of the American Bar Association and a Committee of Publishers and Associations

This product is not a substitute for legal advice.

> —Disclaimer required by Texas statutes

Using Self-Help Law Books

Before using a self-help law book, you should realize the advantages and disadvantages of doing your own legal work and understand the challenges and diligence that this requires.

The Growing Trend

Rest assured that you will not be the first or only person handling your own legal matter. For example, in some states, more than 75% of the people in divorces and other cases represent themselves. Because of the high cost of legal services, this is a major trend, and many courts are struggling to make it easier for people to represent themselves. However, some courts are not happy with people who do not use attorneys and refuse to help them in any way. For some, the attitude is, "Go to the law library and figure it out for yourself."

We write and publish self-help law books to give people an alternative to the often complicated and confusing legal books found in most law libraries. We have made the explanations of the law as simple and easy to understand as possible. Of course, unlike an attorney advising an individual client, we cannot cover every conceivable possibility.

Cost/Value Analysis Whenever you shop for a product or service, you are faced with various levels of quality and price. In deciding what product or service to buy, you make a cost/value analysis on the basis of your willingness to pay and the quality you desire.

When buying a car, you decide whether you want transportation, comfort, status, or sex appeal. Accordingly, you decide among choices such as a Neon, a Lincoln, a Rolls Royce, or a Porsche. Before making a decision, you usually weigh the merits of each option against the cost.

When you get a headache, you can take a pain reliever (such as aspirin) or visit a medical specialist for a neurological examination. Given this choice, most people, of course, take a pain reliever, since it costs only pennies; whereas a medical examination costs hundreds of dollars and takes a lot of time. This is usually a logical choice because it is rare to need anything more than a pain reliever for a headache. But in some cases, a headache may indicate a brain tumor, and failing to see a specialist right away can result in complications. Should everyone with a headache go to a specialist? Of course not, but people treating their own illnesses must realize that they are betting, on the basis of their cost/value analysis of the situation, that they are taking the most logical option.

The same cost/value analysis must be made when deciding to do one's own legal work. Many legal situations are very straightforward, requiring a simple form and no complicated analysis. Anyone with a little intelligence and a book of instructions can handle the matter without outside help.

But there is always the chance that complications are involved that only an attorney would notice. To simplify the law into a book like this, several legal cases often must be condensed into a single sentence or paragraph. Otherwise, the book would be several hundred pages long and too complicated for most people. However, this simplification necessarily leaves out many details and nuances that would apply to special or unusual situations. Also, there are many ways to interpret most legal questions. Your case may come before a judge who disagrees with the analysis of our authors.

Therefore, in deciding to use a self-help law book and to do your own legal work, you must realize that you are making a cost/value analysis. You have decided that the money you will save in doing it yourself outweighs the chance that your case will not turn out to your satisfaction. Most people handling their own simple legal matters never have a problem, but occasionally people find that it ended up costing them more to have an attorney straighten out the situation than it would have if they had hired an attorney in the beginning. Keep this in mind while handling your case, and be sure to consult an attorney if you feel you might need further guidance.

Local Rules   The next thing to remember is that a book which covers the law for the entire nation, or even for an entire state, cannot possibly include every procedural difference of every jurisdiction. Whenever possible, we provide the exact form needed; however, in some areas, each county, or even each judge, may require unique forms and procedures. In our state books, our forms usually cover the majority of counties in the state or provide examples of the type of form that will be required. In our national books, our forms are sometimes even more general in nature but are designed to give a good idea of the type of form that will be needed in most locations. Nonetheless, keep in mind that your state, county, or judge may have a requirement, or use a form, that is not included in this book.

You should not necessarily expect to be able to get all of the information and resources you need solely from within the pages of this book. This book will serve as your guide, giving you specific information whenever possible and helping you to find out what else you will need to know. This is just like if you decided to build your own backyard deck. You might purchase a book on how to build decks. However, such a book would not include the building codes and permit requirements of every city, town, county, and township in the nation; nor would it include the lumber, nails, saws, hammers, and other materials and tools you would need to actually build the deck. You would use the book as your guide, and then do some work and research involving such matters as whether you need a permit of some kind, what type and grade of wood is available in your area, whether to use hand tools or power tools, and how to use those tools.

Before using the forms in a book like this, you should check with your court clerk to see if there are any local rules of which you should be aware or local forms you will need to use. Often, such forms will require the same information as the forms in the book but are merely laid out differently or use slightly different language. They will sometimes require additional information.

Changes in the Law

Besides being subject to local rules and practices, the law is subject to change at any time. The courts and the legislatures of all fifty states are constantly revising the laws. It is possible that while you are reading this book, some aspect of the law is being changed.

In most cases, the change will be of minimal significance. A form will be redesigned, additional information will be required, or a waiting period will be extended. As a result, you might need to revise a form, file an extra form, or wait out a longer time period. These types of changes will not usually affect the outcome of your case. On the other hand, sometimes a major part of the law is changed, the entire law in a particular area is rewritten, or a case that was the basis of a central legal point is overruled. In such instances, your entire ability to pursue your case may be impaired.

Introduction

Going through a divorce is probably one of the most common—and most traumatic—encounters with the legal system. Paying a divorce lawyer can be one of the most expensive single bills to pay, and must be done at a time when you are least likely to have extra funds. In a contested divorce case, it is not uncommon for the parties to run up legal bills over $10,000. This book is designed to enable you to obtain a divorce without hiring a lawyer. Even if you do hire a lawyer, this book will help you work with him or her more effectively, which can also reduce your legal fees.

This is not a law school course, but a practical guide to get you through the system as easily as possible. Legal jargon has nearly been eliminated. For ease of understanding, this book uses the term *spouse* to refer to your husband or wife (whichever applies), and the terms *child* and *children* are used interchangeably.

Keep in mind that different judges—as well as courts in different counties—may have their own particular (if not peculiar) procedures and ways of doing things. The court clerk's office can often tell you if they have any special forms or requirements. Court clerks cannot give legal advice, but they can tell you what the particular court or judge requires.

The first two chapters of this book will give you an overview of the law and the legal system. Chapters 3, 4, and 5 will help you decide if you want an attorney and if you even really want a divorce. The remaining chapters will show you which forms you need, how to fill out the forms, and what procedures to follow. There is a glossary to help clarify some of the legal terms.

You will also find two appendices in the back of the book. Appendix A contains selected portions of the Texas law dealing with various aspects of divorce. Although these provisions are discussed in the book, it is sometimes helpful to read the law exactly as the legislature wrote it.

Finally, Appendix B contains the forms you will complete. You will not need to use all of the forms. This book will tell you which forms you need, depending upon your situation. Some forms may need to be changed to fit your particular circumstance.

Be sure to read "Introduction to Legal Forms" in Chapter 6 before you use any of the forms in this book.

Marriage Ins and Outs

Several years (or maybe only months) ago, you made a decision to get married. This chapter will discuss, in a very general way, what you got yourself into and how you can get yourself out.

MARRIAGE

Marriage is frequently referred to as a contract. It is a legal contract, and for many, it is also a religious contract. This book will deal only with the legal aspects. The wedding ceremony involves the bride and groom reciting certain vows, which are actually mutual promises about how they will treat each other. There are also legal papers signed, such as a marriage license and a marriage certificate. These formalities create certain rights and obligations for the husband and wife. Although the focus at the ceremony is on the emotional and romantic aspects of the relationship, the legal reality is that financial and property rights are being created. It is these financial and property rights and obligations that cannot be broken without a legal proceeding. Unfortunately, most people do not fully realize that these rights and obligations are being created until it comes time for a divorce.

DIVORCE

A divorce is the most common method of terminating or breaking the marriage contract. In Texas, a divorce may also be referred to as a *dissolution of marriage,* although the technical legal term is *divorce.* In a divorce, the court declares the marriage contract broken, divides the parties' property and debts, and determines the custody, support, and visitation for any children the parties may have.

Grounds

Traditionally, a divorce could only be granted under certain very specific circumstances, such as for *adultery* or *mental cruelty.* Today, a divorce may be granted simply because one or both of the parties want one.

Residency Requirement

There are two basic residency laws you need to be aware of. First, either you or your spouse must live in Texas for at least six months immediately before filing a petition with the court. Second, you must be a resident of the county in which you file the **Original Petition for Divorce** for at least ninety days before filing the petition.

ANNULMENT

The basic difference between a divorce and an annulment is that a divorce says, *this marriage is broken*, while an annulment says, *there never was a marriage.* An annulment is more difficult and often more complicated to prove, so it is not used very often. Annulments are only possible in a few circumstances, usually where one party deceived the other. If you decide that you want an annulment, you should consult an attorney. If you are seeking an annulment for religious reasons and need to go through a church procedure (rather than, or in addition to, a legal procedure), you should consult your priest or minister.

A divorce is generally easier to get than an annulment. All you need to prove to get a divorce is that your marriage is broken. You prove this by simply saying it. To accomplish this, the **Original Petition for Divorce** (discussed in Chapter 7) reads as follows.

The marriage has become insupportable because of discord or conflict of personalities between the parties that destroys the legitimate ends of the marriage relationship and prevents any reasonable expectation of reconciliation.

However, in order to get an annulment, you will need to prove more. This proof will involve introducing various documents into evidence and having other people come to testify at the court hearing.

Grounds for Annulment

Annulments can only be granted under one of the following ten circumstances.

1. If one of the parties was too young to get married. In Texas, both parties must be at least 18 years old to get married, unless the underage person has parental consent and is at least 14.

2. If one of the parties is guilty of *fraud*. An example of fraud would be if one party just got married in order to have the right to inherit from the other, with no intention of ever living together as husband and wife.

3. If one party was under duress when he or she got married. *Duress* means that the person was being threatened or was under some kind of pressure, so that he or she did not get married voluntarily.

4. If one party did not have the *mental capacity* to get married. This means the person was suffering from mental illness or mental disability (such as being severely retarded) to such an extent that the person did not understand he or she was getting married, or possibly did not even understand the concept of marriage.

5. If one party was already married to another person. This might occur if one party married, mistakenly believing that the divorce from his or her previous spouse was final.

6. If the marriage is *incestuous*. Texas law prohibits marriage between certain family members, such as brother and sister, aunt and nephew, or uncle and niece.

7. If one party was under the influence of alcohol or narcotics at the time of the marriage.

8. If one party, for physical or mental reasons, was *permanently impotent* at the time of the marriage and did not inform the other party of the impotency.

9. If one party was divorced within thirty days of the marriage, and did not inform the other party of the divorce or the other party could not have reasonably discovered the divorce.

10. If the marriage ceremony took place within seventy-two hours of the issuance of the marriage license.

If your spouse wants to stop an annulment, there are several arguments he or she could make to further complicate the case. There are no Texas statutes outlining the proper procedures to follow to obtain an annulment (although many of the procedures governing a suit for divorce apply to a suit for an annulment).

Annulments are much less common than divorces. The annulment procedure can be extremely complicated, and should not be attempted without consulting a lawyer.

LEGAL SEPARATION

Texas does not permit a *legal separation*. This procedure is available in some states, and is used to divide the property and provide for child support in cases where the husband and wife live separately, but remain married. This is usually used to break the financial rights and obligations of a couple whose religion does not permit divorce. Some states refer to this procedure as *divorce from bed and board*. It is an old procedure that is gradually fading out. It is possible to obtain child support without getting a divorce, but that procedure is beyond the scope of this book.

The Legal System

This chapter will give you a general introduction to the legal system. There are things you need to know in order to obtain a divorce (or help your lawyer get the job done) and to get through any encounter with the legal system with minimum stress. These are some of the realities of our system. If you do not learn to accept these realities, you will experience a great deal of stress and frustration.

THEORY VERSUS REALITY

Our legal system is a system of rules. There are basically three types of rules.

1. *Rules of Law.* These are the basic substance of the law, such as a law telling a judge how to divide your property.

2. *Rules of Procedure.* These outline how matters are to be handled in the courts, such as requiring court papers to be in a certain form or filed within a certain time.

3. *Rules of Evidence.* These set forth the manner in which facts are to be proven.

The theory is that these rules allow each side to present evidence most favorable to that side, and an independent person or persons (the judge or jury) will be able to figure out the truth. Then, certain legal principles will be applied to that truth, which will give a fair resolution to the dispute between the parties. These legal principles are supposed to be relatively unchanging, so everyone knows what will happen in any given situation and can plan their lives accordingly. This will provide order and predictability to society. Any change in the legal principles is supposed to occur slowly, so the expected behavior in society is not confused from day to day.

Unfortunately, the system does not actually work this way. What follows are only some of the problems in the real legal system.

The System Is Not Perfect

Contrary to how it may seem, legal rules are not made just to complicate the system and confuse everyone. They are attempts to make the system as fair and just as possible. They have been developed over several hundred years, and in most cases, they do make sense.

Unfortunately, efforts to find fairness and justice have resulted in a complex set of rules. The legal system affects every person's life in important ways. It is not a game. However, it can be compared to a game in some ways. The rules are designed to apply to all people, in all cases. Sometimes the rules do not seem to give a fair result in a certain situation, but the rules are still followed. Just as a referee can make a bad call, so can a judge. There are also cases where one side wins by cheating.

Judges Do Not Always Follow the Rules

This is a shocking discovery for many young lawyers. After spending three years in law school learning legal theory, and after spending countless hours preparing for a hearing and having all of the law on your side, you find that the judge is not going to pay any attention to legal theories or the law. Many judges make decisions simply based on what they think seems fair under the circumstances. This concept is actually being taught in some law schools now.

Unfortunately, what seems fair to a particular judge may depend upon his or her personal ideas and philosophy. For example, there is nothing in the divorce laws that gives one parent priority in child custody; however, a vast majority of judges believe that a child is generally better off with his or her mother. All other things being equal, these judges will find a way to justify awarding custody to the mother.

The System is Often Slow Even lawyers get frustrated with how long it can take to get a case completed. Whatever your situation, things will take longer than you expect. Patience is required to get through the system with a minimum amount of stress. Do not let your impatience or frustration show. No matter what happens, remain calm and be courteous. Be polite to the judge, to the court clerks, to any lawyers involved, and even to your spouse. (On the other hand, if you and your spouse can agree on everything, it is possible to complete the divorce process in about three weeks.)

No Two Cases are Alike Just because your friend's case went a certain way does not mean your case will have the same result. The judge can make a difference, and more often, the circumstances will make a difference. Just because your coworker makes the same income as you and has the same number of children, you cannot assume you will be ordered to pay the same amount of child support. There are usually other circumstances your coworker does not tell you about and possibly does not understand.

Half the People Lose Remember, there are two sides to every legal issue, and there is usually only one winner. Do not expect to have every detail go your way. If you leave anything to the judge to decide, you can expect to have some things go your spouse's way.

DIVORCE LAW AND PROCEDURE

To most people (including lawyers), the law appears very complicated and confusing. Fortunately, many areas of the law can be broken down into simple and logical steps. Divorce is one of those areas.

The Players As was mentioned before, the legal system can often be compared to a game, and just like a game, it is important to know the players.

The judge. The judge has the power to decide whether you can get divorced, how your property will be divided, who will get custody of the children, and how much will be paid for child support. The judge is the last person you want to anger. In general, judges have large caseloads, and like it best when your case can be concluded quickly and without hassle. This means that the more you and your spouse agree upon, and the more complete your paperwork is, the happier the judge will be.

Most likely, your only direct contact with the judge will be at the final hearing, which may last as little as five minutes. (See the section on "Courtroom Manners" in Chapter 6 for more about how to deal with the judge.)

The judge's administrative assistant. The judge's administrative assistant sets the hearings for the judge, and can frequently answer many of your questions about the procedure and what the judge would like or requires. Not surprisingly, you do not want to make an enemy of the administrative assistant. This means that you do not call him or her often and do not ask too many questions. A few questions are okay. You may want to start off saying that you just want to make sure you have everything in order for the judge.

Be friendly and courteous, even if the administrative assistant is rude. The judge's administrative assistant has a large caseload just like the judge and may be suffering from stress, or may just be a nasty person. However, you will get farther by being nice than by arguing with or complaining to him or her.

The court clerk. Where the administrative assistant usually only works for one judge, the court clerk handles the files for all of the judges. The clerk's office is the central place where all of the court files are kept. The clerk files your court papers and keeps the official records of your divorce.

Most people who work in the clerk's office are friendly and helpful. While they cannot give you legal advice (such as telling you what to say in your court papers), they can help explain the system and the procedures (such as telling you what type of papers must be filed). The clerk has the power to accept or reject your papers, so you do not want to anger the clerk, either. If the clerk tells you to change something in your papers, just change it. Do not argue or complain.

If you anger the judge, his or her administrative assistant, or the clerk, any one of them can delay your divorce or cause you a number of problems—so be polite, courteous, and friendly to all of these people. It never hurts to engage in a little small talk or to express your sympathy or understanding for all of the rude people they have to deal with and for their heavy workload.

Lawyers. Lawyers serve as guides through the legal system. They try to guide their own client while trying to confuse, manipulate, or out-maneuver their opponent. In dealing with your spouse's attorney (if he or she has one), try to be polite. You will not get anywhere by being antagonistic or by arguing. Generally, the lawyer is just doing his or her job by trying to get the best results for his or her client.

Some lawyers are truly nasty people. These lawyers simply cannot be reasoned with, and you should not try. If your spouse gets one of these lawyers, it may be a good idea for you to get a lawyer as well.

A lawyer can sometimes get you through the legal system faster, while helping you avoid the potential dangers along the way. Chapter 5 will provide more information about whether you need a lawyer.

This book. This book will serve as your guide through the court system. In most cases, the dangers along the way are relatively small. If you were on trial for a crime or for seriously injuring someone, there is no question that you would need a lawyer. However, that is not the case with seeking a divorce. If you start getting lost or the dangers seem to be getting worse, you can always hire a lawyer to come to your aid.

The Law   The law relating to divorce, as well as to any other area or topic, comes from two sources. The first source is the Texas statutes, which are the laws passed by the Texas legislature. This book is designed so that you will not need to look up the law.

The other source of law is the past decisions of the Texas courts. These are much more difficult to locate and follow. For most situations, the law is clearly spelled out in the statutes, so the past court decisions are not all that important. However, if you wish to learn more about how to find these court decisions, see the section on "Legal Research" later in this chapter.

The law is really very simple in most divorce cases. You will need to show the following three things:

1. that your marriage has become *insupportable* (this is done simply by stating this fact—your marriage is broken and cannot be saved);

2. how your property should be divided between you and your spouse; and,

3. who should have custody of your children (if any) and how they should be supported.

The Procedure The basic uncontested divorce process may be viewed as a five-step process.

1. File court papers asking the judge to grant a divorce (which includes dividing your property and deciding how the children will be cared for).

2. Notify your spouse that you are filing for divorce.

3. File papers explaining what you and your spouse have agreed upon with regard to property division and child custody.

4. Obtain a hearing date.

5. Attend a hearing with the judge and have the judge sign a decree granting the divorce.

These steps are now examined in a little more detail, and later chapters will explain how to carry them out.

Petition for divorce. This is nothing more than a written request for the judge to grant you a divorce, divide your property, and determine child support and custody. Petition forms are provided in Appendix B of this book. Full instructions are provided in later chapters. Once the petition is completed, it is taken to the court clerk to be filed.

Notifying your spouse. After you have prepared the petition, you need to officially notify your spouse. Even though your spouse may already know that you are filing for divorce, you still need to have him or her officially notified. This is done by having a copy of your petition delivered to your spouse, which may be accomplished in various ways.

Obtaining a hearing date. Once all of your paperwork is in order and has been filed, you need to set a date for a hearing. A *hearing* is simply a meeting with the judge so that he or she can give you a divorce. You usually set this up with the court clerk when you file your petition.

The hearing. Finally, you go to the hearing. The judge will review the papers you have submitted and any additional information you have. He or she will make decisions about whether to grant the divorce, how your property should be divided, who should have custody of your children, and how the children are to be supported. If you and your spouse agree on these matters, the judge will simply approve your agreement.

The judge can order the husband and wife into mediation when the parties are having a difficult time reaching agreement on the major issues. *Mediation* is a process that involves a third party (the *mediator*) who does not have an interest in the outcome of the divorce. The mediator meets with the parties and assists the parties in resolving any differences they may have between them. The mediator may offer suggestions, point out weaknesses and strengths of each party's position, and advise the parties as to how courts might resolve their differences. The suggestions and advice offered by the mediator are not binding upon the parties.

Marriage counseling can be ordered if the judge has reason to believe that the marriage can be saved. However, this is an extremely rare situation. The judge can also direct the state Department of Human Resources to conduct a study and provide the judge with a custody recommendation.

LEGAL RESEARCH

This book has been designed so that you do not need to do legal research. However, if your case becomes complicated or you simply have an interest in checking into the divorce law in Texas, this section will give you some guidance.

Texas Statutes and Codes

The main source of information on Texas divorce law is the Texas statutes and codes. This is a set of volumes that contain the laws passed by the Texas legislature. Some volumes are labeled "Statutes" and others are labeled "Codes." *Supplements* are issued each year. A set can usually be found at the public library. Check to be sure they have the most recent set.

You will primarily be concerned with Chapter 6 of the *Family Code* contained within the Texas statutes and codes, although you can look for other subjects in the index volume.

Case Law

In addition to the laws passed by the legislature, law is also made by the decisions of the judges in various cases each year. To find this *case law,* you will need to go to a law library. Each county has a law library connected with the court—ask the court clerk where the library in your county is located. Also, law schools have libraries that may be open to the public.

Do not be afraid to ask the librarian for assistance. Librarians cannot give you legal advice, but they can tell you where the books are located, and they might even be kind enough to give you a short course on legal research.

Texas Statutes and Codes Annotated

The *Texas Statutes Annotated* and the *Texas Codes Annotated* are numerous volumes that contain the Texas statutes and Texas codes, followed by summaries (or *annotations*) of court cases that discuss each section of the statutes.

Example:

If you are looking for information about division of property, you would find Section 7.001 of the Texas Family Code. This would give you the exact language of the statute, which would be followed by summaries of court opinions explaining the alimony statute.

Texas Digest

The *Texas Digest* is a set of volumes that gives short summaries of cases, and is the place where you can find the court's full written opinion. The information in the digest is arranged alphabetically by subject. Find the chapter on "Divorce," then look for the headings of the subject you want.

South Western Reporter

The *South Western Reporter* is where the appeals courts publish their written opinions on the cases they hear. There are two series of the *South Western Reporter*, the older cases being found in the *South Western Reporter* (abbreviated S.W.) and newer cases being found in the *South Western Reporter 2d Series* (abbreviated S.W.2d).

Example:

If the digest tells you that the case of *Woody v. Woody* is located at 371 S.W.2d 576, you can find the case by going to Volume 371 of the *South Western Reporter 2d Series*, and turning to page 576. In its opinion, the court will discuss what the case was about, what questions of law were presented for consideration, and what the court decided and why.

Texas Jurisprudence

Texas Jurisprudence is a legal encyclopedia. You simply look up the subject you want ("Family Law/Dissolution of Marriage") in alphabetical order, and it gives you a summary of the law on that subject. It will also refer to specific court cases that can then be found in the *South Western Reporter*. *Texas Jurisprudence* deals specifically with Texas cases. More general legal encyclopedias that cover the entire United States are *American Jurisprudence* (abbreviated Am. Jur. and Am. Jur. 2d) and *Corpus Juris Secundum* (abbreviated C.J.S.).

Texas Rules of Course

The *Texas Rules of Court* are the rules that are applied in the various courts in Texas. They also contain some approved forms. These rules mainly deal with forms and procedures. You would be primarily concerned with the *Rules of Civil Procedure*.

Other Sources   Three books you may want to ask for at the law library are *Family Law Practice Manual*, by the Family Law Section of the State Bar of Texas; *Texas Family Law*, by Loy M. Simpkins; and, *O'Conner's Texas Rules—Civil Trial*, by Texas Lawyer.

Internet   The following are some Internet resources that may be helpful in your research.

Texas State Government in General   www.state.tx.us

Comptroller of Public Accounts   www.window.state.tx.us

Texas Administrative Code/   www.sos.state.tx.us
    Texas Register

Texas Legislature Online (Statutes,   www.capitol.state.tx.us
    Codes, Bills, Legislative Committees)

Texas Judicial Server   www.courts.state.tx.us

General/All-Purpose Legal Directory   www.texaslawyer.com

Effects of Divorce and Its Alternatives

Getting a divorce is one of the most emotionally stressful events in a person's life. It will have an impact on several aspects of your life and can change your entire lifestyle. Before you begin the process of getting a divorce, you need to take some time to think about how it will affect your life. This chapter helps you examine these things and offers alternatives in the event you want to try to save your relationship. Even if you feel absolutely sure that you want a divorce, you should still read this chapter so you are prepared for what may follow.

LEGAL DIVORCE

In emotional terms, the legal aspect is the easiest part of divorce. It is simply the breaking of your matrimonial bonds—the termination of your marriage contract and partnership. The stress created here is caused by going through a court system procedure and having to deal with your spouse as you go through it. When compared to the other aspects of divorce, the legal divorce does not last as long. However, the legal divorce can be the most confrontational and emotionally explosive stage.

There are generally three matters to be resolved through the legal divorce:

1. the divorce of two people (this gives each the legal right to marry someone else);

2. the division of their property (and responsibility for debts); and,

3. the care and custody of their children.

Although it is theoretically possible for the legal divorce to be concluded within a few months, the legalities most often continue for years. This is mostly caused by the emotional aspects leading to battles over the children.

SOCIAL AND EMOTIONAL DIVORCE

Divorce will have a tremendous impact on your social and emotional life. The impact will continue long after you are legally divorced.

Lack of Companionship

Even if your relationship is quite stormy, you are probably still accustomed to having your spouse around. You may be able to temporarily put aside your problems and at least somewhat support each other in times of mutual adversity (such as in dealing with a death in the family, the illness of your child, or hurricane damage to your home). You may also feel a little more secure at night knowing that you are not alone in the house.

Even if your marriage is miserable, you may still notice a little emptiness, loneliness, or solitude after the divorce. It may not be that you miss your spouse in particular, but you just miss another person being around.

Grief

Divorce may be viewed as the death of a marriage—or maybe the funeral ceremony for the death of a marriage. As with the death of anyone or anything you have been close to, you will feel a sense of loss. This aspect can take you through all of the normal feelings associated with grief, such as guilt, anger, denial, and acceptance.

You will get angry and frustrated over the years you have "wasted." You will feel guilty because you "failed to make the marriage work." You will find yourself saying, "I can't believe this is happening to me." For months or even years, you will spend a lot of time thinking about your marriage. It can be extremely difficult to put it all behind you and get on with your life.

The Single's Scene—Dating

If you want to avoid solitary evenings in front of the television, you will find yourself trying to get back into the single's scene. This will probably involve a change in friends, as well as a change in lifestyle.

You may find that your current friends, who may all be married, no longer find that you, as a single person, fit in with their circle. Gradually, or even quickly, you may find yourself dropped from their guest list. Now, you have to start making an effort to meet single people at work, going out on the town, and even dating. This experience can be very frightening, tiring, and frustrating after years of being away from this lifestyle. It can also be very difficult if you have custody of the kids.

FINANCIAL DIVORCE

The financial divorce can be a very long and drastic adjustment. Divorce has a significant financial impact in almost every case. Many married couples are just able to make ends meet. After getting divorced, there are suddenly two rent or mortgage payments, two electric bills, and so on. For the spouse without custody, there is also child support to be paid. For at least one spouse (and often for both), money becomes even tighter than it was before the divorce.

Also, once you have divided your property, each of you will need to replace the items the other person got to keep. If she got the bedroom furniture and the pots and pans, he will need to buy his own. If he got the television and the sofa, she will need to buy her own.

CHILDREN AND DIVORCE

The effect upon your children and your relationship with them can be the most painful and long-lasting aspect of divorce. Your family life will be permanently changed, as there will no longer be a family. Even if you remarry, stepparents rarely bring back that same family feeling. Your relationship with your children may become strained as they work through their feelings of blame, guilt, disappointment, and anger.

This strain may continue for many years. Your children may even need professional counseling. Also, as long as there is child support and visitation involved, you will be forced to have at least some contact with your ex-spouse.

ALTERNATIVES TO DIVORCE

By the time you have purchased this book and read this far, you have probably already decided that you want a divorce. However, if what you have just read and thought about has changed your mind or made you want to make a last effort to save your marriage, there are a few things you can try. These are only very basic suggestions. Details and other suggestions can be offered by professional marriage counselors.

Talk to Your Spouse

Choose the right time (not when your spouse is trying to unwind after a day at work or is trying to quiet a screaming baby) and talk about your problems. Try to establish a few ground rules for the discussion.

- Each person must talk about how he or she feels, instead of making accusations that may start an argument.

- Each person listens while the other speaks (no interrupting).

- Each person must say something that he or she likes about the other and about the relationship.

As you talk, you may want to discuss such things as where you would like your relationship to go, how it has changed since you got married, and what can be done to bring you closer together.

Change Your Thinking

Many people get divorced because they will not change something about their outlook or their lifestyle. Then, once they get divorced, they find they have made that same change they resisted for so long.

Example:

George and Wendy were unhappy in their marriage. They did not seem to share the same lifestyle. George felt overburdened with responsibility and was bored. He wanted Wendy to be more independent and outgoing, meet new people, handle the household budget, and go out with him more often. However, Wendy was more shy and reserved. She was not confident in her ability to find a job and succeed in the business world. She preferred to stay at home.

Wendy wanted George to give up some of his frequent nights out with the guys, to help with the cooking and laundry, to stop leaving messes for her to clean up, and to stop bothering her about going out all the time. Neither would try change, and eventually, all of the little things built up into a divorce.

After the divorce, Wendy was forced to get a job to support herself. She made friends at work, and goes out with them two or three nights a week. She is successful and happy at her job, and she is quite competent at managing her own budget.

George now has his own apartment, and has to cook his own meals (something he finds he enjoys) and do his own laundry. He has also found it necessary to clean up his own messes and keep the place neat, especially if he is going to entertain guests. George has even thought about inviting Wendy over for dinner and a quiet evening at his place. Wendy has been thinking about inviting George out for a drink after work with her friends.

Both George and Wendy have changed in exactly the way the other had wanted. It is too bad they did not make these changes before they got divorced. If you think some change may help, give it a try. You can always go back to a divorce if things do not work out.

Counseling   Counseling is not the same as giving advice. A counselor should not be telling you what to do. A counselor's job is to assist you in figuring out what you really want to do. A counselor's job is mostly to ask questions that will get you thinking.

Actually, just talking things out with your spouse is a form of self-counseling. The only problem is that it is difficult to remain objective and nonjudgmental. You both need to be able to calmly analyze what the problems are and discuss possible solutions.

Very few couples seem to be able to do this successfully, which is why there are professional marriage counselors. As with doctors and lawyers, good marriage counselors are best discovered by word of mouth. You may have friends who can direct you to someone who helped them. You can also check with your family doctor or your clergy person for a referral, or even check the telephone Yellow Pages under "Marriage and Family Counselors" or some similar category.

You can see a counselor either alone or with your spouse. It may be a good idea to see a counselor even if you are going through with the divorce.

Another form of individual counseling is talking to a close friend. Just remember the difference between counseling and giving advice. Do not let your friend tell you what you should do.

Trial Separation   Before going through the time, expense, and trouble of getting a divorce, you and your spouse may want to try just getting away from each other for awhile. This can be as simple as taking separate vacations or as complex as actually moving into separate households for an indefinite period of time.

This may give each of you a chance to think about how you will like living alone, how important or trivial your problems are, and how you really feel about each other.

COLLABORATIVE LAW

If you and your spouse agree that ending your marriage is the solution, but need help figuring out how to divide your property, calculate child support, and establish a visitation schedule, you may wish to use a process called *collaborative law*. Collaborative law is a process by which spouses hire lawyers who will work with them to come to a written agreement regarding all of these issues without involving the courts. After a written agreement has been made, it will be signed by the spouses and their lawyers, and presented to the court to legally dissolve the marriage and make the agreement an order of the court.

Once the process is started, if the spouses cannot come to an agreement, they can file a petition for divorce in the court. However, the attorneys who worked with them during the collaborative law process cannot represent them in the court case.

CHECKLIST FOR CONSIDERING THE IMPACT OF DIVORCE

The following questions will help you understand if you are truly ready for a divorce.

❑　Is divorce the solution?

❑　Will talking to my spouse help resolve our problems?

❑　Why do I want a divorce?

❑　Can my spouse and I change our relationship and avoid divorce?

❑　Have my spouse and I tried counseling to resolve our problems?

❑　Will my spouse and I get along better if we have a trial separation?

❑　How will a divorce affect my social life?

❑　Am I emotionally prepared to go through the divorce process?

❑　Am I emotionally prepared to live without the companionship of my spouse?

❑　How will a divorce affect my financial situation?

❑　How will a divorce impact my children emotionally and financially?

Evaluating Your Situation

The following things should be done or considered before you begin the divorce process, as you evaluate your situation.

RELATIONSHIP WITH YOUR SPOUSE

First, you need to evaluate your situation with respect to your spouse. Have you both already agreed to get a divorce? If not, what kind of reaction do you expect from him or her? His or her expected reaction can determine how you proceed. If he or she reacts in a rational manner, you can probably use the simplified or uncontested procedure. However, if you expect an extremely emotional and possibly violent reaction, you will need to take steps to protect yourself, your children, and your property. You will have to start out expecting to use the contested procedure.

Unless you and your spouse have already decided together to get a divorce, you do not want your spouse to know you are thinking about filing for divorce. This is a defense tactic, although it may not seem that way at first.

If your spouse thinks you are planning a divorce, he or she may do things to prevent you from getting a fair result. These things include withdrawing money from bank accounts, hiding information about income, and hiding assets. Do not let on that you are planning to file for divorce until you have collected all of the information you will need and are about to file with the court, or until you are prepared to protect yourself from violence, if necessary.

– Warning –

Tactics such as withdrawing money from bank accounts and hiding assets are dangerous. If you try any of these things, you risk looking like the bad guy before the judge. This can result in anything from having disputed matters resolved in your spouse's favor, to being ordered to produce the assets or being jailed for contempt of court.

Theoretically, the system would prefer that you keep evidence of the assets (such as photographs, sales receipts, or bank statements) to present to the judge if your spouse hides them. Then, your spouse will be the bad guy and risk being jailed. However, once your spouse has taken assets and hidden them, or sold them and spent the money, even a contempt order may not get the money or assets back.

If you determine that you need to get the assets in order to keep your spouse from hiding or disposing of them, be sure you keep them in a safe place. Do not dispose of them. If your spouse claims you took them, you can explain to the judge why you were afraid that your spouse would dispose of them and that you merely got them out of his or her reach.

FINANCIAL INFORMATION

It is extremely important that you collect all of the financial information you can get. This information should include originals or copies of the following:

❑   your most recent income tax return (and your spouse's, if you filed separately);

❑   the most recent W-2 tax forms for yourself and your spouse;

❑   any other income reporting papers (such as interest, stock dividends, etc.);

❑   your spouse's most recent pay stub, hopefully showing year-to-date earnings (otherwise, try to get copies of all pay stubs since the beginning of the year);

❑   deeds to real estate and titles to cars, boats, or other vehicles;

❑   your and your spouse's will;

❑   life insurance policies;

❑   stocks, bonds, or other investment papers;

❑   pension or retirement fund papers and statements;

❑   health insurance card and papers;

❑   bank account or credit union statements;

❑   your spouse's Social Security number and driver's license number;

❑   names, addresses, and phone numbers of your spouse's employer, close friends, and family members;

❑   credit card statements, mortgage documents, and other credit and debt papers;

❑   a list of vehicles, furniture, appliances, tools, etc., owned by you and your spouse (see the next section in this chapter on "Property and Debts" for forms and a detailed discussion of what to include);

❑   copies of bills or receipts for recurring, regular expenses, such as electric, gas, other utilities, and car insurance;

❏   copies of bills, receipts, insurance forms, or medical records for any unusual medical expenses (including recurring or continuous medical conditions) for yourself, your spouse, or your children; and,

❏   any other papers showing what you and your spouse earn, own, or owe.

Make copies of as many of these papers as possible and keep them in a safe and private place (where your spouse will not find them). Try to make copies of new papers as they come in, especially as you get close to filing court papers and as you get close to a court hearing.

PROPERTY AND DEBTS

This section is designed to help you get a rough idea of where things stand regarding the division of your property and debts, and to prepare you for completing the court papers you will need to file. The following sections deal with the questions of child support, custody, and visitation. If you are still not sure whether you want a divorce, these sections may help you to decide.

Property   Texas characterizes property possessed by either spouse during marriage as community property or separate property. *Separate property* is property owned by a spouse before marriage, property acquired during the marriage by gift or inheritance, and funds recovered by a spouse for personal injuries. All other property of the spouses is *community property*. Each spouse automatically owns one-half of the community property, and generally is entitled to that one-half upon divorce.

This section assists you in completing the **PROPERTY INVENTORY**. (see form 1, p.165.) This form is a list of all of your property and key information about that property. You will notice that this form is divided into nine columns, designated as follows.

Column (1):   Check the box in this column (S) if that piece of property is separate property. This is property that either you or your spouse acquired before you were married, that was given to you or your spouse separately, or that was inherited by you or your spouse separately. It also includes money one of you received for a personal injury claim.

Column (2): In this column, describe the property. (A discussion regarding what information should go in this column will follow.)

Column (3): Write in the serial number, account number, or other number that will help clearly identify that piece of property.

Column (4): This is for the current market value of the property. *Market value* is the amount of money that a buyer is willing to pay for property in a particular area based upon other sales of similar property. For example, if a person owns a three-bedroom house in Dallas, the market value of the house would be determined by reviewing the selling price of other three-bedroom homes located in Dallas—not Houston.

Column (5): This shows how much money is owed on the property, if any.

Column (6): Subtract the balance owed from the value. This shows how much the property is worth to you (your *equity*).

Column (7): This column shows the current legal owner of the property. (H) designates the husband, (W) the wife, and (J) is for jointly owned property (in both of your names).

Column (8): This column is for those pieces of property you expect the husband will keep.

Column (9): This column is for the property you expect the wife will keep.

Use the **PROPERTY INVENTORY** to list your property, including the following.

Cash. List the name of the bank, credit union, or other lending institution, and the account number for each account. This includes savings and checking accounts, as well as certificates of deposit

(CDs). The balance of each account should be listed in the columns entitled "Value" and "Equity." (Leave the "Balance Owed" column blank.) Make copies of the most recent bank statements for each account.

Stocks and bonds. All stocks, bonds, or other *paper investments* should be listed. Write down the number of shares and the name of the company or other organization that issued them. Also, copy any notation such as *common* or *preferred* stock or shares. This information can be obtained from the stock certificate itself or from a statement from the stock broker. Make a copy of the certificate or the statement.

Real estate. List each piece of property you and your spouse own. The description might include a street address for the property, a subdivision name and lot number, or anything that lets you know what piece of property you are referring to. There probably will not be an identification number, although you might use the county's tax number. Real estate (or any other property) may be in both of your names (joint), in your spouse's name alone, or in your name alone. The only way to know for sure is to look at the deed to the property. (If you cannot find a copy of the deed, try to find mortgage papers or payment coupons, homeowners insurance papers, or a property tax assessment notice.) The owners of property are usually referred to on the deed as the *grantees*.

In assigning a value to the property, consider the market value, which is how much you could probably sell the property for. This might be what similar houses in your neighborhood have sold for recently. You might also consider how much you paid for the property or how much the property is insured for. *Do not* use the tax assessment value, as this is usually considerably lower than the market value.

Vehicles. This category includes cars, trucks, motor homes, recreational vehicles (RVs), motorcycles, boats, trailers, airplanes, and any other means of transportation for which the state requires a title and registration. Your description should include the following information (which can usually be found on the title or on the vehicle itself):

✪ year it was made;

✪ make (the name of the manufacturer, such as Ford, Honda, Chris Craft, etc.);

- ✪ model (for example, Mustang)—the model may be a name, a number, a series of letters, or a combination of these; and,

- ✪ serial number/vehicle identification number (VIN) (this is most likely found on the vehicle, as well as on the title or registration).

Make a copy of the title or registration. Regarding a value, you can go to the public library and ask to look at the blue book for cars, trucks, or whatever you are looking for. A *blue book* (which can actually be any color) gives the average values for used vehicles. Your librarian can help you find what you need.

Another source is the classified advertising section of a newspaper, which you can use to see what similar vehicles are selling for. You might also try calling a dealer to see if they can give you a rough idea of the value. Be sure you take into consideration the condition of the vehicle.

Furniture. List all furniture as specifically as possible. You should include the type (such as sofa, coffee table, etc.), the color, and if you know it, the manufacturer, line name, or style. Furniture usually will not have a serial number, although if you find one be sure to write it on the list. Just estimate a value, unless you know what it is worth.

Appliances, electronic equipment, and yard machines. This category includes things such as refrigerators, lawn mowers, and power tools. Again, estimate a value, unless you are familiar enough with them to simply know what they are worth. There are too many different makes, models, accessories, and age factors to be able to figure out a value otherwise. These items will probably have a make, model, and serial number on them. You may have to look on the back, bottom, or other hidden place for the serial number, but try to find it.

Jewelry and other valuables. You do not need to list inexpensive or costume jewelry. You can plan on keeping your own personal watches, rings, etc. However, if you own an expensive piece, you should include it in your list, along with an estimated value. Be sure to include silverware, original art, gold, coin collections, and so on. Again, be as detailed and specific as possible.

Life insurance with cash surrender value. Any life insurance policy that you may cash in or borrow against, and that therefore has value, should be listed. If you cannot find a cash surrender value in the papers you have, you can call the insurance company and ask.

Other big ticket items. This is simply a general reference to anything of significant value that does not fit into one of the categories already discussed. Examples might be a portable spa, an above-ground swimming pool, golf clubs, guns, pool tables, camping or fishing equipment, farm animals, or machinery.

Pensions and military benefits. The division of pensions, as well as military and other retirement benefits, can be a complicated matter. Whenever these types of benefits are involved, you will need to consult an attorney or a certified public accountant (CPA) to determine the value of the benefits and how they should be divided. (Be sure to read the section in Chapter 11 on "Pension Plans.")

What not to list. You will not need to list your clothing and other personal effects. Pots and pans, dishes, and cooking utensils ordinarily do not need to be listed, unless they have some unusually high value.

Once you have completed your list, go back through it and try to determine who should end up with each item. The ideal situation is for both you and your spouse to go through the list together and divide things fairly. However, if this is not possible, you will need to offer a reasonable settlement to the judge. Consider each item and make a check mark in either column (8) or (9) to designate whether that item should go to the husband or wife. You may make the following general assumptions.

- Your separate property will go to you.

- Your spouse's separate property will go to your spouse.

- You should get the items that only you use.

- Your spouse should get the items only used by your spouse.

- The remaining items should be divided, evening out the total value of all the community property and taking into consideration who would really want that item.

To somewhat equally divide your property (referring only to marital property), you first need to know the total value of your property. First of all, do not count the value of the separate property. Add the remaining amounts in the "Equity" column of the **PROPERTY INVENTORY**, which will give you an approximate value of all community property.

Your spouse may own property that is his or her separate property, either because he or she owned it prior to the marriage or inherited the property during the marriage. If community property has been used to reduce debt, you may have the right to receive reimbursement for the *economic contribution* made during the marriage. The measurement of the economic contribution is defined to refer to the equity in the property. If you believe this is an issue in your particular situation, you may wish to seek the services of an experienced attorney or accountant to properly value the amount of your economic contribution to your spouse's separate property.

When it comes time for the hearing, you and your spouse may be arguing over some or all of the items on your list. This is when you will be glad that you made copies of the documents relating to the property on your list. Arguments over the value of property may need to be resolved by hiring appraisers to set a value. However, you will have to pay the appraiser a fee. Dividing your property will be discussed further in later chapters.

Texas law requires that when property is divided in a divorce, the tax consequences of the property division be taken into consideration. In the past, spouses divided property without calculating how much income tax would have to be paid in order to divide the property. For example, spouses would often allocate investments to one spouse and retirement plan assets to the other spouse. The gain on the sale of the investment assets would be subject to tax, but at the rate applicable to capital gains. Currently, this rate is much less than the ordinary income tax rates. The full value of the retirement assets would be subject to tax at ordinary income tax rates. After the taxes are paid, the division of property may end up being significantly unequal. It must be clear to the court that the parties have taken into account this inequality caused by the taxes, and have either made a compensating property distribution or specifically agreed to the inequality.

Debts   This section relates to the **DEBT INVENTORY**, which will list your debts. (see form 2, p.167.) Although there are cases where, for example, the wife gets a car but the husband is ordered to make the payments, generally, whoever gets the property also gets the debt owed on that property. This seems to be a fair arrangement in most cases. On the **DEBT INVENTORY**, you will list each debt owed by you or your spouse.

As with separate property, there is also *separate debt*. This is any debt incurred before you were married that is yours alone. The **DEBT INVENTORY** contains a column for "S" that should be checked for each separate debt. You will be responsible for your separate debts and your spouse will be responsible for his or hers.

To complete the **DEBT INVENTORY** (form 2), list each debt as follows.

Column (1):   Check if this is a separate debt.

Column (2):   Write in the name and address of the creditor (the bank, company, or person to whom the debt is owed).

Column (3):   Write in the account, loan, or mortgage number.

Column (4):   Write in any notes to help identify what the loan was for (such as Christmas gifts or vacation).

Column (5):   Write in the amount of the monthly payment.

Column (6):   Write in the balance still owed on the loan.

Column (7):   Write in the date (approximately) when the loan was made.

Column (8):   Note whether the debt is in the husband's name (H), the wife's name (W), or jointly in both names (J).

Columns (9) & (10):   These columns note who will be responsible for the debt after the divorce. As with your property, each of you will keep your separate debts, and the remainder should be divided, first taking into consideration who will keep the property the loan was for, and then equally dividing the remaining debt.

CHILD CUSTODY AND VISITATION

As with everything else in divorce, things are ideal when both parties can agree on the question of custody of the children. Generally, the judge will accept any agreement you reach, provided it does not appear that your agreement will cause harm to your children.

In Texas, child custody is formally referred to in the statutes as *managing conservatorship*.

NOTE: *Throughout this book, "child custody" and "managing conservatorship" are used interchangeably and mean the same thing.*

In Texas, any divorce involving minor children is technically considered two separate legal matters: (1) a *divorce* and (2) a *suit affecting the parent-child relationship*. These will be joined together in your petition and will be discussed more in Chapter 7.

With respect to child custody, the Texas law makes two significant statements.

> *1. It is the policy of this state to assure that children will have frequent and continuing contact with parents who have shown the ability to act in the best interest of the child, to provide a stable environment for the child, and to encourage parents to share in the rights and responsibilities of raising their children after the parents have separated or dissolved their marriage.*

> *2. The court shall apply the [child custody] guidelines without regard to the sex of the parents or the child.*

In spite of this modern philosophy voiced by the Texas courts and legislature, you will find that most judges are from the old school of thought on this subject and believe that (all things being equal) a young child is better off with the mother. Because of these statements in the law, the judge may go to great lengths to find that all things are not equal in order to justify his or her decision to award custody to the mother. It happens day after day throughout the state, and it is a reality you may have to deal with.

The Texas law also states that the court may appoint the parents as *joint managing conservators* (commonly referred to as *joint custody*) of the child in its decree only if the judge finds that the appointment of both parents is in the *best interests* of the child. Best interests of the child generally means the judge will review the facts and circumstances, and make a decision that is most favorable to the child and not necessarily his or her parent. In other words, the judge puts the interests of the child first. To determine the best interests of the child, the judge will consider:

- whether the physical, psychological, or emotional needs and development of the child will benefit from the appointment of joint custodians;

- the ability of the parents to put the welfare of the child first and reach agreement on what is in the child's best interests;

- whether each parent can encourage and accept a positive relationship between the child and the other parent;

- whether both parents took a role in raising the child prior to the divorce;

- the physical distance between the homes of the parents;

- the preference of a child 12 years of age or older with regard to joint custody;

- whether there is a history of family violence involving the parents of the child; and,

- any other factor the judge believes is relevant.

While joint custody is a great idea in concept, it is usually not a very practical one. Very few parents can put aside their anger at each other to agree on what is best for their child. Joint custody merely leads to more fighting. Even if joint custody is ordered, a child can only have one primary residence. The judge may still decide which parent the child will mainly live with, as well as how decisions regarding things such as education and medical care will be made.

PARENTING PLANS

In 2005, the Texas legislature passed new legislation that has a major impact on all divorce actions in which children are involved. Parents who are seeking a divorce must present the court with a detailed agreement called a *parenting plan*. The court will not enter a temporary or final order in a divorce action unless a **PARENTING PLAN** is submitted to the court. Section 153.601 of the Texas Family Code defines a parenting plan as a:

> *temporary or final court order that sets out the rights and duties of parents in a suit affecting the parent-child relationship and includes provisions relating to conservatorship, possession of and access to a child, and child support and a dispute resolution process to minimize future disputes.*

In the past, parents often used a document called a *standard possession order*. Under the new law, parents can still use a standard possession order as a basic framework for the **PARENTING PLAN**, but must include several other items. The law requires that each **PARENTING PLAN** submitted to the court must:

- establish the rights and duties of each parent with respect to the child;

- minimize the child's exposure to harmful parental conflicts;

- provide for the child's changing needs as the child grows and matures, in a way that minimizes the need for further modifications to the final **PARENTING PLAN**; and,

- provide for a dispute resolution process or other voluntary dispute resolution procedure before requesting enforcement or modification of the terms and conditions of the **PARENTING PLAN** through court action.

In addition, in providing for a dispute resolution process, each **PARENTING PLAN** *must* include the following two statements.

1. "Preference shall be given to carrying out the parenting plan."

2. "The parties shall use the designated process to resolve disputes."

Finally, each **PARENTING PLAN** must have the following two documents attached to it.

1. A verified statement of income determined in accordance with the child support guidelines.

2. A verified statement that the **PARENTING PLAN** is proposed in good faith and is in the best interests of the child.

Parents are encouraged to work together to create a **PARENTING PLAN** that is specific and flexible. If the parents cannot agree on the terms of a **PARENTING PLAN**, each parent may submit his or her own proposed **PARENTING PLAN**, or the court can appoint a *parenting coordinator* to assist the parents with resolving issues related to parenting or other family issues affecting the conclusion of the divorce action. The role of the parenting coordinator is to act as a mediator and help the parents work together to create a fair **PARENTING PLAN** that is in the best interests of the child.

Specific provisions of a **PARENTING PLAN** include:

○   name, address, and telephone number of mother;

○   name, address, and telephone number of father;

○   names, birthdates, and residence address of the children;

○   parent responsible for designating primary residence of children;

○   parent responsible for paying child support;

○   amount of child support and frequency of payments (weekly, biweekly, semimonthly, or monthly);

○   whether or not a wage withholding order will be entered;

○   parent that will maintain health insurance for children;

○   payment of uninsured medical expenses;

- ✪ rights and duties of parents;

- ✪ special provisions regarding rights of parents;

- ✪ detailed schedule of visitation; and,

- ✪ general provisions regarding parenting times.

The importance of a **PARENTING PLAN** cannot be overstated. The courts expect that parents will set aside their personal feelings toward one another, take an active role in planning for their children's future, and come to an agreement that puts the children first. Parents are most familiar with their children's schedules, routines, school and social interests, and emotional stability. Parents also recognize the limitations of their own schedules and routines.

The Texas legislature has not created a **PARENTING PLAN** form. Form 3 is a basic **PARENTING PLAN** that is similar to those used in many other states. It may be a difficult and painful process to talk with your spouse about the **PARENTING PLAN** and come to an agreement. If your spouse is not willing to work with you, you can request that the court appoint a parenting coordinator to help you and your spouse resolve the differences you have about the **PARENTING PLAN**. If you and your spouse still cannot come to an agreement, you can file your own proposed **PARENTING PLAN** with the court and request that the court adopt your **PARENTING PLAN**. Keep in mind, however, that your spouse has the right to file his or her own proposed **PARENTING PLAN**.

Typically, it is easier to prepare the **PARENTING PLAN** as a separate document. If this is the case, it is very important that the final decree of divorce contain the following language.

> *The parenting plan is attached to this Decree and is incorporated for all purposes.*

If that language is not included in the **DECREE**, the **PARENTING PLAN** cannot be enforced by a contempt charge against the parent who does not comply with its terms.

The following items should be considered for inclusion in the **PARENTING PLAN** either initially or when the children become older:

- summer camp;

- restriction of smoking by parent in presence of children;

- restriction of alcohol consumption by parent in presence or possession of children;

- supervised parenting time;

- restriction on who may or may not be allowed to spend the night when the children are present;

- use of cell phones by children;

- curfews;

- unchaperoned or international travel;

- control of children's savings accounts;

- pets;

- telephone access to children by parent during periods of non-possession;

- mail access to children by parent during periods of nonpossession;

- separate bedrooms for children;

- visitation by grandparents, aunts, uncles, etc. if parent cannot exercise scheduled visitation;

- makeup visitation for periods missed by parent because of illness or other reason; and,

- Scheduled dates for review, and if necessary, amendment of **PARENTING PLAN**.

NOTE: *When signing the* **PARENTING PLAN** *from p.169, cross out Petitioner or Respondent by your name—whichever you are not. (You will probably cross out Respondent).*

Letting the Court Decide

If you and your spouse cannot agree on how these matters will be handled, you will be leaving this important decision to the judge. The judge cannot possibly know your child as well as you and your spouse, so it makes sense for you to work this out yourselves. Otherwise, you are leaving the decision to a stranger.

If the judge must decide the question of custody, he or she will consider the following factors:

❂ which parent is most likely to allow the other to visit with the child;

❂ the love, affection, and other emotional ties existing between the child and each parent;

❂ the ability and willingness of each parent to provide the child with food, clothing, medical care, and other material needs;

❂ the length of time the child has lived with either parent in a stable environment;

❂ the permanence, as a family unit, of the proposed custodial home (relating to whether one of the parties will be getting remarried immediately after the divorce, or more often, to change of custody petitions at a later date);

❂ the moral fitness of each parent;

❂ the mental and physical health of each parent;

❂ the home, school, and community record of the child;

❂ the preference of the child, providing the child is of sufficient intelligence and understanding; and,

❂ any other fact the judge decides is relevant.

It is difficult to predict the outcome of a custody battle. There are too many factors and individual circumstances to make such a guess. The only exception is where one parent is clearly unfit and the other can prove it.

Drug abuse is probably the most common charge against a spouse, but unless there has been an arrest and conviction, it is difficult to prove to a judge. In general, do not charge your spouse with being unfit unless you can prove it. Judges are not impressed with unfounded allegations, and they can do more harm than good.

In Texas, the law contains a model **STANDARD POSSESSION ORDER** addressed in Appendix B of this book. (see form 23, p.239.) (Texas Family Code (Tex. Fam. Code), Section (Sec.) 153.316.) This sets forth the terms of visitation for the parent who does not have custody of the child. This is the order that a judge will generally use to establish visitation rights if you and your spouse do not agree on a **PARENTING PLAN**, or if the judge does not accept either parent's proposed **PARENTING PLAN**.

If your children are older (not infants), it may be a good idea to seriously consider their preference for who they want to live with. If their preference is your spouse, your fairness and respect for their wishes may benefit you in the long run. Just be sure that you keep in close contact with them and visit them often.

CHILD SUPPORT

Once again, the judge will probably go along with any agreement you and your spouse reach, as long as he or she is satisfied that the child will be adequately cared for. The following information and the **CHILD SUPPORT GUIDELINES WORKSHEET** (form 4, p.185) will help you get an idea of the proper amount of child support. The **CHILD SUPPORT GUIDELINES WORKSHEET** consists of one main page, followed by Schedules A, B, C, and D. The schedules are used to help you complete the form. Using this form will give you a rough idea of the amount of child support to expect. Where an agreement cannot be reached, the next section demonstrates the procedure that will be used.

How Child Support is Determined

Generally, there are two factors used to determine the proper amount of support to be paid: (1) the needs of the child and (2) the financial ability of the parents to meet those needs. In Texas, the presumption is that the spouse who does not have physical custody of the child will be ordered to pay child support. This presumption assumes that the parent with custody will be spending resources of his or her own to provide shelter, food, and so on for the child.

The **CHILD SUPPORT GUIDELINES WORKSHEET** is simply to be used as a guideline for you to determine how much support would probably be ordered under the guidelines. The judge will take the following steps to determine the proper amount of support.

- ✪ You and your spouse each provide proof of your gross income.

- ✪ Taxes and other deductions are allowed to determine each of your *net resources*.

- ✪ The number of children you have is used to establish the percentage of net resources to be paid by the *noncustodial parent* (the *obligor*). This is done by reading the chart.

- ✪ The net resources of the noncustodial parent (the obligor) are multiplied by the percentage obtained from the chart to arrive at the amount of support to be paid by the parent without custody.

Of course, if payment of child support would create an economic hardship on the obligor and the custodial parent has sufficient resources to support the child, the judge may deviate from the guidelines and decrease the amount of child support to be paid by the obligor.

Gross income. The first thing you will need to do is determine your *gross income.* This is basically your income before any deductions for taxes, Social Security, etc. The following money sources are considered part of gross income:

- ✪ gross salary or wages;

- ✪ overtime, commissions, bonuses, allowances, tips;

✪ business income from self-employment, partnerships, corporations, and independent contracts (gross receipts minus ordinary and necessary expenses);

✪ disability benefits;

✪ workers' compensation;

✪ unemployment compensation;

✪ pension, retirement, or annuity payment;

✪ Social Security benefits;

✪ alimony received from a previous marriage;

✪ interest, dividends, and royalty income;

✪ income from trusts or estates;

✪ rental income (gross receipts minus ordinary and necessary expenses—but not depreciation);

✪ gains derived from dealings in property, unless the gain is non-recurring; and,

✪ reimbursed expenses to the extent they reduce living expenses (such as a rent allowance, or the value of an apartment, provided by your employer).

These categories are all listed in Schedule A of the **CHILD SUPPORT GUIDELINES WORKSHEET**. Fill out the Schedule A portion of form 4 as follows.

◈ Fill in the amounts for yourself and your spouse in Schedule A.

◈ Write in the totals on the line for "Step 1" on the first page of the form.

If you voluntarily reduce your income or quit your job, the judge can refuse to recognize the reduction or loss of income. This is called *imputed income*. This is income you do not really have, but are considered capable of having. The only exception is where you are required to take such an action to stay home and care for your child. If this question comes up, the judge will decide whether you needed to stay home, so be ready to explain your reasons.

Net resources. Net resources are determined by subtracting certain deductions (listed in Schedule B) from your gross income. The following deductions are allowed:

- ✪ federal income taxes (amount of the deduction will be based on withholding for a single person claiming one personal exemption and the standard deduction);

- ✪ Social Security and Medicare (FICA) or self-employment taxes;

- ✪ mandatory union dues (where you must pay dues to keep your job); and,

- ✪ health insurance payments for coverage of the children.

To fill out Schedule B of the **Child Support Guidelines Worksheet**, follow these steps.

- ◈ Fill in these deductions on Schedule B.

- ◈ Total the deductions, then write the totals on the line for "Step 2" on the first page.

- ◈ Your gross income minus these deductions will give your net resources. The same process should be used to determine your spouse's net resources. Write these figures in on the line for "Step 3" on the first page.

Once you determine the obligor's net resources, turn to the child support guidelines table, which is Schedule C of the **Child Support Guidelines Worksheet**.

⬥ Find the number of children who will receive support, and read across to get the percentage to be applied to the obligor's net resources. Enter this percentage in "Step 4."

⬥ Multiply the obligor's net resources by this percentage, which will give you the amount of child support.

Example:

If the obligor's net resources are $3,200 and there are two children who must be supported, the guideline amount of child support would be $800 per month ($3,200 x 25%).

There are several factors that may change the amount of child support ordered according to the guidelines explained above. The judge has the right to adjust the amount of support after taking into account the factors listed in Schedule D. Review Schedule D to determine whether any of the items listed apply to your situation.

In addition to child support payments, Texas law assumes that the court will order the parent who must pay child support to provide medical support, generally in the form of health insurance coverage, for the child. If the parent who is receiving child support provides health insurance for the child, the other parent must reimburse the paying parent for the amount of health insurance premium for the child.

ALIMONY

Texas law provides that temporary alimony, called *temporary support*, can be paid to a spouse after an **ORIGINAL PETITION FOR DIVORCE** has been filed, ending when the divorce becomes final. However, in order for temporary support to be ordered, it must be clearly shown that the receiving spouse is in financial need of such support.

Texas law also permits a court to authorize the payment of postdivorce alimony, called *maintenance*. The basic requirements are as follows.

✪ The parties must have been married at least ten years.

✪ The party seeking maintenance:

- lacks sufficient property to provide for his or her minimum needs because of an incapacitating physical or mental disability;

- is the custodian of a child who requires care because of a physical or mental disability; or,

- lacks the ability to earn sufficient income to provide a minimum level of support for him- or herself.

The amount of monthly maintenance cannot be more than $2,500 or 20% of the payor's income, whichever amount is less. Maintenance cannot be paid for longer than three years. It ends upon the death of either party or when the party receiving maintenance remarries.

Courts have the ability to enter withholding orders to ensure that the maintenance is paid. The court can enter an order directing that the payor's employer withhold the amount of maintenance from the payor's earnings and pay such amount to the agency designated by the court.

A request for maintenance should be included in the **ORIGINAL PETITION FOR DIVORCE**.

CHECKLIST FOR PARENTING PLAN

❏   Current addresses and telephone numbers of mother and father

❏   Calculation of child support and frequency of payment

❏   Wage withholding order

❏   Payment for health insurance

❏   Payment/apportionment of uninsured medical expenses

❏   Rights and duties of mother

❏   Rights and duties of father

❏   Special issues requiring agreement of both parents

❏   Visitation schedule

    ❏   Weekends

    ❏   Weekdays

    ❏   Spring Break

    ❏   Summer Vacation

Holidays

❏   Christmas (or other major religious holiday)

❏   Thanksgiving

❏   Father's Day

❏   Mother's Day

❏   Child's birthday

Special visitation provisions

❑ Additional parenting time

❑ Makeup for missed visitation

❑ General rules regarding visitation

❑ Place of pickup and return

❑ Child's personal effects

❑ Persons permitted to pick up and return child

❑ Notification provisions

❑ Special provisions regarding visitation as child attains certain ages

❑ Dispute resolution procedure

❑ Verified statement of income

❑ Verified statement of good faith and best interests of children

CHECKLIST FOR PROPERTY DIVISION, CUSTODY, AND ALIMONY

❏ Collect financial information, including assets and debts

❏ Identify property that is your separate property, your spouse's separate property, and community property

❏ Complete a **PROPERTY INVENTORY**

❏ Prepare a proposal regarding division of property

❏ When making the property division proposal, consider the tax consequences of the division

❏ Determine whether you and your spouse can put your personal differences aside and serve as joint custodians of your children

❏ Determine whether the best interests of your children would be served by living with you

❏ Draft a **PARENTING PLAN** to share with your spouse or propose to the court (use the *Checklist for Parenting Plan*)

❏ Calculate child support in accordance with the attorney general's guidelines

❏ Determine whether you qualify for alimony

❏ Determine whether you need temporary alimony until the divorce is final

Lawyers

Whether or not you need an attorney will depend upon many factors, including how comfortable you feel handling the matter yourself, whether your situation is more complicated than usual, how much opposition you get from your spouse, and whether your spouse has an attorney. It may also be advisable to hire an attorney if you encounter a judge with a hostile attitude or if your spouse gets a lawyer who wants to fight. There are no court-appointed lawyers in divorce cases, so if you want an attorney, you will have to hire one.

A very general rule is that you should consider hiring an attorney whenever you reach a point where you no longer feel comfortable representing yourself. This point will vary greatly with each person, so there is no easy way to be more definite.

A more appropriate question is, *do you want a lawyer?* The next section will discuss some of the pros and cons of hiring a lawyer, as well as some of the things you may want to consider in making this decision.

DECIDING IF YOU WANT A LAWYER

One of the first questions you will want to consider, and most likely the reason you are reading this book, is, *how much will an attorney cost?* Attorneys come in all ages, shapes, sizes, sexes, racial and ethnic groups—and price ranges. For a very rough estimate, you can expect an attorney to charge anywhere from $150 to $1,000 for an uncontested divorce, and from $800 and up for a contested divorce. Lawyers usually charge an hourly rate for contested divorces, ranging from about $75 to $300 per hour. Most new (and therefore, less expensive) attorneys would be quite capable of handling a simple divorce, but if your situation became more complicated, you would probably prefer a more experienced lawyer.

Advantages to Hiring a Lawyer

Some advantages to hiring a lawyer include the following.

✪ Judges and other attorneys may take you more seriously if you have an attorney represent you. Most judges prefer both parties to have attorneys. They feel this helps the case move in a more orderly fashion, because both sides will know the procedures and relevant issues. Persons representing themselves often waste a lot of time on matters that have absolutely no bearing on the outcome of the case.

✪ A lawyer will serve as a *buffer* between you and your spouse. This can lead to a quicker passage through the system by reducing the chance for emotions to take control and confuse the issues.

✪ Attorneys prefer to deal with other attorneys for the same reasons listed above. However, if you become familiar with this book and conduct yourself in a calm and proper manner, you should have no trouble. (Proper courtroom manners are discussed in Chapter 6.)

✪ You can let your lawyer worry about all of the details. By having an attorney, you only need to become generally familiar with the contents of this book. It will be your attorney's job to file the proper papers in the correct form, and to deal with the court clerk, the judge, the process server, your spouse, and your spouse's attorney.

✪ Lawyers provide professional assistance with problems. In the event your case is complicated or suddenly becomes complicated, it is an advantage to have an attorney who is familiar with your case. It can also be comforting to have a lawyer you can turn to for advice and to get your questions answered.

Advantages to Representing Yourself

Some advantages to representing yourself include the following.

✪ Sometimes judges feel more sympathetic toward a person not represented by an attorney. This may result in the unrepresented person being allowed a certain amount of leeway with the procedural rules.

✪ The procedure may be faster. Two of the most frequent complaints about lawyers received by the bar association involve delay in completing the case and failure to return phone calls. Most lawyers have a heavy caseload, which sometimes results in cases being neglected for various periods of time. If you are following the progress of your own case, you will be able to push it along the system diligently.

✪ Selecting any attorney is not easy. As the next section shows, it is hard to know whether you are selecting an attorney you will be happy with.

Middle Ground

You may want to look for an attorney who will be willing to accept an hourly fee to answer your questions and give you help as you need it. This way, you will save some legal costs, but still get professional assistance.

SELECTING A LAWYER

Selecting a lawyer is a two-step process. First, you need to decide with which attorneys to make an appointment. Then, you need to decide if you want to hire one of those attorneys.

Finding a Lawyer

There are several ways to go about finding a lawyer.

Ask a friend. A common, and frequently the best, way to find a lawyer is to ask someone you know to recommend one to you. This is especially helpful if the lawyer represented your friend in a divorce or other family law matter.

Use a lawyer referral service. You can find a referral service by looking in the Yellow Pages phone directory under "Attorney Referral Services" or "Attorneys." This is a service, usually operated by a bar association, that is designed to match a client with an attorney handling cases in the area of law the client needs. The referral service does not guarantee the quality of work, or the level of experience or ability, of the attorney. Finding a lawyer this way will at least connect you with one who is interested in divorce and family law matters.

Check the Yellow Pages. Check under the heading for "Attorneys" in the Yellow Pages phone directory. Many lawyers and law firms place display ads here, indicating their areas of practice and educational backgrounds. Look for firms or lawyers that indicate they practice in areas such as divorce, family law, or domestic relations.

Ask another lawyer. If you have used the services of an attorney in the past for some other matter (for example, a real estate closing, traffic ticket, or will), you may want to call and ask if he or she could refer you to an attorney whose ability in the area of family law is respected.

Search the Internet. The Internet sites **www.lawyers.com**, **www.martindale.com**, and **www.attorneystore.com** may be useful as you search for a lawyer that can help you.

Evaluating a Lawyer

From your search, you should select three to five lawyers worthy of further consideration. Your first step will be to call each attorney's office. Explain that you are interested in seeking a divorce, and ask the following questions.

- ✪ Does the attorney (or firm) handle this type of matter?

- ✪ How much can you expect it to cost?

- ✪ How soon can you get an appointment?

If you like the answers you get, ask if you can speak to the attorney. Some offices will permit this, but others will require you to make an appointment. Make the appointment if that is what is required. Once you get in contact with the attorney (either on the phone or at the appointment), ask the following questions.

- ✪ How much will it cost?

- ✪ How will the fee be paid?

- ✪ How long has the attorney been in practice?

- ✪ How long has the attorney been in practice in Texas?

- ✪ What percentage of the attorney's cases involve divorce cases or other family law matters? (Do not expect an exact answer, but you should get a rough estimate that is at least 20%.)

- ✪ How long will it take? (Do not expect an exact answer, but the attorney should be able to give you an average range and discuss things that may make a difference.)

If you get acceptable answers to these questions, it is time to ask yourself the following questions about the lawyer.

- ✪ Do you feel comfortable talking to the lawyer?

- ✪ Is the lawyer friendly toward you?

- ✪ Does the lawyer seem confident in him- or herself?

- ✪ Does the lawyer seem to be straightforward with you and able to explain things so you understand?

If you get satisfactory answers to all of these questions, you probably have a lawyer you will be able to work with. Most clients are happiest with an attorney they feel comfortable with.

WORKING WITH A LAWYER

In general, you will work best with your attorney if you keep an open, honest, and friendly attitude. You should also consider the following suggestions.

Ask Questions

If you want to know something or if you do not understand something, ask your attorney. If you do not understand the answer, tell your attorney and ask him or her to explain it again. There are many points of law that even many lawyers do not fully understand, so you should not be embarrassed to ask questions.

Many people who say they had a bad experience with a lawyer either did not ask enough questions or had a lawyer who would not take the time to explain things to them. If your lawyer is not taking the time to explain what he or she is doing, it may be time to look for a new lawyer.

Give Your Lawyer Complete Information

Anything you tell your attorney is confidential. An attorney can lose his or her license to practice if he or she reveals information without your permission—so do not hold back. Tell your lawyer everything, even if it does not seem important to you. There are many things that seem unimportant to a non-attorney, but can change the outcome of a case.

Also, do not hold something back because you are afraid it will hurt your case. It will definitely hurt your case if your lawyer does not find out about it until he or she hears it in court from your spouse's attorney. If your lawyer knows in advance, he or she can plan to eliminate or reduce damage to your case.

Accept Reality

Listen to what your lawyer tells you about the law and the system. It will do you no good to argue with your attorney about the law or the system not working the way you think it should. If your lawyer tells you that the judge cannot hear your case for two weeks, do not demand that he or she set a hearing tomorrow.

By refusing to accept reality, you are only setting yourself up for disappointment. It is not your attorney's fault that the system is not perfect or that the law does not say what you would like it to say.

Be Patient   Try to be patient with the system (which is often slow, as was discussed earlier) and with your attorney. Do not expect your lawyer to return your phone call within an hour. Your lawyer may not even be able to return your call the same day. Most lawyers are very busy and often overworked. It is rare that an attorney can maintain a full caseload and still make each client feel as if he or she is the only client.

Talk to the Secretary   Your lawyer's secretary can be a valuable source of information, so be friendly and get to know him or her. The secretary will often be able to answer your questions, and you will not get a bill for this time.

Let Your Attorney Deal with Your Spouse   It is your lawyer's job to communicate with your spouse or with your spouse's lawyer. Let your lawyer do his or her job. Many lawyers have clients who lose or damage their cases when they decide to say or do something on their own.

Be on Time   Be on time—both to appointments with your lawyer and to court hearings.

Keep Your Case Moving   Many lawyers operate on the old principle of the *squeaking wheel gets the oil*. Work on a case tends to get put off until a deadline is near, an emergency develops, or the client calls. There is a reason for this. Many lawyers take more cases than can be effectively handled in order to earn the income they desire. Your task is to become a squeaking wheel that does not squeak so much that it becomes annoying. Whenever you talk to your lawyer, ask the following questions.

- ✪ What is the next step?

- ✪ When do you expect it to be done?

- ✪ When should I talk to you next?

If you do not hear from the lawyer when you expect, call him or her the following day. Do not remind your lawyer that he or she did not call—just ask how things are going.

Save Money   Of course, you do not want to spend unnecessary money for an attorney. The following are a few things you can do to avoid excess legal fees.

✪ Do not make unnecessary phone calls to your lawyer.

✪ Give information to the secretary whenever possible.

✪ Direct your question to the secretary first. He or she will refer your question to the attorney, if necessary.

✪ Plan your phone calls so you can get to the point and take less of your attorney's time.

✪ Do some of the legwork yourself. For example, pick up and deliver papers yourself. Ask your attorney what you can do to assist with your case.

✪ Be prepared for appointments. Have all related papers with you, plan your visit to get to the point, and make an outline of what you want to discuss and what questions you want to ask.

Pay Your Attorney Bill When It is Due

No client gets prompt attention like a client who pays his or her lawyer on time. However, you are entitled to an itemized bill, showing what the attorney did and how much time it took. Many attorneys will have you sign an agreement that states how you will be charged, what is included in the hourly fee, and what is extra. Review your bill carefully. There are numerous stories of people paying an attorney $500 or $1,000 in advance, only to have the attorney make a few phone calls to the spouse's lawyer, then ask for more money. If your attorney asks for $500 or $1,000 in advance, be sure that you and the lawyer agree on what is to be done for this fee. For $500, you should at least expect to have a petition prepared, filed with the court, and served on your spouse (although the filing and service fees will probably be extra).

FIRING YOUR LAWYER

If you find that you no longer can work with your lawyer, or do not trust your lawyer, it is time to either go at it alone or get a new attorney. You will need to send your lawyer a letter stating that you no longer desire his or her services and are discharging him or her from your case. Also, state that you will be coming by his or her office the following day to pick up your file.

The attorney does not have to give you his or her own notes or other work in progress, but he or she must give you the essential contents of your file (such as copies of papers already filed or prepared and billed for, as well as any documents you provided). If your attorney refuses to give you your file for any reason, contact the Texas Bar Association about filing a complaint or grievance against the lawyer. Of course, you will need to settle any remaining charges.

CHECKLIST FOR HIRING A LAWYER

Ask yourself the following questions to help determine whether you need a lawyer.

- ❏ Am I comfortable reading the law and completing court papers without help?

- ❏ Am I comfortable speaking up for myself?

- ❏ Am I intimidated by judges or lawyers?

The following questions should be considered when deciding which lawyer to hire.

- ❏ Does the lawyer have experience in divorce, child custody, and child support cases?

- ❏ Does the lawyer have a good reputation in the community?

- ❏ Does the lawyer have any special credentials?

- ❏ How much will the attorney charge and when must the fee be paid?

- ❏ How long will the case take from start to finish?

- ❏ Does the attorney keep you informed of what is happening in the case?

- ❏ Does the attorney answer your questions?

General Procedures

Once you have decided that you want to proceed with a divorce, forms must be prepared and filed with the court. Most of the information you have collected, such as asset and debt information, as well as estimates of child support, will not be included in the initial forms filed with the court. However, this information is very important for you to have a general idea of what you will be asking the court to award to you when the divorce is final.

INTRODUCTION TO LEGAL FORMS

The forms in this book are modeled after forms widely used by attorneys in Texas. Court clerks and judges are familiar with these forms and are not likely to object to them. The forms in this book are legally correct; however, one occasionally encounters a troublesome clerk or judge who is very particular about how he or she wants the forms. If you encounter any problem with the forms in this book being accepted by the clerk or judge, you can try one or more of the following.

✪ Ask the clerk or judge what is wrong with your form, then try to change it to suit the clerk or judge.

✪ Ask the clerk or judge if the local bar association has forms available. If forms are available, find out where you can get them, and then use them. The instructions in this book will still help you to fill them out.

✪ Consult an attorney.

Although the instructions in this book will tell you to type in certain information, it is not absolutely necessary to use a typewriter. If typing is not possible, you can print the information required in the forms. Just be sure your handwriting can be easily read, or the clerk may not accept your papers for filing.

Each form in this book is referred to by both the title of the form and a form number. Be sure to check the form number, because some of the forms have similar titles. The form number is found in the top outside corner of the first page of each form. Also, a list of the forms, by both number and name, is found at the beginning of Appendix B.

You will notice that most of the forms in Appendix B of this book have the same heading. The forms without this heading are not filed with the court, but are for your use only. The top portion of these court forms will all be completed in the same manner.

The heading at the very top of the form states which court your case is filed in. Complete the following steps to fill in the heading.

◈ Type in, on the right hand side of the heading, the number of the *judicial district* and the *county* in which the court is located. (You can either look in the phone book or call the court clerk's office to find out your court's district number.)

◈ Next, type your full name and your spouse's on the lines at the left side of the form, below the words, "In the Matter of the Marriage of." Do not use nicknames or shortened versions of the names. You should use the names as they appear on your marriage license, if possible.

✦   If you have minor children, include the words "And in the interests of" under your and your spouse's names, and type the names of the children under that phrase.

You will not be able to type in a *case number* at the top until after you file your petition with the clerk. The clerk will assign a case number and will write it on your petition and any other papers you file with it. You must include the case number on all papers you file later.

When completed, the top portion of your forms should look something like the following.

NO. _____

IN THE MATTER OF	§	IN THE DISTRICT COURT
THE MARRIAGE OF	§	
	§	
_____Rhett Butler_____	§	
	§	
AND	§	
	§	
Scarlett O' Hara Butler	§	_Thirteenth_ JUDICIAL DISTRICT
	§	
AND IN THE INTERESTS OF	§	
	§	
_____	§	
	§	
_____, and	§	
	§	
_____	§	
MINOR CHILDREN	§	___Windy___ COUNTY, TEXAS

FILING WITH THE COURT CLERK

Once you have decided which forms you need and have them all prepared, it is time to file your case with the court clerk. First, make at least three copies of each form (the original for the clerk, one copy for yourself, one for your spouse, and one extra just in case the clerk asks for two copies or you decide to hire an attorney later).

Filing is actually about as simple as making a bank deposit, although some additional information will help things go smoothly. Call the court clerk's office. You can find the phone number under the county government section of your phone directory. Ask the clerk the following questions (along with any other questions that come to mind).

○ Where is the clerk's office located?

○ What are their hours?

○ How much is the filing fee for a dissolution of marriage?

○ Does the court have any special forms that need to be filed with the petition? (If there are special forms that do not appear in this book, then you will need to go down to the clerk's office and pick them up. There may be a fee, so be sure to ask.)

○ How many copies of the petition and other forms need to be filed with the clerk?

Next, take your petition and any other forms you determine you need to the clerk's office. The clerk handles many different types of cases, so be sure to look for signs telling you which office or window to go to. You should be looking for signs that say something similar to *Family Court*, *Family Section*, or *Filing*. If it is too confusing, ask someone where you file a petition for divorce.

Once you have found the right place, simply hand the papers to the clerk and say, "I would like to file this." The clerk will examine the papers, then do one of two things—either accept it for filing (and either collect the filing fee or direct you to where to pay it) or tell you that something is not correct.

If you are told something is wrong, ask the clerk to explain to you what is wrong and how to correct the problem. Although clerks are not permitted to give legal advice, the types of problems they spot are usually very minor things that they can tell you how to correct. It is often possible to figure out how to correct it from the way they explain what is wrong.

NOTIFYING YOUR SPOUSE

If you and your spouse are in agreement about everything, you do not need to worry about the information in this section. Your spouse will sign a **WAIVER OF CITATION** (form 11, p.207) and file this with the court. However, if you and your spouse are not in agreement, you are required to notify your spouse that you have filed for divorce. This gives your spouse a chance to respond to your petition. If you are unable to find your spouse, you will also need to read Chapter 10.

Notice of Filing the Petition
The usual way to notify your spouse that you filed for a divorce is called *personal service*, which is where the sheriff or someone else designated by the judge personally delivers the papers to your spouse.

Personal service is usually requested in the **ORIGINAL PETITION**. A separate paragraph is included in the petition, and contains the residence or business address where you want service to be attempted on your spouse. The fee for personal service will be included in the original filing fee for the petition. When you ask the clerk for information about the filing fee for the petition, also ask what the additional fee is for personal service. The filing fee for the petition can range from $150 to $185. The fee for personal service can range from $40 to $60 if done by the sheriff or constable, and $50 to $70 if done by a private process server.

A sheriff's deputy will personally deliver the papers to your spouse. The deputy will fill out a form to verify that the papers were delivered (including the date and time they were delivered), and will file a copy of that form with the court clerk.

Other Notices
Once your spouse has been served with the petition, you may simply mail him or her copies of any papers you file later. All you need to do is sign a statement (called a **CERTIFICATE OF SERVICE**) that you mailed copies to your spouse. Some of the forms in this book will have a **CERTIFICATE OF SERVICE** for you to complete. If any form you file does not contain one, you will need to complete the **CERTIFICATE OF SERVICE**. (see form 25, p.247.)

Follow these steps to complete the **Certificate of Service**:

◈ Complete the top portion according to the instructions in the first section of this chapter on page 61.

◈ Type in the name or title of the papers being sent on the first line of the main paragraph.

◈ Type in your spouse's name (or your spouse's attorney's name if he or she has an attorney) on the second line in that paragraph.

◈ Indicate how the papers are being sent (mail or hand-delivery) by crossing out whichever does not apply.

◈ Type in the date the papers are being sent. Be sure to deliver or mail them on the date you provide.

◈ Sign your name on the line marked "Name." This form is to be filed with the court clerk as your proof that you sent a copy to your spouse or your spouse's attorney.

Preliminary or temporary matters. When a hearing date is obtained on preliminary matters or temporary orders, you will need to notify your spouse of the date of the hearing. This is generally done by sending a letter to your spouse by personal delivery or certified mail. A **Notice of Hearing for Temporary Orders** (form 24, p.245) may be used when temporary alimony or temporary child support is requested from the court.

Complete the **Notice of Hearing for Temporary Orders** as follows.

◈ Fill in the heading as instructed on page 61.

◈ Type in your spouse's name, the address of the court, and the date and time of the hearing on the appropriate lines in the main paragraph.

The judge will sign the form, and a copy will be sent to your spouse.

General matters. A general **NOTICE OF HEARING** (form 30, p.257) is included in Appendix B and can be changed to fit the particular circumstances, such as whether it is a hearing on a motion, a final hearing, and so on. Fill it in the same way as the **NOTICE OF HEARING FOR TEMPORARY ORDERS**, except indicate the purpose of the hearing on the last line of the main paragraph.

SETTING A COURT HEARING

When you file your petition, the clerk will generally assign a hearing date that is sixty days from the date of filing. If there are any preliminary matters that require a hearing, the judge's clerk will assign a hearing date.

When you get a hearing date, be sure to ask the clerk where the hearing will be held. You will need the street address of the courthouse, as well as the room number, floor, or other location within the building.

COURTROOM MANNERS

There are certain rules of procedure that are used in court. These are really the rules of good conduct or good manners, and are designed to keep things orderly. Many of the rules are written down, although some are unwritten customs that have just developed over many years. They are not difficult, and most of them make sense. Following these suggestions will make the judge respect you for your maturity and professional manner, and possibly even make him or her forget for a moment that you are not a lawyer. It will also increase the likelihood that you will get the things you request.

Show Respect for the Judge

Do not do anything to make the judge angry at you, such as arguing with him or her. Be polite, and call the judge *Your Honor* when you speak to him or her, such as *Yes, Your Honor,* or *Your Honor, I brought proof of my income.* Although many lawyers address judges as *Judge,* this is not proper. Many of the rules relate to showing respect for the court. This means wearing appropriate clothing, such as a coat and tie for men and a dress for women. This especially means no T-shirts, blue jeans, shorts, or revealing clothing.

Listen to the Judge

Any time the judge is talking, you need to be listening carefully. Even if the judge interrupts you, stop talking immediately and listen.

Only One Person Can Talk at a Time

Each person is allotted his or her own time to talk in court. The judge can only listen to one person at a time, so do not interrupt your spouse when it is his or her turn. As difficult as it may be, stop talking if your spouse interrupts you. (Let the judge tell your spouse to keep quiet and let you have your say.)

Talk to the Judge, Not to Your Spouse

Many people get in front of a judge and begin arguing with each other. They actually turn away from the judge, face each other, and begin arguing as if they are in the room alone. This generally has several negative results. The judge cannot understand what either one is saying, since they both start talking at once. They both look like fools for losing control, and the judge gets angry with both of them. Whenever you speak in a courtroom, look only at the judge. Try to pretend that your spouse is not there. Remember, you are there to convince the judge that you should have certain things. You do not need to convince your spouse.

Talk Only When It is Your Turn

The usual procedure is for you to present your case first. When you are done saying all you came to say, your spouse will have a chance to say whatever he or she came to say. Let your spouse have his or her say. When he or she is finished, you will get another chance to respond to what has been said.

Stick to the Subject

Many people cannot resist the temptation to get off track and start telling the judge all the problems with their marriage over the past twenty years. This just wastes time and aggravates the judge. Stick to the subject and answer the judge's questions simply and to the point.

Keep Calm

Judges like things to go smoothly in their courtrooms. They do not like shouting, name calling, crying, or other displays of emotion. Generally, judges do not like family law cases because they get too emotionally charged. Give your judge a pleasant surprise by keeping calm and focusing on the issues.

Show Respect for Your Spouse

Even if you do not respect your spouse, act like you do. All you have to do is refer to your spouse as *Mr. Smith* or *Ms. Smith* (using his or her correct name, of course).

NEGOTIATING SETTLEMENTS

It is beyond the scope and ability of this book to fully present a course in negotiation techniques. However, a few basic rules may be of some help.

Ask for More Than You Want

Asking for more than you want always gives you some room to compromise by giving up a few things and ending up with close to what you really want.

Property. With property division, this means you will review your **PROPERTY INVENTORY** (form 1, p.165) and decide which items you really want, would like to have, and do not care much about. Also, try to figure out which items your spouse really wants, would like to have, and does not care much about. At the beginning, you will say that you want certain things. Your list will include:

- ✪ everything you really want;

- ✪ everything you would like to have;

- ✪ the things you do not care about; and,

- ✪ the things you think your spouse really wants or would like to have.

Once you find out what is on your spouse's list, you begin trading items. Generally, you try to give your spouse things that he or she really wants and that you do not care about, in return for your spouse giving you the items you really care about and would like to have.

Child custody. Generally, child custody tends to be something that cannot be negotiated. It is more often used as a threat by one of the parties in order to get something else, such as more of the property or lower child support. If the real issue is one of these other matters, do not be concerned by a threat of a custody fight. In these cases, the other party probably does not really want custody and will not fight for it. If the real issue is custody, you will not be able to negotiate for it and will end up letting the judge decide anyway.

Child support. If you will be receiving child support, you should first work out what you think the judge will order based upon the child support guidelines discussed in Chapter 4. Then, you should ask for more and negotiate down to what the guidelines call for. If your spouse will not settle for something very close to the guidelines, give up trying to work it out and let the judge decide.

When you negotiate child support, you should also negotiate whether you or your spouse will be entitled to report the child on the federal income tax return as a dependent. The exemption for your child can make a significant difference in the amount of federal income tax you pay. When you and your spouse agree on who will claim the child on his or her income tax return, the appropriate form supplied by the Internal Revenue Service should be signed by each spouse and filed with the tax return of the spouse claiming the exemption. Use the **Release of Claim to Exemption for Child of Divorced or Separated Parents** to make the claim. (see form 33, p.265.)

Let Your Spouse Start the Bidding	A general negotiation rule is that the first person to mention a dollar figure loses. Whether it is a child support figure or the value of a piece of property, try to get your spouse to name the amount he or she thinks it should be first. If your spouse starts with a figure close to what you had in mind, it will be much easier to get to your figure. If your spouse begins with a figure far from yours, you know how far in the other direction to begin your bid.
Give Your Spouse Time to Think and Worry	Your spouse is probably just as afraid as you about the possibility of losing to the judge's decision and would like to settle. Do not be afraid to state your final offer, then walk away. Give your spouse a day or two to think it over. Maybe he or she will call back and make a better offer. If not, you can always reconsider and make a different offer in a few days. Do not be too willing to do this, or your spouse may think you will give in even more.
Know Your Bottom Line	Before you begin negotiation, try to set a point that you will not go beyond. If you have decided that there are four items of property that you absolutely must have, and your spouse is only willing to agree to let you have three, it is time to end the bargaining session and go home.

Remember What You Have Learned

By the time you have read this far, you should be aware of two things.

1. The judge will roughly divide your property equally.

2. The judge will probably come close to the guidelines in assigning child support.

This awareness should give you an approximate idea of how things will turn out if the judge is asked to decide these issues, and it should help you set your bottom line on them.

Texas has recently enacted *collaborative law* statutes addressing divorce, child support, and custody. These statutes are a means by which parties and their attorneys can develop their own solutions to the issues presented by the divorce, including spousal maintenance, property division, custody, visitation, and support of minor children of the marriage. Collaborative law involves the written agreement of both spouses and their attorneys to work toward resolution of the issues, and, failing agreement, withdrawal of the attorneys from further involvement in the case, and the hiring of new attorneys.

While these statutes do not directly affect individuals who are representing themselves in a divorce, they illustrate the strong sentiment of the Texas legislature and Texas courts to resolve cases prior to trial. Many times, when individuals represent themselves, the courts will suggest that mediation rather than trial be used as the method to resolve the issues between the parties.

CHECKLIST FOR GENERAL PREPARATION

❑   Complete all of the necessary forms

❑   Check with the county clerk to find out what the filing fee is

❑   Make extra copies of the forms to have a copy for your file and a copy give to your spouse

❑   Have your spouse sign a **WAIVER OF CITATION** or notify your spouse that you have filed for divorce

❑   If you have to notify your spouse, make sure you have a current address for him or her

❑   If there needs to be a hearing for temporary alimony, temporary custody, or temporary child support, prepare the appropriate **NOTICE OF HEARING**

❑   Familiarize yourself with the court's procedures and how to behave in the courtroom

Uncontested Divorce Procedure

This chapter provides a general overview of the standard, uncontested divorce procedure. Chapter 8 discusses contested divorce procedures in detail.

CONTESTED OR UNCONTESTED DIVORCE

For purposes of this book, a *contested* case is where you and your spouse will be doing your arguing in court, and will be leaving the decision to the judge. An *uncontested* case is where you will do your arguing and deciding before court, and the judge will only be approving your decision.

Example:

A new client comes in, saying she wants to file for divorce. She has discussed it with her husband, and it will be a *simple, uncontested* divorce. Once the papers are filed, the husband and wife begin arguing over a few items of property. The lawyer then spends a lot of time negotiating with the husband. After much arguing, an agreement is finally reached. The case will proceed in the court as *uncontested*, but only after a lot of contesting out of court.

You probably will not know if you are going to have a contested case until you try the uncontested route and fail. Therefore, the following sections are presented mostly to assist you in attempting the uncontested case. Chapter 8 specifically discusses the contested case.

There are actually two ways that a case can be considered *uncontested*. One is where you and your spouse reach an agreement on every issue in the divorce. To be in this situation, you must be in agreement on the following points:

❂   how your property is to be divided;

❂   how your debts are to be divided;

❂   which of you will have custody of the children; and,

❂   how much child support is to be paid by the person who does not have custody.

The other type of uncontested case is where your spouse simply does not respond to the petition. If you have your spouse served by the sheriff (as described in Chapter 6), and he or she does not respond, you will need to file certain forms.

To begin your divorce case, you should file an **ORIGINAL PETITION FOR DIVORCE** with the court clerk. Various forms of the petition are included in Appendix B for your use, depending on what particular circumstances apply. (see forms 5–10.) This will be discussed in greater detail later in this chapter.

It may be necessary to file other forms either with your petition or prior to the final hearing. The following forms will be prepared in advance, but will not be filed until the final hearing.

❑   **DECREE OF DIVORCE** (form 17, 18, or 19)

❑   **STATEMENT OF EVIDENCE** (form 21 or 22)

❑   **ORDER WITHHOLDING FROM EARNINGS FOR CHILD SUPPORT** (if you have children) (form 20)

The following sections give instructions for when you need each form, and how to complete it.

PETITION FOR DIVORCE

An **ORIGINAL PETITION FOR DIVORCE** must be completed in all cases. The petition is simply the paper you file with the court to begin your case and to ask the judge to give you a divorce. The particular form to be used will depend upon your particular circumstances. For instance, forms 5, 6, 7, or 8 will be used if there are no minor children involved. The differences between these forms deal with the way by which you notify your spouse and whether you request temporary alimony.

Use form 5 if you and your spouse are in agreement about everything. (see form 5, p.191.) If form 5 is used, you must also file a **WAIVER OF CITATION**. (see form 11, p.207.)

Use form 6 if you request that your spouse be notified of the divorce case by personal service (discussed in Chapter 6). (see form 6, p.193.)

Use form 7 if you cannot locate your spouse. (see form 7, p.195.) This is discussed in greater detail in Chapter 10.

Use form 8 if you are asking the court to order your spouse to pay you temporary alimony until the divorce becomes final. (see form 8, p.197.) Paragraph II of form 8 provides for personal service of the petition. If your spouse cannot be located, this form must be adapted (using the language contained in paragraph II of form 8), and you must use the procedure discussed in Chapter 10.

Use form 9 if you and your spouse have minor children and you are asking the court to order your spouse to pay temporary child support until the divorce becomes final. (see form 9, p.199.) Paragraph II of form 9 provides for personal service of the petition. If your spouse cannot be located, form 10 should be used following the procedure outlined in Chapter 10. (see form 10, p.203.)

When there are minor children involved but you do not request that the judge order temporary child support, form 9 should be changed to delete the request for temporary orders. This generally occurs when you and your spouse have made arrangements between yourselves regarding the payment of child support.

A temporary **PARENTING PLAN** should be submitted with any **ORIGINAL PETITION FOR DIVORCE** filed with the court that involves a request for temporary custody of the children.

No matter which form you use, if you are requesting that your spouse pay alimony (called *maintenance* in Texas) after the **DECREE OF DIVORCE** (see forms 17–19) is entered by the court, you must adapt your **ORIGINAL PETITION FOR DIVORCE** to include a request for maintenance. The added language is included on pages 83–84.

Maintenance after a **DECREE OF DIVORCE** is only possible in a few narrow situations. You will notice that there are alternative paragraphs that can be used for each of these situations. Choose the paragraph that best suits your situation. Pages 83–84 also have the wording that must be added to your **DECREE OF DIVORCE** if the judge grants your request for maintenance.

To complete any of the **ORIGINAL PETITION FOR DIVORCE** forms, use the following instructions.

- ◈ Complete the top portion of the form according to the instructions in Chapter 6, page 61.

- ◈ Fill in your name, Social Security number, age, and county of residence as the "Petitioner" in the spaces in the top paragraph beneath the heading.

- ◈ Fill in your spouse's name, Social Security number, age, and county of residence (if known) as "Respondent" in the appropriate spaces in the same paragraph.

- ◈ In paragraph I, fill in the county of your residence for the past six months.

◈ In paragraph II, choose how notice is to be given to your spouse. (It is already designated in forms 6, 7, 9, and 10.)

◈ In paragraph III, indicate the date and place of your marriage, and the date on which you and your spouse stopped living together. If you and your spouse have not separated, cross out the words in the brackets.

◈ In paragraph IV, state the name, birth date, residence, and Social Security number of each minor child, if there are any (forms 9 and 10 only).

◈ If you are requesting that your name be changed back to what it was prior to your marriage, indicate your full name as you wish it to be after your divorce in paragraph VI.

◈ In paragraph VII, you must state whether or not a protective order has been entered against one of the parties to the divorce. If a protective order has been entered, you must supply the court with a copy of the order.

◈ On the last page, sign your name under "Respectfully submitted," and type your name, address, and phone number on the lines provided.

Miscellaneous Petition Requirements

If you are requesting that temporary support be paid until the divorce becomes final, you will need to provide the court with convincing evidence of your spouse's income. This can often be obtained from the documents you collected to complete the **PROPERTY INVENTORY**. (see form 1, p.165.)

If you have no convincing evidence of income, the best procedure is to obtain a *subpoena duces tecum* for employment records. An **ATTACHMENT TO SUBPOENA** (form 28, p.253) is an exhibit that identifies the records you need. You will request that a subpoena be issued when you file the **ORIGINAL PETITION FOR DIVORCE** and attach the **ATTACHMENT TO SUBPOENA** to it. This will be discussed in greater detail in Chapter 8.

If you are requesting that temporary support be paid, you should include a **NOTICE OF HEARING** (form 30, p.257) with your petition. This will be completed by the court clerk when you file your **ORIGINAL PETITION FOR DIVORCE**.

If you are asking that the court order maintenance to be paid after the divorce becomes final, you will need to request this and provide the court with convincing evidence that you cannot support yourself and need the assistance from your spouse.

Your **ORIGINAL PETITION FOR DIVORCE** is now ready for filing. Take it to the courthouse and follow the procedure for filing as explained in Chapter 6.

WAIVER OF CITATION

If your spouse agrees to everything that you are asking the court to do, your spouse should file a **WAIVER OF CITATION** (form 11, p.207) with the court.

Follow these directions to complete the **WAIVER OF CITATION**.

- ◈ Complete the top portion of the form according to the instructions in Chapter 6, page 61.

- ◈ Type in your spouse's name in the blank space in the first paragraph.

- ◈ Type in your spouse's name and address in the second paragraph.

- ◈ Have your spouse sign the line directly under "Respectfully submitted" in the presence of a notary public. Have the notary public complete the rest of the form.

The **WAIVER OF CITATION** should not be signed and dated before the date on which the **ORIGINAL PETITION FOR DIVORCE** is filed with the court. The **WAIVER OF CITATION** can be filed with the court at any time after the **ORIGINAL PETITION FOR DIVORCE** is filed.

ANSWER

If you and your spouse agree on everything and your spouse files a **WAIVER OF CITATION**, you do not need to file a **RESPONDENT'S ORIGINAL ANSWER**. (see form 13, p.211.) However, if your spouse does not agree with everything, a **RESPONDENT'S ORIGINAL ANSWER** should be filed with the court.

Complete the **RESPONDENT'S ORIGINAL ANSWER** as follows.

◈ Complete the top portion of the form according to the instructions in Chapter 6, page 61.

◈ Type in your spouse's name in the blank space in the first paragraph.

◈ Type in your spouse's name, address, and phone number where indicated at the bottom of the form.

◈ Have your spouse sign the line directly under the words "Respectfully submitted."

◈ Have your spouse sign the line directly under the statement on the alternative dispute resolution.

MARITAL SETTLEMENT AGREEMENT

If you and your spouse agree on the division of your assets, you may prepare a **MARITAL SETTLEMENT AGREEMENT**. (see form 26, p.249.) This spells out how your property and debts will be divided.

Complete the **MARITAL SETTLEMENT AGREEMENT** as follows.

◈ Complete the top portion according to the instructions in Chapter 6, page 61.

◈ Type in your name, your spouse's name, and your Social Security numbers, ages, and counties of residence in the appropriate spaces in the first (unnumbered) paragraph.

◈ In paragraph I, type in the county in which you have resided for the ninety days preceding the date when you filed the petition.

◈ Type in the date of your marriage, the city and state where you were married, and the date of your separation in paragraph II. If you and your spouse have not separated, cross out the words in the brackets.

◈ In paragraph V, list the items of property to be kept by the person designated as the *Petitioner* (this is the person whose name appears first in the case style heading, which will probably be you). Be as specific as possible in describing the items. You do not need to include every little item in the house, but you should include all major items.

◈ In paragraph VI, list the items the *Respondent* (your spouse) will keep.

◈ In paragraph VII, list the debts the petitioner will pay.

◈ In paragraph VIII, list the debts the respondent will pay.

◈ After the paragraph beginning with the word "WHEREFORE," type in you and your spouse's names, addresses, and telephone numbers where indicated.

◈ Take this form to a notary public, and sign your names before the notary. The notary public will complete the rest of the form. There are two notary spaces on the last page of this form, one for you and one for your spouse. This is so both you and your spouse do not need to go to the notary at the same time (or to the same notary).

This form should be filed with the court prior to the day you are scheduled to have a hearing on your petition.

TEMPORARY SUPPORT

If temporary support has been requested, the court will set a hearing on your request. Your spouse should be sent a **NOTICE OF HEARING FOR**

TEMPORARY ORDERS. (see form 24, p.245.) See the section on "Notifying Your Spouse" in Chapter 6 for more information about this form. You should have **TEMPORARY ORDERS** ready at the hearing. (see form 15 or form 16.) Use form 16 if there are no children involved. Use form 15 if you are also seeking temporary child support. To complete either form 15 or form 16, you must do the following.

◈ Complete the top portion according to the instructions in Chapter 6, page 61.

◈ Fill in your name and your spouse's name where appropriate.

◈ Fill in the name of the parent who will have custody of the children.

Leave the amount and timing of the support payments blank, as the judge will decide these questions at the hearing. You should attach the **STANDARD POSSESSION ORDER** (form 23, p.239) to the **TEMPORARY ORDERS** form in order to govern visitation rights. After the **TEMPORARY ORDERS** form is signed, you will need to send a copy to your spouse.

DECREE OF DIVORCE

A **DECREE OF DIVORCE** (forms 17, 18, and 19) will be completed in all cases. You should complete as much of the form as possible before the hearing. The form is designed so that you can complete it at the hearing according to what the judge decides on each issue. You can complete any items that you and your spouse have agreed upon ahead of time. Give your spouse a copy of the **DECREE OF DIVORCE** before the hearing, so that he or she can tell the judge that he or she is aware of it and agrees with what it says.

If your spouse has waived citation, you may go to the courthouse on the day of your hearing and *prove up* your petition. Generally, a prove-up consists of testimony in the form of restating the principal allegations of your petition. Take your time, and recite to the judge the most important points of the petition and what it is that you are asking the court to do—grant you a divorce, divide your property, and change your name (if requested).

If maintenance was awarded, be sure to follow the instructions on page 83 and add the appropriate provisions from page 83–84 to the **DECREE OF DIVORCE**.

If your spouse has not responded by filing a **WAIVER OF CITATION** or a **RESPONDENT'S ORIGINAL ANSWER**, you may bring to the hearing a **DEFAULT CERTIFICATE** (form 27, p.251) if your spouse was served in person. Bring a **STATEMENT OF EVIDENCE** (form 22 if you have children or form 21 if you do not) if your spouse was served by publication. If your spouse was served by publication and children are involved, the court will have appointed an *attorney ad litem* to represent the interests of the children. This attorney ad litem generally will be present at the prove-up and will also sign the **STATEMENT OF EVIDENCE**. If child support is ordered by the court, bring with you an **ORDER WITHHOLDING FROM EARNINGS FOR CHILD SUPPORT**. (see form 20, p.231.)

After the **DECREE OF DIVORCE**, **STATEMENT OF EVIDENCE**, and **ORDER WITHHOLDING FROM EARNINGS FOR CHILD SUPPORT** are signed by the judge, fill in any blanks left by the judge for you to complete. Have several copies conformed by the court clerk. *Conformed* copies are ones that have the judge's stamped signature on it. The clerk will keep the original, and you should get at least two conformed copies.

In addition to the **DECREE OF DIVORCE**, **STATEMENT OF EVIDENCE**, and **ORDER WITHHOLDING FROM EARNINGS FOR CHILD SUPPORT**, you will need to complete and provide to the court what is often referred to as the *Austin Form*, or the **REPORTING FORM FOR SUITS AFFECTING THE PARENT-CHILD RELATIONSHIP AND DIVORCE**. (form 32, p.261.)

Mail a conformed copy of the **DECREE OF DIVORCE** to your spouse by registered mail. Send a copy of the **ORDER WITHHOLDING EARNINGS FOR CHILD SUPPORT** to your spouse's employer by certified mail. The Child Support Office may have additional forms that you may need to complete and file with it. You should be sure to check with this office as to what additional forms you need to complete to make certain that the child support order is correctly implemented.

Each county will have its own child support office. It is typically located in the courthouse near the family courts. Also, the attorney general for Texas has a child support division.

ORDER WITHHOLDING FROM EARNINGS FOR CHILD SUPPORT

An **ORDER WITHHOLDING FROM EARNINGS FOR CHILD SUPPORT** (form 20, p.231) must be completed whenever child support is ordered. This is an order to the employer of the person required to make the payment, requiring the employer to deduct the payment from the person's paycheck and send it to the Child Support Office. This form can be completed prior to the final hearing and presented to the judge for signature.

Follow these instruction to complete the **ORDER WITHHOLDING FROM EARNINGS FOR CHILD SUPPORT**.

- ◈ Complete the top portion of the form according to the instructions in Chapter 6, page 61.

- ◈ Type in the name, address, Social Security number, and driver's license number of the person who must pay support (you or your spouse) on the lines for "Obligor."

- ◈ Type in the name, address, Social Security number, and driver's license number of the person who will receive support (you or your spouse) on the lines for "Obligee."

- ◈ Type in the name, address, Social Security number, driver's license number, birth date, and birthplace of each child who will receive support on the appropriate lines.

- ◈ Type in the appropriate amount of earnings to be withheld by using line (1), (2), (3), or (4) on the second page of this form.

- ◈ Type in the name and address of the agency to which the support payments must be mailed. Also, include the child support account number that has been assigned. The information necessary to complete this section can be obtained from the court clerk.

- ◈ Leave this form with the judge's clerk, who will process it or direct you to where you should take it.

STATEMENT REGARDING HEALTH INSURANCE COVERAGE FOR CHILDREN

A statement regarding health insurance coverage or medical assistance received by a child must be provided to the court before a hearing for temporary orders or before a final decree of divorce is entered. A **STATEMENT OF HEALTH CARE FOR CHILDREN** (form 31, p.259) should be filed as an attachment to the **ORIGINAL PETITION FOR DIVORCE**.

SPECIAL PROVISIONS FOR MAINTENANCE (ALIMONY)

If you are asking that your spouse pay maintenance after the **DECREE OF DIVORCE** is entered by the court, you must adapt your **ORIGINAL PETITION FOR DIVORCE** (forms 5–10), following these instructions (for words or phrases in brackets "{ }," select one of the choices).

◈ Add this paragraph: *Petitioner requests the Court to order Respondent to pay maintenance to Petitioner for a reasonable period after the divorce is granted.*

◈ Add one (and only one) of the following paragraphs.

    a. *Respondent was convicted of {received deferred adjunction for} an offense that also constitutes an act of family violence under Section 71.01, Family Code, and the offense occurred {within two years before the date on which this suit was filed} {during the pendency of this suit}.*

    b. *Petitioner would show the Court that the parties have been married more than 10 years, and that Petitioner is unable to support {himself} {herself} due to an incapacitating physical or mental disability. Petitioner requests the Court to order Respondent to pay maintenance to Petitioner for an indefinite period of time for as long as the disability continues.*

    c. *Petitioner would show the Court that the parties have been married more than 10 years, and that Petitioner lacks sufficient property, including property to be distributed to Petitioner under the Texas Family code, to provide for Petitioner's minimum reasonable needs.*

If you added paragraph "c," then you will need to add one or both of the following paragraphs.

- *Petitioner is the custodian of a child who requires substantial care and personal supervision because a physical or mental disability makes it necessary, taking into consideration the needs of the child, that Petitioner not be employed outside the home.*

- *Petitioner clearly lacks earning ability in the labor market adequate to provide support for Petitioner's minimum reasonable needs.*

Decree of Divorce

If maintenance was ordered by the judge, you must adapt your **Decree of Divorce** (forms 17–19), following these instructions (for words or phrases in brackets "{ }," select one of the choices).

◈ Add one or both of the following paragraphs.

a. *The Court finds that Respondent {was convicted of} {received deferred adjudication for} an offense that also constitutes an act of family violence under Section 71.01, Family Code, and the offense occurred {within two years before the date on which this suit was filed} {during the pendency of this suit}.*

b. *The Court finds that the parties have been married more than 10 years, and that Petitioner lacks sufficient property, including property to be distributed to Petitioner under the Texas Family Code, to provide for Petitioner's minimum reasonable needs.*

If you added paragraph "b," then you will also need to add one or more of the following paragraphs.

- *The Court finds that Petitioner is unable to support {himself} {herself} through appropriate employment due to an incapacitating physical or mental disability.*

- *The Court finds that Petitioner is the custodian of a child who requires substantial care and personal supervision because a physical or mental disability makes it necessary, taking into consideration the needs of the child, that Petitioner not be employed outside the home.*

- *The Court finds that Petitioner clearly lacks earning ability in the labor market adequate to provide support for Petitioner's minimum reasonable needs.*

◈ Add the following paragraph (filling in the amounts and dates).

IT IS ORDERED AND DECREED that RESPONDENT is obligated to pay and shall pay to PETITIONER maintenance of $_____ per month, in two equal payments of $_____ each, with the first payment of $_____ being due and payable on the ___ day of _____, _____, and like payments being due and payable on the _____ and _____ days of each month thereafter until the date of the earliest occurrence of one of the following events:

1. Death of Petitioner.

2. _____, _____.

3. Petitioner is cohabitating with another person in a permanent place of abode on a continuing, conjugal basis.

4. Further order of this Court regarding maintenance.

CHECKLIST FOR UNCONTESTED DIVORCE

❑ Prepare the necessary forms for an uncontested divorce, including:

  ❑ **PETITION FOR DIVORCE**

  ❑ **WAIVER OF CITATION** (signed by your spouse)

  ❑ Alternative methods to notify your spouse if he or she has not signed a **WAIVER OF CITATION**

  ❑ **APPLICATION FOR TEMPORARY ORDERS OF ALIMONY OR CHILD SUPPORT**

❑ Make sure your spouse has filed an **ANSWER** in response to your **PETITION FOR DIVORCE**

❑ Prepare a **MARITAL SETTLEMENT AGREEMENT** dividing your assets and liabilities with your spouse

❑ Prepare an **ORDER FOR TEMPORARY SUPPORT**

❑ Prepare a **DECREE OF DIVORCE** that includes:

  ❑ Division of property

  ❑ Award of alimony

  ❑ **PARENTING PLAN**

    ❑ Child support

    ❑ **ORDER WITHHOLDING FROM EARNINGS FOR CHILD SUPPORT** (if necessary)

    ❑ Child visitation

    ❑ Parental rights and responsibilities

chapter 8

Contested Divorce Procedure

Sometimes, despite your best efforts and beliefs that your spouse will be cooperative during the divorce process, your spouse may surprise you and not cooperate from the outset, or perhaps during the divorce proceedings, he or she suddenly becomes uncooperative. At that point, the manner in which you approach the divorce process must change. Your goal is to protect your rights and interests, and the rights and interests of your children. These goals should be kept in mind and not compromised simply to make things easier for your spouse.

PROCEDURE DIFFERENCES FROM UNCONTESTED DIVORCE

This book cannot turn you into a trial lawyer. It can be very risky to try to handle a contested case yourself, although it has been done. There are several differences between a contested and an uncontested case. First, in an uncontested case, the judge will usually go along with whatever you and your spouse have worked out. In a contested case, you need to prove that you are entitled to what you are asking for. This means you will need a longer time for the hearing, you will need to present papers as evidence, and you may need to have witnesses testify for you.

Second, you may have to do some extra work to get the evidence you need, such as sending out subpoenas or even hiring a private investigator.

Also, you will need to pay extra attention to assure that your spouse is properly notified of any court hearings and that he or she is sent copies of any papers you file with the court clerk.

When it becomes apparent that you have a contested divorce, it is probably time to consider hiring an attorney, especially if the issue of child custody is involved. If you are truly ready to go to war over custody, it is an extremely important matter to you and you probably want to get professional assistance. You can predict a contested case when your spouse is seriously threatening to fight you every inch of the way, or when he or she hires an attorney.

On the other hand, you should not assume that you need an attorney just because your spouse has hired one. Sometimes it will be easier to deal with the attorney than with your spouse. The attorney is not as emotionally involved and may see your settlement proposal as reasonable. Discuss things with your spouse's attorney first and see if things can be worked out. You can always hire your own lawyer if your spouse's is not reasonable. Just be very cautious about signing any papers until you are certain you understand what they mean. You may want to have an attorney review any papers prepared by your spouse's lawyer before you sign them.

Aside from deciding if you want a lawyer, there are two main procedural differences between the uncontested and the contested divorce. First, you will need to be more prepared for the hearing. Second, you will not prepare the **DECREE OF DIVORCE** until after the hearing with the judge. This is because you will not know what to put in the **DECREE OF DIVORCE** until the judge decides the various matters in dispute.

COLLECTING INFORMATION

If there is a dispute over property, the judge may require an *Inventory and Appraisement* form from you and one from your spouse. (This form can be obtained from the judge, clerk, or law library.) You may be able to use a signed copy of the **Property Inventory** (form 1, p.165) and the **Debt Inventory** (form 2, p.167) instead.

If your spouse has indicated that he or she will not cooperate at all and will not provide an *Inventory and Appraisement*, you may have to try to get the information yourself. You can go to the hearing and tell the judge that your spouse will not cooperate, but the judge may just issue an order requiring your spouse to provide information (or be held in contempt of court) and continue the hearing to another date. It may help to speed things up if you are able to get the information yourself and have it available at the hearing. This will require that you get subpoenas issued.

Subpoenas   Before you send a subpoena to your spouse's employer, bank, or accountant, you need to let your spouse know what you are about to do. The thought that you are about to get these other people involved in your divorce may be enough to get your spouse to cooperate. If your spouse calls and says that he or she will give you the information, give him or her a few days to follow through. Ask when you can expect to receive the *Inventory and Appraisement*. Offer to send your spouse another blank copy if needed.

If your spouse sends a completed *Inventory and Appraisement* as promised, do not send the subpoena. If your spouse does not follow through, go ahead with the subpoena. You can send out subpoenas to as many people or organizations as you need, but you will need to use the following procedure for each subpoena.

Request the clerk that give you a form for a subpoena for employment records. This form will eventually be sent to whomever you want to get information from. If you were able to do a good job making copies of important papers while preparing to file for divorce, you should have the information you need to figure out where you need to send subpoenas.

Your spouse's income information can be obtained from his or her employer. Stock and bond information can be obtained from his or her stockbroker, bank account balances from the bank, auto loan balances from the lender, and so on. You can have subpoenas issued to any or all of these places, but do not overdo it.

Concentrate on income information (especially if you are asking for child support or expect to pay child support) and information on the major property items. It may not be necessary to send out subpoenas if you already have recent copies of the papers relating to these items. You can always show the judge the copies of your spouse's pay stubs, W-2 tax statements, or other papers at the hearing.

An **ATTACHMENT TO SUBPOENA** (form 28, p.253) is an exhibit that you may wish to attach to the subpoena. An **AFFIDAVIT FOR BUSINESS RECORDS** (form 29, p.255) can be provided to the person you seek records from. If completed and signed before a notary, it allows him or her to verify the records as being authentic and avoid having to appear for a deposition or hearing.

Next, have the sheriff personally serve the subpoena to the person or place named in the subpoena. The sheriff will need at least one extra copy of the subpoena and a check for the service fee. The employer, bank, and so on should send you the requested information. If the employer calls you and says you must pay for copies, ask him or her how much they will cost, and send a check or money order (if the amount is not too high and you do not already have some fairly recent income information).

If the employer does not provide the information, you can try sending a letter to the employer saying, "*unless you provide the information requested in the subpoena in seven days, a motion for contempt will be filed with the circuit court.*" This may scare the employer into sending you the information. The sheriff will have also filed an affidavit verifying when the subpoena was served.

There are more procedures you could go through to force the employer to give the information, but it probably is not worth the hassle and you would probably need an attorney to help you with it.

At the final hearing, you can tell the judge that your spouse refused to provide income information, and that the subpoena was not honored by the employer. The judge may do something to help you out, or he or she may advise you to see a lawyer.

Interrogatories   There is also a procedure in which you send written questions to your spouse that he or she must answer in writing and under oath. These written questions are called *interrogatories*. If your spouse did not file an *Inventory and Appraisement*, he or she probably will not answer the interrogatories, which would leave you no better off. However, if you would like to try this, you may be able to locate the forms you would need at the clerk's office or law library.

Once you collect the necessary information, you can prepare for the hearing.

PROPERTY AND DEBTS

Generally, the judge will look at your property and debts, and will try to divide them fairly. This does not mean they will necessarily be divided fifty-fifty. What you want to do is offer the judge a reasonable solution that looks fair.

It is time to review the **PROPERTY INVENTORY** (form 1, p.165) and the **DEBT INVENTORY** (form 2, p.167) you prepared earlier. For each item or property, note which of the following categories it fits into (it may fit into more than one):

- ✪ you really want it;

- ✪ you would like to have it;

- ✪ you do not care either way;

- ✪ your spouse really wants it;

- ✪ your spouse would like to have it; or,

- ✪ your spouse does not care either way.

Now, start a list of what each of you should end up with, using these categories. You will eventually end up with a list of things you can probably get with little difficulty (you really want them and your spouse does not care), those that you will fight over (you both really want them), and those that need to be divided but can probably be easily divided equally (you both do not really care).

At the hearing, the judge will probably try to get you to work out your disagreements, but he or she will not put up with arguing for very long. In the end, the judge will arbitrarily divide the items you cannot agree upon, or may order you to sell those items and divide the money you get equally.

On the few items that are really important to you, it may be necessary for you to try to prove why you should get them. It will help if you can convince the judge of one or more of the following.

- ✪   You paid for the item out of your own earnings or funds.

- ✪   You are the one who primarily uses that item.

- ✪   You use the item in your employment, business, or hobby.

- ✪   You are willing to give up something else you really want in exchange for that item. (Of course, you will try to give up something from your *do not care* or your *like to have* list.)

- ✪   The item is needed for your children (assuming you will have custody).

The best thing you can do is make up a list of how you think the property should be divided. Make it a reasonably fair and equal list, regardless of how angry you are at your spouse. Even if the judge changes some of it to appear fair to your spouse, you will most likely get more of what you want than if you do not offer a suggestion.

NOTE: *This is not an exception to the negotiating rule of letting your spouse make the first offer, because at this point you are no longer just negotiating with your spouse. You are now negotiating with the judge. You are trying to impress the judge with your fairness—not trying to convince your spouse.*

Separate Property

Special problems arise if a claim of *separate property* becomes an issue. This may be your spouse trying to get your separate property or you trying to get property you feel your spouse is wrongly claiming to be separate. Basically, separate property is property either of you had before you were married and kept separate.

It is also a good idea to have any papers that prove the property you claim to be separate property is actually separate property. These would be papers showing that:

✪ you bought the item before you were married (such as dated sales receipts);

✪ you were given or inherited the item as your own property (such as certified copies of wills and probate court papers); or,

✪ you got the property by exchanging it for property you had before you got married, or for property you received as a gift or through an inheritance (such as a statement from the person you made the exchange with, or some kind of receipt showing what was exchanged).

If you want to get at assets your spouse is claiming are separate assets, you will need to collect the following types of evidence:

✪ papers showing that you helped pay for the asset (such as a check that you wrote or bank statements showing that your money went into the same account that was used to make payments on the asset);

Example:

Suppose your spouse purchased a house before you got married. During your marriage, you made some of the mortgage payments with your own checking account (you will have cancelled checks, hopefully with the mortgage account number on them, to prove this). At other times, you deposited some of your paychecks into your spouse's checking account. Your spouse wrote checks from that account to pay the mortgage (again, there should be some bank records and cancelled checks that show this was done). Since you contributed to the payments on the house, you can claim some of the value of the house as a marital asset.

❂ papers showing that you paid for repairs of the asset (if you paid for repairs on the home or a car your spouse had before you were married, you can claim part of the value); and,

❂ papers showing the asset was improved or increased in value during your marriage.

Example 1:

Your spouse owned the house before you were married. During your marriage, you and your spouse added a family room to the house. This will enable you to make a claim for some of the value of the house.

Example 2:

Your spouse owned the house before you were married. The day before you got married, the house was worth $85,000. Now the house is appraised at $115,000. You can claim part of the $30,000 of increased value.

During the hearing, the judge will announce who gets what items. Make a list of this as the judge tells you. Then, complete the **DECREE OF DIVORCE** according to what the judge says. Once you have completed the **DECREE OF DIVORCE**, the judge will sign the judgment and return a copy to you. You should send a copy to your spouse.

CHILD CUSTODY AND VISITATION

Generally, if you are the wife, the odds start out in favor of you getting custody. However, do not depend upon the odds. Start out by reviewing the guidelines the judge will use to decide the custody question. These can be found in Chapter 4. For each item listed in that section, write down an explanation of how that item applies to you. This will be your argument when you have your hearing with the judge.

Many custody battles revolve around the moral fitness of one or both of the parents. If you become involved in this type of a custody fight, you should consult a lawyer. Charges of moral unfitness (such as illegal drug use, child abuse, or immoral sexual conduct) can require long court hearings involving the testimony of many witnesses, as well as possibly the employment of private investigators. For such a hearing, you will require the help of an attorney who knows the law, knows what questions to ask witnesses, and understands the rules of evidence.

However, if the only question is whether you or your spouse has been the main caretaker of the child, you can always have friends, neighbors, and relatives come into the hearing (if they are willing to help you out) to testify on your behalf. It may not be necessary for you to have an attorney. On the other hand, if you need to subpoena unwilling witnesses to testify, you should have an attorney.

The judge's decision regarding custody will have to be put into the **DECREE OF DIVORCE**. Read Chapter 7, pages 83–84 for instructions on preparing the **DECREE OF DIVORCE**.

CHILD SUPPORT

In Texas, as in most states, the question of child support is mostly a matter of a mathematical calculation. Getting a fair child support amount depends upon the accuracy of the income information presented to the judge. If you feel fairly sure that the information your spouse presents is accurate or that you have obtained accurate information about his or her income, there is not much to argue about. The judge will simply take the income information provided, use the formula to calculate the amount to be paid, and order that amount to be paid.

In most cases, there will not be much room to argue about the amount of child support, so there is usually no need to get an attorney. If you claim your spouse has not provided accurate income information, it will be up to you to prove this to the judge by showing the income information you have obtained from your spouse's employer or other source of income.

The only areas open for argument are whatever special needs are claimed by the party asking for child support. For instance, your child may be enrolled in special athletic, music, arts, or other programs that require extra fees, dues, and the like. The importance of maintaining this consistency in the child's life after the divorce may lead the court to award additional payments for these expenses.

Additionally, the parent requesting child support may show that additional money is required to maintain the current residence of the parent and the child to keep the child in the current school district. Once again, it will be necessary for that party to provide proof of the cost of these special needs by producing billing statements, receipts, or other papers to show the amount of these needs.

The judge's decision regarding child support will have to be put into the **DECREE OF DIVORCE**. Be sure to read Chapter 7 for instructions on preparing the **DECREE OF DIVORCE**.

CHECKLIST FOR CONTESTED DIVORCE PREPARATION

❏ Decide whether you can you handle a contested divorce action or if you need a lawyer

❏ Determine whether you need additional information about assets and debts. If so, determine whether:

  ❏ your will spouse provide it voluntarily

  ❏ you need to have the court issue a subpoena to obtain information regarding assets, debts, and your spouse's income

  ❏ you need to have a subpoena issued to obtain business records (if your spouse owns or operates a business)

  ❏ you need to prepare interrogatories to obtain information about your spouse's financial or personal affairs for purposes of property division, child support, or child visitation

❏ Categorize property as your separate property, your spouse's separate property, or community property

The Court Hearing

Whether the divorce is contested or uncontested, there must be a hearing before the judge in order to have him or her approve the property division, child custody, visitation, and child support agreed to between the parties. Just as the state issues a formal recognition of the beginning of a marriage by requiring a marriage license, the state issues a formal recognition of the termination of a marriage by requiring a formal **DECREE OF DIVORCE**.

PREPARATION

It is very important that you follow all of the procedures exactly and that you have all of the proper paperwork gathered together prior to the hearing. Adequate preparation will not only make the hearing go smoothly, but will also impress the judge. This may be to your benefit if your spouse is unprepared and becomes uncooperative.

Setting a Hearing Date

The first step in preparing for the final hearing is to get a hearing date set. See Chapter 6, page 65 for instructions on setting a hearing date.

Notifying Your Spouse

Now that you have a hearing date set with the judge, you will need to notify your spouse of when the hearing will be held. Even if you can easily call your spouse on the phone and notify him or her of the hearing, it is also a good idea to send a formal notice of the hearing by regular or certified mail.

What Papers to Bring

Bring your copies (if available) of the following papers to the hearing:

❑   your **ORIGINAL PETITION FOR DIVORCE**;

❑   any papers you may have showing that your spouse was properly notified of the divorce;

❑   any papers you may have to support your claim that certain property can be awarded to you (including copies of your most recent pay stub, federal income tax return, and W-2 forms);

❑   any papers showing your spouse's income or property;

❑   your **MARITAL SETTLEMENT AGREEMENT**, if you have one that has not yet been filed with the court; and,

❑   your proposed **DECREE OF DIVORCE**.

THE HEARING

The judge may start the hearing by summarizing what you are there for, then ask you and your spouse if you have any additional evidence to present. The judge may then ask each of you any questions he or she may have. The judge will review the papers you filed with the clerk, and will probably ask you whether you understand and agree with what is in the papers. The judge will also ask you to explain why you are getting divorced. Answer honestly.

If you have any information that is different and more current than what is in the *Inventory and Appraisement* forms that may have been filed with the court, you should mention to the judge that you have more current information. You will then give a copy of whatever papers you have to show the changed situation (such as a current pay stub showing an increase in pay or a current bank statement showing a new balance).

If there are any items that you and your spouse have not yet agreed upon, tell the judge what these items are. Refer to Chapter 8 relating to the contested divorce for more information about how to handle these unresolved issues. Be prepared to make a suggestion as to how these matters should be settled and to explain to the judge why your suggestion is the best solution.

If the judge asks for any information that you have not brought with you, tell the judge that you do not have it with you, but you will be happy to provide him or her with the information by the end of the following day. Just be sure you get the papers to the judge.

At the end of the hearing, the judge will tell you if he or she is going to grant you a divorce and accept your settlement agreement. It would be very unusual not to grant the divorce and accept your agreement. You will then tell the judge that you have prepared a proposed **Decree of Divorce**, and hand him or her the original. Refer back to Chapter 7 regarding how to prepare the **Decree of Divorce** form.

You should have two extra copies of the **Decree of Divorce** with you, one for yourself and one for your spouse. You should also bring two envelopes, one addressed to yourself and one addressed to your spouse, and two stamps. This is in case the judge wants to review the **Decree of Divorce** and mail it to you later, instead of signing it at the hearing.

If the judge wants you to make any changes in the **Decree of Divorce**, make a careful note of exactly what the judge wants (ask the judge to explain it again if you did not understand the first time), then tell the judge that you will make the correction and deliver it the following day. If the change requested is a small one, you might even be able to write in the change by hand at the hearing.

If child support or alimony is to be paid, you will also need to bring a third copy of the **Decree of Divorce** and an original, as well as four copies of the **Order Withholding From Earnings for Child Support**. (see form 20, p.231.) The judge will sign the **Order Withholding From Earnings for Child Support** at the hearing. The four copies are for you, your spouse, the attorney general's office, and the Child Support Enforcement Office (which also gets the additional copy of the judgment). (See the next section regarding child support agencies.)

When the hearing is over, thank the judge and leave. The judge will sign the original **DECREE OF DIVORCE** and send it to the court clerk's office to be entered in the court's file. Take the copies of the judgment and withholding order to the clerk. The clerk will write in the date and use a stamp with the judge's name on each copy to authenticate them.

If any serious problems develop at the hearing (such as your spouse's attorney starts making a lot of technical objections or the judge gives you a hard time), just tell the judge you would like to continue the hearing so you can retain an attorney. Then go get one.

Child Support Agencies

There are two child support agencies you need to be aware of if you and your spouse have children.

The *Child Support Office* (CSO) is the agency that processes the child support payments. The spouse responsible to pay the support (or his or her employer) will make payments to the CSO. The CSO then cashes that check and issues a check to the spouse entitled to receive support. The CSO keeps the official records of what has and has not been paid.

The *Child Support Enforcement Division* is responsible for enforcing the payment of child support to custodial parents receiving welfare (Aid to Families with Dependent Children) and others who request their services.

The secretary of state maintains a website that has links to the attorney general's office that is responsible for the collection of child support. This website provides the most current information regarding how to contact the Child Support Office in your area. The website is found at **www.sos.state.tx.us**.

The website for the Texas attorney general is located at **www.oag. state.tx.us**.

If you are to receive support and you would like to use the enforcement services of this office, you will need to contact your local Child Support Enforcement Division. This may not be necessary if your spouse goes on a withholding order immediately and keeps his or her job. However, if some payments are missed, you may call the Child Support Enforcement Division at any time and ask for their assistance.

Remarriage   If you are planning to get married again after you get divorced, you should be aware that Texas law prohibits you from marrying for thirty-one days after the date of your **Decree of Divorce**. There are two exceptions to this thirty-one day waiting period: (1) if you are remarrying the person you just divorced and (2) if you obtain a waiver from the judge *for good cause shown*. (Tex. Fam. Code, Sec. 6.902.)

When You Cannot Find Your Spouse

If your spouse has run off and you have no idea of where he or she might be, you cannot have the sheriff deliver a copy of your petition to your spouse. Instead of personal service, use a method of giving notice called *service by publication*. You will need to follow the steps listed below very carefully.

THE DILIGENT SEARCH

The court will only permit service by publication when you cannot locate your spouse. This also includes the situation in which the sheriff has tried several times to personally serve your spouse, but it appears that your spouse is hiding to avoid being served. First, you will have to show that you cannot locate your spouse by letting the court know what you have done to try to find him or her—your diligent search. In making this search, you should try the following.

- ✪ Check the phone book and directory assistance in the area where you live.

- ✪ Check directory assistance in the area where you last knew your spouse lived.

✪ Ask friends and relatives who might know where your spouse is living.

✪ Check with the post office where he or she last lived to see if there is a forwarding address. (You can ask by mail if it is too far away.)

✪ Check records of the tax collector and property assessor to see if your spouse owns property.

✪ Write to the Department of Motor Vehicles to see if your spouse has any car registrations.

✪ Check with any other sources you know that may lead you to a current address (such as landlords, prior employers, and so on).

If you do come up with a current address, go back to personal service by the sheriff, but if not, continue with this procedure.

PREPARING AND FILING COURT PAPERS

Once you have made your search, notify the court. This is done by filing the **AFFIDAVIT FOR CITATION BY PUBLICATION**. (see form 12, p.209.) All this form does is tell the court what you have done to try to locate your spouse and ask for permission to publish your notice. (If your spouse lives in another state and you have his or her address, you may use this procedure.)

To complete the **AFFIDAVIT FOR CITATION BY PUBLICATION**:

◈ Complete the top portion of the form according to the instructions in Chapter 6, page 61.

◈ Type your name in the blank in the first two paragraphs.

◈ Type in the name of your spouse in the fourth paragraph.

◈ Type in the date.

◈   Sign your name on the "Signed" line at the end of the form in front of a notary public.

◈   Give the form to a notary public to complete.

PUBLISHING

The clerk will arrange for publication. The notice need only be published once. Get a copy of the paper and check to be sure it was printed correctly. If you find an error, notify the newspaper immediately.

Special Circumstances

Unique situations in which you must file additional papers with the court often present themselves. These situations can range from an inability to pay court costs to obtaining protective orders from the court to protect yourself or your children from a violent spouse. Many times there may be minimal or no filing fees required to be paid with the papers. You should check with your local county clerk regarding this issue.

WHEN YOU CANNOT AFFORD COURT COSTS

There is an **AFFIDAVIT OF INABILITY TO PAY COURT COSTS** (see form 14, p.213) for use when you cannot afford to pay the filing fee and other costs associated with the divorce.

Complete the **AFFIDAVIT OF INABILITY TO PAY COURT COSTS** as follows.

❖ Complete the top portion according to the instructions in Chapter 6, page 61.

❖ Type in your name in the first (unnumbered) paragraph.

◈ Complete numbered paragraphs 1 through 8 with as much detail as possible.

◈ Sign on the line marked "Affiant" in the presence of a notary public.

◈ The notary public will then date and sign the form. The form is now ready for filing.

PROTECTING YOURSELF, YOUR CHILDREN, AND YOUR PROPERTY

Some people have two special concerns when preparing to file for a divorce—fear of physical attack by their spouse and fear that their spouse will try to take the marital property and hide it. There are additional legal papers you can file if you feel you are in either of these situations.

Protecting Yourself

If you fear violence from your spouse, contact the court clerk's office and ask for information and assistance in filing papers to prevent domestic violence. This subject is covered in the Texas Family Code, beginning with Section 3.581.

Protecting Your Children

If you are worried that your spouse may try to kidnap your children, you should make sure that the day care center, baby-sitter, relative, or whomever you leave the children with at any time, is aware that you are in the process of a divorce and that the children are only to be released to you personally (not to your spouse or to any other relative or friend).

To prevent your spouse from taking the children out of the United States, you can apply for a passport for each child. Once a passport is issued, the government will not issue another. Get their passports and lock them up in a safe-deposit box. This will not prevent them from being taken to Canada or Mexico, where passports are not currently required (a rule that is changing), but will prevent them from being taken overseas.

You can also file a motion to prevent the removal of the children from the state and to deny passport services. Forms for this motion are discussed at the beginning of Appendix B, in the section titled "Where To Find Additional Forms."

If your spouse is determined and resourceful, there is no guaranteed way to prevent the things discussed in this chapter from happening. All you can do is put as many obstacles in his or her way as possible, and prepare for him or her to suffer legal consequences for acting improperly.

Protecting Your Property

If you genuinely fear that your spouse will try to remove money from bank accounts and try to hide important papers showing what property you own, you may want to take this same action before your spouse can. However, you can make a great deal of trouble for yourself with the judge if you do this to try to get these assets for yourself.

Make a complete list of any property you do take, and be sure to include these items in your *Inventory and Appraisement* form. You may need to convince the judge that you only took these items temporarily, in order to preserve them until a **DECREE OF DIVORCE** is entered.

Also, do not spend any cash you take from a bank account, or sell or give away any items of property you take. Any cash should be placed in a separate bank account, without your spouse's name on it, and be kept separate from any other cash you have.

Any papers, such as deeds, car titles, or stock or bond certificates, should be placed in a safe-deposit box without your spouse's name on it. The idea is not to take these things for yourself, but to get them in a safe place so your spouse cannot hide them and deny they ever existed.

TEMPORARY SUPPORT AND CUSTODY

If your spouse has left you with the children, the mortgage, and the monthly bills, and is not helping you out financially, you may want to consider asking the court to order the payment of support for you and the children during the divorce procedure. Of course, if you were the only person bringing in income and have been paying all the bills, do not expect to get any temporary support.

You will need to use one of the petition forms that include a request for temporary support (forms 8, 9, or 10) and a **TEMPORARY ORDER** form (forms 15 and 16). These are discussed in greater detail in Chapter 7.

TAXES

As you are no doubt aware, the United States' income tax code is complicated and ever-changing. For this reason, it is impossible to give detailed legal advice with respect to taxes in a book such as this. Any such information could easily be out of date by the time of publication. Therefore, it is strongly recommended that you consult your accountant, lawyer, or whomever prepares your tax return about the tax consequences of a divorce. A few general concerns are discussed in this chapter to give you an idea of some of the tax questions that can arise. Be sure to read the following section on alimony, because unusual property settlements are asking for tax problems.

Taxes and Property

You and your spouse may be exchanging titles to property as a result of your divorce. Generally, there will not be any tax to pay as the result of such a transfer. However, whomever gets a piece of property will be responsible to pay any tax that may become due upon sale.

The Internal Revenue Service (IRS) has issued numerous rulings about how property is to be treated in divorce situations. You need to be especially careful if you are transferring any tax shelters or other complicated financial arrangements.

Taxes and Alimony

Alimony can cause the most tax problems of any aspect of divorce. The IRS is always making new rulings on whether an agreement is really alimony or is really property division. The basic rule is that alimony is treated as income to the person receiving it and as a deduction for the person paying it. Therefore, in order to manipulate the tax consequences, many couples try to show something as part of the property settlement instead of as alimony, or the reverse. As the IRS becomes aware of these tax games, it issues rulings on how it will view a certain arrangement.

Taxes and Child Support

If you are simply talking about the regular, periodic payment of cash, the IRS will probably not question that it is alimony. However, if you try to call it property settlement, you may run into problems. The important thing is to consult a tax expert if you are considering any unusual or creative property settlement or alimony arrangements.

There are simple tax rules regarding child support.

✪ Whoever has custody gets to claim the children on his or her tax return (unless both parents file a special IRS form agreeing to a different arrangement each year).

✪ The parent receiving child support does not need to report it as income.

✪ The parent paying child support cannot deduct it.

If you are sharing physical custody, the parent with whom the child lives for the most time during the year is entitled to claim the child as a dependent. However, the parties can agree otherwise by filing IRS Form 8332, **Release of Claim to Exemption for Child of Divorced or Separated Parents**. (see form 33, p.265.) Follow the instructions on the form for completing and filing it.

PENSION PLANS

Pension plans (retirement plans) belonging to you and your spouse are marital assets. They may be very valuable assets. If you and your spouse are young and have not been working very long, you may not have pension plans worth worrying about. Also, if you have both worked and have similar pensions plans, it may be best just to include a provision in your settlement agreement stating that "each party shall keep his or her own pension plan." However, if you have been married a long time, and one of you worked while the other stayed home to raise the children, the pension plan may be worth a lot of money and may be necessary to see you through retirement. If you and your spouse cannot agree on how to divide a pension plan, you should see an attorney. The valuation of pension plans and how they are to be divided is a complicated matter that you should not attempt without legal assistance.

SOCIAL SECURITY BENEFITS

When you get divorced, you may be eligible to collect retirement benefits under Social Security if you have been married to your former spouse for at least ten years. If you are at least age 62 and if your former spouse is entitled to or is receiving benefits, you may collect benefits on his or her Social Security record. If your former spouse dies, you can receive benefits as a widow or widower if your marriage lasted ten years or more. Benefits paid to you if you are 60 years or older will not affect the benefit rates for other survivors receiving benefits on your former spouse's record.

NOTE: *Although you may be entitled to benefits as a divorced spouse, if you remarry, you will lose entitlement to Social Security benefits under your former spouse's benefit record.*

During your marriage, if you have been unable to work at a full-time job, and therefore been unable to accumulate a significant retirement record with Social Security, you may want to have this taken into consideration in the marital property settlement. You may suggest that additional property be awarded to you upon divorce to compensate for this loss of benefits in the future.

Many times, individuals who are self-employed prefer to report a profit or loss from their business rather than report wages on which they must pay FICA and Medicare taxes. While this action may save payments for taxes, it will have a detrimental impact on future retirement benefits.

PATERNITY

Under Texas law, a man is presumed to be the legal father of a child if he was married to the mother at the time of the child's birth. If the parents are not married at the time of the child's birth, it is important to establish a child's paternity.

Paternity means fatherhood. When paternity is established, a child can become eligible for child support and benefits such as Social Security, veterans' benefits, and health care. Additionally, because many health problems can be inherited from parents, it is important for a child to know the family medical history of his or her mother and father.

The primary reason a mother wants to establish paternity is to obtain a court order requiring the father to pay child support. A father can ask the court to establish paternity to give him the right to visit with and be involved in the life of his child.

Paternity can be established in two ways. First, both parents can sign an *Acknowledgment of Paternity* (AOP) form. The AOP form can be signed at the hospital at the time the baby is born. Alternatively, the AOP form can be signed, certified, and filed with the Bureau of Vital Statistics.

If an AOP form is not signed by the father, a suit can be brought against the alleged father to establish paternity by court order. Typically, the court will order a paternity test. A paternity test is a genetic test that identifies the similarities between the DNA of the child and the DNA of the father. There are numerous laboratories that offer paternity testing.

GRANDPARENTS' RIGHTS

Many times, grandparents want to have visitation with their grandchild. Texas does not recognize an independent right of grandparents to have court-ordered visitation with the grandchild unless the parent of the grandchild has been incarcerated, has been declared incompetent, has died, or does not have actual or court-ordered possession or visitation of the child. Generally, Texas courts believe that parents will act in the best interests of their child, which includes fostering a relationship between the child and grandparents. The courts will rarely interfere with the parents' decisions in this regard. Grandparents must rely on the parents to facilitate and foster a relationship with their grandchildren.

Glossary

A

acknowledgment. A statement, written or oral, made before a person authorized by law to administer oaths (such as a notary public).

adult. In Texas, a person 18 years of age or older.

affiant. The legal term for the person who signs an affidavit.

affidavit. A person's written statement of facts, signed under oath before a person authorized to administer oaths (such as a notary public or court clerk).

alimony. *See maintenance.*

annulment. A legal procedure by which a marriage is declared invalid.

answer. The title of a legal pleading that responds to a petition, usually by either admitting or denying the allegations in the petition.

C

certificate of service. A written statement that you mailed papers to a party or person involved in a lawsuit.

child custody. Physical possession of a child.

child support. An amount of money paid to the parent who has custody of a child to be used for the benefit of the child, for things such as food, clothing, shelter, and medical care.

community property. Property acquired by spouses during their marriage.

conservator. A parent who has the responsibility of making decisions regarding his or her child.

conservatorship. *See child custody.*

creditor. A person or institution to whom money is owed.

D

debtor. A person or institution who owes money.

decree. The final judgment of a court.

deposition. The posing of verbal questions to one party, who is required to answer verbally under oath, usually before a court reporter.

E

equitable distribution. A way to divide marital property, the goal of which is to treat the parties fairly under the circumstances.

execute. To sign a legal document in the legally required manner (e.g., before witnesses or a notary public), thereby making it effective.

F

final judgment. The order of the court at the end of a trial or pursuant to a settlement agreement.

G

gross income. Income before deductions for taxes and Social Security.

H

homestead. Real estate that is a person's primary place of residence.

I

institution. As used in this book, any type of business entity (e.g., corporation, partnership, limited liability company), organization, or other entity other than an individual person.

instrument. A legal term for a document.

interrogatories. Written questions sent by one party to the other that must be answered in writing under oath.

irretrievably broken. A legal way of saying that a marriage is broken and cannot be repaired.

J

joint conservatorship. *See joint custody.*

joint custody. Where both parents share the responsibility of making decisions regarding their child.

joint tenancy. A way for two or more people to own property, so that when one owner dies, his or her interest in the property passes automatically to the remaining owner or owners.

M

maintenance. Money paid by one spouse to help support the other spouse.

managing conservator. The parent who has primary responsibility for making decisions regarding his or her child.

marital assets. Assets that are considered the property of both parties to a marriage.

marital property agreement. An agreement between spouses that spells out how property and debts will be divided.

mediation. The process in which a neutral person helps disputing parties communicate and promotes reconciliation, settlement, or understanding between them.

motion. A party's written or oral request that the judge take a certain action.

N

net resources. Gross income minus certain deductions, such as federal income tax, Social Security or self-employment taxes, mandatory union dues, and health insurance coverage for the children.

nonmarital assets. Assets that are considered the separate property of only one party to a marriage. Generally, these are assets that were acquired before the marriage, or acquired by one party during the marriage as a separate gift or inheritance.

notary public. A person who is legally authorized by the state to acknowledge signatures on legal documents.

P

parenting plan. Document that sets forth in detail residence, visitation, and support of children, and rights, duties, and obligations of parents with respect to the children.

pay-on-death account. A financial account, such as a bank account or certificate of deposit, which is payable to a certain person upon the death of the account holder.

personal property. All property other than land and things permanently attached to the land (such as buildings).

personal service. The process where a sheriff or someone else designated by the judge personally delivers copies of papers that have been filed with the court.

petition. The title of the legal pleading that begins a divorce case.

prove-up. Consists of testimony in court, giving the judge primary facts stated in the petition and the agreement made between the parties regarding child support, visitation and custody, and the division of marital property.

R

recording. The process of filing a deed, mortgage, or other legal document affecting title to land with the court clerk's office.

S

shared custody. *See joint custody.*

sole custody. One parent is given the sole legal right to make decisions regarding his or her child.

standard possession order. The basic guidelines for child visitation and possession under Texas law.

subpoena. An order from a court that a person appear before the court or at a deposition to give testimony.

subpoena duces tecum. A particular type of subpoena that requires the person to bring certain, specified documents, records, or other items to the court or deposition.

T

temporary support. Payments ordered by the court to support the spouse or child until the divorce is finalized.

tenancy by the entirety. This is essentially the same as joint tenancy, but it can only occur between a husband and wife. Upon the death of one spouse, the property automatically passes to the surviving spouse.

tenancy in common. A way for two or more people to own property, where if one of the owners dies, his or her interest in the property passes to his or her heirs (not to the other co-owners).

title. A document that proves ownership of property.

W

waiver of citation. Agreement of a party that personal service is not required.

Texas Family Code

The following are portions of the *Texas Family Code* relating to various aspects of divorce. These are not all of the provisions relating to divorce, but only some of the more significant ones. Comments that are not part of these laws are in brackets "[ ]." For more information, refer to the most recent version of the *Texas Family Code*. This can be found at many public libraries and at all law libraries. Remember, the title on these books will be *Vernon's Texas Codes Annotated*. Look for the volume marked "Family Code."

TITLE 1. THE MARRIAGE RELATIONSHIP

SUBTITLE B. PROPERTY RIGHTS AND LIABILITIES

CHAPTER 3. MARITAL PROPERTY RIGHTS AND LIABILITIES

SUBCHAPTER A. GENERAL RULES FOR SEPARATE AND COMMUNITY PROPERTY

Sec. 3.001. Separate Property

A spouse's separate property consists of:
(1)   the property owned or claimed by the spouse before marriage;
(2)   the property acquired by the spouse during marriage by gift, devise, or descent; and
(3)   the recovery for personal injuries sustained by the spouse during the marriage, except any recovery for loss of earning capacity during marriage.

Sec. 3.002. Community Property

Community property consists of the property, other than separate property, acquired by either spouse during marriage.

Sec. 3.003. Presumption of Community Property

(a)   Property possessed by either spouse during or on dissolution of marriage is presumed to be community property.
(b)   The degree of proof necessary to establish that property is separate property is clear and convincing evidence.

Sec. 3.005. Gifts Between Spouses

If one spouse makes a gift of property to the other spouse, the gift is presumed to include all the income and property that may arise from that property.

Sec. 3.006.   Proportional Ownership of Property by Marital Estates

If the community estate of the spouses and the separate estate of a spouse have an ownership interest in property, the respective ownership interests of the marital estates are determined by the rule of inception of title.

Sec. 3.007.   Property Interest in Certain Employee Benefits

(a)   A spouse who is a participant in a defined benefit retirement plan has a separate property interest in the monthly accrued benefit the spouse had a right to receive on normal retirement age, as defined by the plan, as of the date of marriage, regardless of whether the benefit had vested.

(b)   The community property interest in a defined benefit plan shall be determined as if the spouse began to participate in the plan on the date of marriage and ended that participation on the date of dissolution or termination of the marriage, regardless of whether the benefit had vested.

(c)   The separate property interest of a spouse in a defined contribution retirement plan may be traced using the tracing and characterization principles that apply to a nonretirement asset.

(d)   A spouse who is a participant in an employer-provided stock option plan or an employer-provided restricted stock plan has a separate property interest in the options or restricted stock granted to the spouse under the plan as follows:

    (1)   if the option or stock was granted to the spouse before marriage but required continued employment during marriage before the grant could be exercised or the restriction removed, the spouse's separate property interest is equal to the fraction of the option or restricted stock in which the numerator is the period from the date the option or stock was granted until the date of marriage and the denominator is the period from the date the option or stock was granted until the date the grant could be exercised or the restriction removed; and

    (2)   if the option or stock was granted to the spouse during the marriage but required continued employment after marriage before the grant could be exercised or the restriction removed, the spouse's separate property interest is equal to the fraction of the option or restricted stock in which the numerator is the period from the date of dissolution or termination of the marriage until the date the grant could be exercised or the restriction removed and the denominator is the period from the date the option or stock was granted until the date the grant could be exercised or the restriction removed.

(e)   The computation described by Subsection (d) applies to each component of the benefit requiring varying periods of employment before the grant could be exercised or the restriction removed.

(f)   The characterization of the marital property interest in an option or restricted stock described by Subsection (d) must be recalculated if, after the initial division of the option or stock, the vesting occurs on a date earlier than the vesting date stated in the original grant of the option or stock. The recalculation required by this subsection must adjust for the shortened vesting period and applies to options and stock granted before and during the marriage.

Sec. 3.008.   Property Interest in Certain Insurance

(a)   Insurance proceeds paid or payable that arise from a casualty loss to property during marriage are characterized in the same manner as the property to which the claim is attributable.

(b)   If a person becomes disabled or is injured, any disability insurance payment or workers' compensation payment is community property to the extent it is intended to replace earnings lost while the disabled or injured person is married. To the extent that any insurance payment or workers' compensation payment is intended to replace earnings while the disabled or injured person is not married, the recovery is the separate property of the disabled or injured spouse.

TITLE 1. THE MARRIAGE RELATIONSHIP

SUBTITLE B. PROPERTY RIGHTS AND LIABILITIES

CHAPTER 3. MARITAL PROPERTY RIGHTS AND LIABILITIES

SUBCHAPTER E.   CLAIMS FOR ECONOMIC CONTRIBUTION AND REIMBURSEMENT

Sec. 3.401.   Definitions

In this subchapter:

    (1)   "Claim for economic contribution" means a claim made under this subchapter.

    (2)   "Economic contribution" means the contribution to a marital estate described by Section 3.402.

    (3)   "Equity" means, with respect to specific property owned by one or more marital estates, the amount computed by subtracting from the fair market value of the property as of a specific date the amount of a lawful lien specific to the property on that same date.

    (4)   "Marital estate" means one of three estates:

        (A)   the community property owned by the spouses together and referred to as the community marital estate;

        (B)   the separate property owned individually by the husband and referred to as a separate marital estate; or

        (C)   the separate property owned individually by the wife, also referred to as a separate marital estate.

    (5)   "Spouse" means a husband, who is a man, or a wife, who is a woman. A member of a civil union or similar relationship entered into in another state between persons of the same sex is not a spouse.

Sec. 3.402.   Economic Contribution

(a)   For purposes of this subchapter, "economic contribution" is the dollar amount of:

    (1)   the reduction of the principal amount of a debt secured by a lien on property owned before marriage, to the extent the debt existed at the time of marriage;

    (2)   the reduction of the principal amount of a debt secured by a lien on property received by a spouse by gift, devise, or descent during a marriage, to the extent the debt existed at the time the property was received;

    (3)   the reduction of the principal amount of that part of a debt, including a home equity loan:
        (A)   incurred during a marriage;
        (B)   secured by a lien on property; and
        (C)   incurred for the acquisition of, or for capital improvements to, property;
    (4)   the reduction of the principal amount of that part of a debt:
        (A)   incurred during a marriage;
        (B)   secured by a lien on property owned by a spouse;
        (C)   for which the creditor agreed to look for repayment solely to the separate marital estate of the spouse on whose property the lien attached; and
        (D)   incurred for the acquisition of, or for capital improvements to, property;
    (5)   the refinancing of the principal amount described by Subdivisions (1)-(4), to the extent the refinancing reduces that principal amount in a manner described by the appropriate subdivision; and
    (6)   capital improvements to property other than by incurring debt.
(b)   "Economic contribution" does not include the dollar amount of:
    (1)   expenditures for ordinary maintenance and repair or for taxes, interest, or insurance; or
    (2)   the contribution by a spouse of time, toil, talent, or effort during the marriage.

Sec. 3.403. Claim Based on Economic Contribution

(a)   A marital estate that makes an economic contribution to property owned by another marital estate has a claim for economic contribution with respect to the benefited estate.
(b)   The amount of the claim under this section is equal to the product of:
    (1)   the equity in the benefited property on the date of dissolution of the marriage, the death of a spouse, or disposition of the property; multiplied by
    (2)   a fraction of which:
        (A)   the numerator is the economic contribution to the property owned by the benefited marital estate by the contributing marital estate; and
        (B)   the denominator is an amount equal to the sum of:
           (i)   the economic contribution to the property owned by the benefited marital estate by the contributing marital estate; and
           (ii)   the contribution by the benefited estate to the equity in the property owned by the benefited estate.
(b-1) the amount of the contribution by the benefited marital estate under subsection (b)(2)(b)(ii) is measured by determining:
    (1)   if the benefited estate is the community property estate:
        (A   the net equity of the community property estate in the property owned by the community property estate as of the date of the first economic contribution to that property by the contributing separate property estate; and
        (B)   any additional economic contribution to the equity in the property owned by the community property estate made by the benefited community property estate after the date described by subdivision (A); or
    (2)   if the benefited estate is the separate property estate of a spouse:
        (A)   the net equity of the separate property estate in the property owned by the separate property estate as of the date of the first economic contribution to that property by the contributing community property estate or the separate property estate of the other spouse; and
        (B)   any additional contribution to the equity in the property owned by the separate property estate made by the benefited separate property estate after the date described by subdivision (A).
(c)   The amount of a claim under this section may be less than the total of the economic contributions made by the contributing estate, but may not cause the contributing estate to owe funds to the benefited estate.
(d)   The amount of a claim under this section may not exceed the equity in the property on the date of dissolution of the marriage, the death of a spouse, or disposition of the property.
(e)   The use and enjoyment of property during a marriage for which a claim for economic contribution to the property exists does not create a claim of an offsetting benefit against the claim.

Sec. 3.404. Application of Inception of Title Rule; Ownership Interest Not Created

(a)   This subchapter does not affect the rule of inception of title under which the character of property is determined at the time the right to own or claim the property arises.
(b)   The claim for economic contribution created under this subchapter does not create an ownership interest in property, but does create a claim against the property of the benefited estate by the contributing estate. The claim matures on dissolution of the marriage or the death of either spouse.

Sec. 3.405. Management Rights

    This subchapter does not affect the right to manage, control, or dispose of marital property as provided by this chapter.

Sec. 3.406. Equitable Lien

(a)   On dissolution of a marriage, the court shall impose an equitable lien on property of a marital estate to secure a claim for economic contribution in that property by another marital estate.
(b)   On the death of a spouse, a court shall, on application for a claim of economic contribution brought by the surviving spouse, the personal representative of the estate of the deceased spouse, or any other person interested in the estate, as defined by Section 3, Texas Probate Code, impose an equitable lien on the property of a benefited marital estate to secure a claim for economic contribution by a contributing marital estate.
(c)   Subject to homestead restrictions, an equitable lien under this section may be imposed on the entirety of a spouse's property in the marital estate and is not limited to the item of property that benefited from an economic contribution.

Sec. 3.407. Offsetting Claims

The court shall offset a claim for one marital estate's economic contribution in a specific asset of a second marital estate against the second marital estate's claim for economic contribution in a specific asset of the first marital estate.

Sec. 3.408. Claim for Reimbursement

(a)   A claim for economic contribution does not abrogate another claim for reimbursement in a factual circumstance not covered by this subchapter. In the case of a conflict between a claim for economic contribution under this subchapter and a claim for reimbursement, the claim for economic contribution, if proven, prevails.

(b)   A claim for reimbursement includes:

(1)   payment by one marital estate of the unsecured liabilities of another marital estate; and

(2)   inadequate compensation for the time, toil, talent, and effort of a spouse by a business entity under the control and direction of that spouse.

(c)   The court shall resolve a claim for reimbursement by using equitable principles, including the principle that claims for reimbursement may be offset against each other if the court determines it to be appropriate.

(d)   Benefits for the use and enjoyment of property may be offset against a claim for reimbursement for expenditures to benefit a marital estate on property that does not involve a claim for economic contribution to the property.

Sec. 3.409. Nonreimbursable Claims

The court may not recognize a marital estate's claim for reimbursement for:

(1)   the payment of child support, alimony, or spousal maintenance;

(2)   the living expenses of a spouse or child of a spouse;

(3)   contributions of property of a nominal value;

(4)   the payment of a liability of a nominal amount; or

(5)   a student loan owed by a spouse.

Sec. 3.410. Effect of Marital Property Agreements

A premarital or marital property agreement, whether executed before, on, or after September 1, 1999, that satisfies the requirements of Chapter 4 is effective to waive, release, assign, or partition a claim for economic contribution under this subchapter to the same extent the agreement would have been effective to waive, release, assign, or partition a claim for reimbursement under the law as it existed immediately before September 1, 1999, unless the agreement provides otherwise.

TITLE 1. THE MARRIAGE RELATIONSHIP

SUBTITLE C. DISSOLUTION OF MARRIAGE

CHAPTER 6. SUIT FOR DISSOLUTION OF MARRIAGE

SUBCHAPTER A. GROUNDS FOR DIVORCE AND DEFENSES

Sec. 6.001.   Insupportability

On the petition of either party to a marriage, a divorce may be decreed without regard to fault if the marriage has become insupportable because of discord or conflict of personalities that destroys the legitimate ends of the marriage relationship and prevents any reasonable expectation of reconciliation.

TITLE 1. THE MARRIAGE RELATIONSHIP

SUBTITLE C. DISSOLUTION OF MARRIAGE

CHAPTER 6. SUIT FOR DISSOLUTION OF MARRIAGE

SUBCHAPTER D. JURISDICTION, VENUE, AND RESIDENCY QUALIFICATIONS

Sec. 6.301.   General Residency Rule for Divorce Suit

A suit for divorce may not be maintained in this state unless at the time the suit is filed either the petitioner or the respondent has been:

(1)   a domiciliary of this state for the preceding six-month period; and

(2)   a resident of the county in which the suit is filed for the preceding 90-day period.

Sec. 6.302.   Suit for Divorce by Nonresident Spouse

If one spouse has been a domiciliary of this state for at least the last six months, a spouse domiciled in another state or nation may file a suit for divorce in the county in which the domiciliary spouse resides at the time the petition is filed.

Sec. 6.303.   Absence on Public Service

Time spent by a Texas domiciliary outside this state or outside the county of residence of the domiciliary while in the service of the armed forces or other service of the United States or of this state is considered residence in this state and in that county.

Sec. 6.304.   Armed Forces Personnel Not Previously Residents

A person not previously a resident of this state who is serving in the armed forces of the United States and has been stationed at one or more military installations in this state for at least the last six months and at a military installation in a county of this state for at least the last 90 days is considered to be a Texas domiciliary and a resident of that county for those periods for the purpose of filing suit for dissolution of a marriage.

Sec. 6.305.   Acquiring Jurisdiction Over Nonresident Respondent

(a)   If the petitioner in a suit for dissolution of a marriage is a resident or a domiciliary of this state at the time the suit for dissolution is filed, the court may exercise personal jurisdiction over the respondent or over the respondent's personal representative although the respondent is not a resident of this state if:

   (1)   this state is the last marital residence of the petitioner and the respondent and the suit is filed before the second anniversary of the date on which marital residence ended; or

   (2)   there is any basis consistent with the constitutions of this state and the United States for the exercise of the personal jurisdiction.

(b)   A court acquiring jurisdiction under this section also acquires jurisdiction over the respondent in a suit affecting the parent-child relationship.

TITLE 1. THE MARRIAGE RELATIONSHIP

SUBTITLE C. DISSOLUTION OF MARRIAGE

CHAPTER 6. SUIT FOR DISSOLUTION OF MARRIAGE

SUBCHAPTER E. FILING SUIT

Sec. 6.401.   Caption

(a)   Pleadings in a divorce or annulment suit shall be styled "In the Matter of the Marriage of _____ and _____."

Sec. 6.402.   Pleadings

(a)   A petition in a suit for dissolution of marriage is sufficient without the necessity of specifying the underlying evidentiary facts if the petition alleges the grounds relied on substantially in the language of the statute.

(b)   Allegations of grounds for relief, matters of defense, or facts relied on for temporary relief that are stated in short and plain terms are not subject to special exceptions because of form or sufficiency.

(c)   The court shall strike an allegation of evidentiary fact from the pleadings on the motion of a party or on the court's own motion.

Sec. 6.403.   Answer

The respondent in a suit for dissolution of a marriage is not required to answer on oath or affirmation.

Sec. 6.404.   [Repealed]

Sec. 6.405.   Protective Order

(a)   The petition in a suit for dissolution of a marriage must state whether a protective order under Chapter 71 is in effect or if an application for a protective order is pending with regard to the parties to the suit.

(b)   The petitioner shall attach to the petition a copy of each protective order issued under Chapter 71 in which one of the parties to the suit was the applicant and the other party was the respondent without regard to the date of the order. If a copy of the protective order is not available at the time of filing, the petition must state that a copy of the order will be filed with the court before any hearing.

Sec. 6.406.   Mandatory Joinder of Suit Affecting Parent-Child Relationship

(a)   The petition in a suit for dissolution of a marriage shall state whether there are children born or adopted of the marriage who are under 18 years of age or who are otherwise entitled to support as provided by Chapter 154.

(b)   If the parties are parents of a child, as defined by Section 101.003, and the child is not under the continuing jurisdiction of another court as provided by Chapter 155, the suit for dissolution of a marriage must include a suit affecting the parent-child relationship under Title 5.

TITLE 1. THE MARRIAGE RELATIONSHIP

SUBTITLE C. DISSOLUTION OF MARRIAGE

CHAPTER 6. SUIT FOR DISSOLUTION OF MARRIAGE

SUBCHAPTER G. ALTERNATIVE DISPUTE RESOLUTION

Sec. 6.603. Collaborative Law

(a)   On a written agreement of the parties and their attorneys, a dissolution of marriage proceeding may be conducted under collaborative law procedures.

(b)   Collaborative law is a procedure in which the parties and their counsel agree in writing to use their best efforts and make a good faith attempt to resolve their dissolution of marriage dispute on an agreed basis without resorting to judicial intervention except to have the court approve the settlement agreement, make the legal pronouncements, and sign the orders required by law to effectuate the agreement of the parties as the court determines appropriate. The parties' counsel may not serve as litigation counsel except to ask the court to approve the settlement agreement.

(c)   A collaborative law agreement must include provisions for:

(1)   full and candid exchange of information between the parties and their attorneys as necessary to make a proper evaluation of the case;

(2)   suspending court intervention in the dispute while the parties are using collaborative law procedures;

(3)   hiring experts, as jointly agreed, to be used in the procedure;

(4)   withdrawal of all counsel involved in the collaborative law procedure if the collaborative law procedure does not result in settlement of the dispute; and

(5)   other provisions as agreed to by the parties consistent with a good faith effort to collaboratively settle the matter.

(d)   Notwithstanding Rule 11, Texas Rules of Civil Procedure, or another rule or law, a party is entitled to judgment on a collaborative law settlement agreement if the agreement:

(1)   provides, in a prominently displayed statement that is boldfaced, capitalized, or underlined, that the agreement is not subject to revocation; and

(2)   is signed by each party to the agreement and the attorney of each party.

(e)   Subject to Subsection (g), a court that is notified 30 days before trial that the parties are using collaborative law procedures to attempt to settle a dispute may not, until a party notifies the court that the collaborative law procedures did not result in a settlement:

(1)   set a hearing or trial in the case;

(2)   impose discovery deadlines;

(3)   require compliance with scheduling orders; or

(4)   dismiss the case.

(f)   The parties shall notify the court if the collaborative law procedures result in a settlement. If they do not, the parties shall file:

(1)   a status report with the court not later than the 180th day after the date of the written agreement to use the procedures; and

(2)   a status report on or before the first anniversary of the date of the written agreement to use the procedures, accompanied by a motion for continuance that the court shall grant if the status report indicates the desire of the parties to continue to use collaborative law procedures.

(g)   If the collaborative law procedures do not result in a settlement on or before the second anniversary of the date that the suit was filed, the court may:

(1)   set the suit for trial on the regular docket; or

(2)   dismiss the suit without prejudice.

(h)   The provisions for confidentiality of alternative dispute resolution procedures as provided in Chapter 154, Civil Practice and Remedies Code, apply equally to collaborative law procedures under this section.

TITLE 1. THE MARRIAGE RELATIONSHIP

SUBTITLE C. DISSOLUTION OF MARRIAGE

CHAPTER 6. SUIT FOR DISSOLUTION OF MARRIAGE

SUBCHAPTER H. TRIAL AND APPEAL

Sec. 6.701.   Failure to Answer

In a suit for divorce, the petition may not be taken as confessed if the respondent does not file an answer.

Sec. 6.702.   Waiting Period

(a)   The court may not grant a divorce before the 60th day after the date the suit was filed. A decree rendered in violation of this subsection is not subject to collateral attack.

(b)   A waiting period is not required before a court may grant an annulment or declare a marriage void other than as required in civil cases generally.

Sec. 6.706.   Change of Name

(a)   In a decree of divorce or annulment, the court shall change the name of a party specifically requesting the change to a name previously used by the party unless the court states in the decree a reason for denying the change of name.

(b)   The court may not deny a change of name solely to keep the last name of family members.

(c)   A change of name does not release a person from liability incurred by the person under a previous name or defeat a right the person held under a previous name.

(d)   A person whose name is changed under this section may apply for a change of name certificate from the clerk of the court as provided by Section 45.106.

Sec. 6.711.   Findings of Fact and Conclusions of Law

(a)   In a suit for dissolution of a marriage in which the court has rendered a judgment dividing the estate of the parties, on request by a party, the court shall state in writing its findings of fact and conclusions of law concerning:

(1)   the characterization of each party's assets, liabilities, claims, and offsets on which disputed evidence has been presented; and

(2)   the value or amount of the community estate's assets, liabilities, claims, and offsets on which disputed evidence has been presented.

(b)   A request for findings of fact and conclusions of law under this section must conform to the Texas Rules of Civil Procedure.

TITLE 1. THE MARRIAGE RELATIONSHIP

SUBTITLE C. DISSOLUTION OF MARRIAGE

CHAPTER 6. SUIT FOR DISSOLUTION OF MARRIAGE

SUBCHAPTER I. REMARRIAGE

Sec. 6.801.   Remarriage

(a)   Except as otherwise provided by this subchapter, neither party to a divorce may marry a third party before the 31st day after the date the divorce is decreed.

(b)   The former spouses may marry each other at any time.

Sec. 6.902.   Waiver of Prohibition Against Remarriage

For good cause shown the court may waive the prohibition against remarriage provided by this subchapter as to either or both spouses if a record of the proceedings is made and preserved or if findings of fact and conclusions of law are filed by the court.

TITLE 1. THE MARRIAGE RELATIONSHIP

SUBTITLE C. DISSOLUTION OF MARRIAGE

CHAPTER 7. AWARD OF MARITAL PROPERTY

Sec. 7.001.   General Rule of Property Division

In a decree of divorce or annulment, the court shall order a division of the estate of the parties in a manner that the court deems just and right, having due regard for the rights of each party and any children of the marriage.

Sec. 7.002.   Division and Disposition of Certain Property Under Special Circumstances

(a)   In addition to the division of the estate of the parties required by Section 7.001, in a decree of divorce or annulment the court shall order a division of the following real and personal property, wherever situated, in a manner that the court deems just and right, having due regard for the rights of each party and any children of the marriage:

(1)   property that was acquired by either spouse while domiciled in another state and that would have been community property if the spouse who acquired the property had been domiciled in this state at the time of the acquisition; or

(2)   property that was acquired by either spouse in exchange for real or personal property and that would have been community property if the spouse who acquired the property so exchanged had been domiciled in this state at the time of its acquisition.

(b)   In a decree of divorce or annulment, the court shall award to a spouse the following real and personal property, wherever situated, as the separate property of the spouse:

(1)   property that was acquired by the spouse while domiciled in another state and that would have been the spouse's separate property if the spouse had been domiciled in this state at the time of acquisition; or

(2)   property that was acquired by the spouse in exchange for real or personal property and that would have been the spouse's separate property if the spouse had been domiciled in this state at the time of acquisition.

(c)   in a decree of divorce or annulment, the court shall confirm the following as the separate property of a spouse if partitioned or exchanged by written agreement of the spouses:

(1)   income and earnings from the spouses' property, wages, salaries, and other forms of compensation received on or after January 1 of the year in which the suit for dissolution of marriage was filed; or

(2)   income and earnings from the spouses' property, wages, salaries, and other forms of compensation received in another year during which the spouses were married for any part of the year.

Sec. 7.003.   Disposition of Retirement and Employment Benefits and Other Plans

In a decree of divorce or annulment, the court shall determine the rights of both spouses in any pension, retirement plan, annuity, individual retirement account, employee stock option plan, stock option, or other form of savings, bonus, profit-sharing, or other employer plan or financial plan of an employee or a participant, regardless of whether the person is self-employed, in the nature of compensation or savings.

Sec. 7.004.   Disposition of Rights in Insurance

In a decree of divorce or annulment, the court shall specifically divide or award the rights of each spouse in an insurance policy.

Sec. 7.005.   Insurance Coverage Not Specifically Awarded

(a)   If in a decree of divorce or annulment the court does not specifically award all of the rights of the spouses in an insurance policy other than life insurance in effect at the time the decree is rendered, the policy remains in effect until the policy expires according to the policy's own terms.

(b)   The proceeds of a valid claim under the policy are payable as follows:

(1)   if the interest in the property insured was awarded solely to one former spouse by the decree, to that former spouse;

(2)   if an interest in the property insured was awarded to each former spouse, to those former spouses in proportion to the interests awarded;

(3)   if the insurance coverage is directly related to the person of one of the former spouses, to that former spouse.

(c)   The failure of either former spouse to change the endorsement on the policy to reflect the distribution of proceeds established by this section does not relieve the insurer of liability to pay the proceeds or any other obligation on the policy.

(d)   This section does not affect the right of a former spouse to assert an ownership interest in an undivided life insurance policy, as provided by Subchapter D, Chapter 9.

Sec. 7.006.   Agreement Incident to Divorce or Annulment

(a)   To promote amicable settlement of disputes in a suit for divorce or annulment, the spouses may enter into a written agreement concerning the division of the property and the liabilities of the spouses and maintenance of either spouse. The agreement may be revised or repudiated before rendition of the divorce or annulment unless the agreement is binding under another rule of law.

(b)   If the court finds that the terms of the written agreement in a divorce or annulment are just and right, those terms are binding on the court. If the court approves the agreement, the court may set forth the agreement in full or incorporate the agreement by reference in the final decree.

(c)   If the court finds that the terms of the written agreement in a divorce or annulment are not just and right, the court may request the spouses to submit a revised agreement or may set the case for a contested hearing.

Sec. 7.007.   Disposition of Claim for Economic Contribution or Claim for Reimbursement

(a)   In a decree of divorce or annulment, the court shall determine the rights of both spouses in a claim for economic contribution as provided by Subchapter E, Chapter 3, and in a manner that the court considers just and right, having due regard for the rights of each party and any children of the marriage, shall:

(1)   order a division of a claim for economic contribution of the community marital estate to the separate marital estate of one of the spouses;

(2)   order that a claim for an economic contribution by one separate marital estate of a spouse to the community marital estate of the spouses be awarded to the owner of the contributing separate marital estate; and

(3)   order that a claim for economic contribution of one separate marital estate in the separate marital estate of the other spouse be awarded to the owner of the contributing marital estate.

(b)   In a decree of divorce or annulment, the court shall determine the rights of both spouses in a claim for reimbursement as provided by Subchapter E, Chapter 3, and shall apply equitable principles to:

(1)   determine whether to recognize the claim after taking into account all the relative circumstances of the spouses; and

(2)   order a division of the claim for reimbursement, if appropriate, in a manner that the court considers just and right, having due regard for the rights of each party and any children of the marriage.

Sec. 7.008.   Consideration of Taxes

In ordering the division of the estate of the parties to a suit for dissolution of a marriage, the court may consider:

(1)   whether a specific asset will be subject to taxation; and

(2)   if the asset will be subject to taxation, when the tax will be required to be paid.

TITLE 1. THE MARRIAGE RELATIONSHIP

SUBTITLE C. DISSOLUTION OF MARRIAGE

CHAPTER 8. MAINTENANCE

SUBCHAPTER A. GENERAL PROVISIONS

Sec. 8.001.   Definitions

In this Chapter:

(1)   "Maintenance" means an award in a suit for dissolution of a marriage of periodic payments from the future income of one spouse for the support of the other spouse.

(2)   "Notice of application for a writ of withholding" means the document delivered to an obligor and filed with the court as required by this chapter for the nonjudicial determination of arrears and initiation of withholding for spousal maintenance.

(3)   "Obligee" means a person entitled to receive payments under the terms of an order for spousal maintenance.

(4)   "Obligor" means a person required to make periodic payments under the terms of an order for spousal maintenance.

(5)   "Writ of withholding" means the document issued by the clerk of a court and delivered to an employer, directing that earnings be withheld for payment of spousal maintenance as provided by this chapter.

TITLE 1. THE MARRIAGE RELATIONSHIP

SUBTITLE C. DISSOLUTION OF MARRIAGE

CHAPTER 8. MAINTENANCE

SUBCHAPTER B.   COURT-ORDERED MAINTENANCE

Sec. 8.051.   Eligibility for Maintenance; Court Order

In a suit for dissolution of a marriage or in a proceeding for maintenance in a court with personal jurisdiction over both former spouses following the dissolution of their marriage by a court that lacked personal jurisdiction over an absent spouse, the court may order maintenance for either spouse only if:

(1)   the spouse from whom maintenance is requested was convicted of or received deferred adjudication for a criminal offense that also constitutes an act of family violence under Title 4 and the offense occurred:

(A)   within two years before the date on which a suit for dissolution of the marriage is filed; or

(B)   while the suit is pending; or

(2)   the duration of the marriage was 10 years or longer, the spouse seeking maintenance lacks sufficient property, including property distributed to the spouse under this code, to provide for the spouse's minimum reasonable needs, as limited by Section 8.054, and the spouse seeking maintenance:

(A)   is unable to support himself or herself through appropriate employment because of an incapacitating physical or mental disability;

(B)   is the custodian of a child who requires substantial care and personal supervision because a physical or mental disability makes it necessary, taking into consideration the needs of the child, that the spouse not be employed outside the home; or

(C)   clearly lacks earning ability in the labor market adequate to provide support for the spouse's minimum reasonable needs, as limited by Section 8.054.

Sec. 8.052. Factors In Determining Maintenance

A court that determines that a spouse is eligible to receive maintenance under this chapter shall determine the nature, amount, duration, and manner of periodic payments by considering all relevant factors, including:

(1)   the financial resources of the spouse seeking maintenance, including the community and separate property and liabilities apportioned to that spouse in the dissolution proceeding, and that spouse's ability to meet the spouse's needs independently;

(2)   the education and employment skills of the spouses, the time necessary to acquire sufficient education or training to enable the spouse seeking maintenance to find appropriate employment, the availability of that education or training, and the feasibility of that education or training;

(3)   the duration of the marriage;

(4)   the age, employment history, earning ability, and physical and emotional condition of the spouse seeking maintenance;

(5)   the ability of the spouse from whom maintenance is requested to meet that spouse's personal needs and to provide periodic child support payments, if applicable, while meeting the personal needs of the spouse seeking maintenance;

(6)   acts by either spouse resulting in excessive or abnormal expenditures or destruction, concealment, or fraudulent disposition of community property, joint tenancy, or other property held in common;

(7)   the comparative financial resources of the spouses, including medical, retirement, insurance, or other benefits, and the separate property of each spouse;

(8)   the contribution by one spouse to the education, training, or increased earning power of the other spouse;

(9)   the property brought to the marriage by either spouse;

(10)   the contribution of a spouse as homemaker;

(11)   marital misconduct of the spouse seeking maintenance; and

(12)   the efforts of the spouse seeking maintenance to pursue available employment counseling as provided by Chapter 304, Labor Code.

Sec. 8.053. Presumption

(a)   Except as provided by Subsection (b), it is presumed that maintenance under Section 8.051(2) is not warranted unless the spouse seeking maintenance has exercised diligence in:

(1)   seeking suitable employment; or

(2)   developing the necessary skills to become self-supporting during a period of separation and during the time the suit for dissolution of the marriage is pending.

(b)   This section does not apply to a spouse who is not able to satisfy the presumption in Subsection (a) because the spouse:

(1)   has an incapacitating physical or mental disability; or

(2)   is the custodian of a child of the marriage of any age who requires substantial care and personal supervision because a physical or mental disability makes it necessary, taking into consideration the needs of the child, that the spouse not be employed outside the home.

Sec. 8.054. Duration of Maintenance Order

(a)   Except as provided by Subsection (b), a court:

(1)   may not order maintenance that remains in effect for more than three years after the date of the order; and

(2)   shall limit the duration of a maintenance order to the shortest reasonable period that allows the spouse seeking maintenance to meet the spouse's minimum reasonable needs by obtaining appropriate employment or developing an appropriate skill, unless the ability of the spouse to provide for the spouse's minimum reasonable needs through employment is substantially or totally diminished because of:

(A)   physical or mental disability;

(B)   duties as the custodian of an infant or young child; or

(C)   another compelling impediment to gainful employment.

(b)   If a spouse seeking maintenance is unable to support himself or herself through appropriate employment because the spouse has an incapacitating physical or mental disability or because the spouse is the custodian of a child of the marriage of any age who has a physical or mental disability, the court may order maintenance for as long as the disability continues. The court may order periodic review of its order, on the request of either party or on its own motion, to determine whether the disability continues to render the spouse unable to support himself or herself through appropriate employment. The continuation of spousal maintenance under these circumstances is subject to a motion to modify as provided by Section 8.057.

Sec. 8.055. Amount of Maintenance
(a)   A court may not order maintenance that requires an obligor to pay monthly more than the lesser of:
    (1) $2,500; or
    (2)   20 percent of the spouse's average monthly gross income.
(b)   The court shall set the amount that an obligor is required to pay in a maintenance order to provide for the minimum reasonable needs of the obligee, considering employment or property received in the dissolution of the marriage or otherwise owned by the obligee that contributes to the minimum reasonable needs of the obligee.
(c)   Department of Veterans Affairs service-connected disability compensation, social security benefits and disability benefits, and workers' compensation benefits are excluded from maintenance.
(d)   For purposes of this chapter, "gross income" means resources as defined in Sections 154.062(b) and (c), regarding any deductions listed in section 154.062(d) and disregarding those benefits excluded under Subsection (c) of this section.

Sec. 8.056. Termination
(a)   The obligation to pay future maintenance terminates on the death of either party or on the remarriage of the obligee.
(b)   After a hearing, the court shall terminate the maintenance order if the obligee cohabits with another person in a permanent place of abode on a continuing, conjugal basis.

Sec. 8.057. Modification of Maintenance Order
(a)   The amount of maintenance specified in a court order or the portion of a decree that provides for the support of a former spouse may be reduced by the filing of a motion in the court that originally rendered the order. A party affected by the order or the portion of the decree to be modified may file the motion.
(b)   Notice of a motion to modify maintenance and the response, if any, are governed by the Texas Rules of Civil Procedure applicable to the filing of an original lawsuit. Notice must be given by service of citation, and a response must be in the form of an answer due on or before 10 a.m. of the first Monday after 20 days after the date of service. A court shall set a hearing on the motion in the manner provided by Rule 245, Texas Rules of Civil Procedure.
(c)   After a hearing, the court may modify an original or modified order or portion of a decree providing for maintenance on a proper showing of a material and substantial change in circumstances of either party. The court shall apply the modification only to payment accruing after the filing of the motion to modify.
(d)   A loss of employment or circumstances that render a former spouse unable to support himself or herself through appropriate employment by reason of incapacitating physical or mental disability that occur after the divorce or annulment are not grounds for the institution of spousal maintenance for the benefit of the former spouse.

Sec. 8.058. Maintenance Arrearages
A spousal maintenance payment not timely made constitutes an arrearage.

Sec. 8.059. Enforcement of Maintenance Order
(a)   The court may enforce by contempt the court's maintenance order or an agreement for the payment of maintenance voluntarily entered into between the parties and approved by the court.
(b)   On the suit to enforce by an obligee, the court may render judgment against a defaulting party for the amount of arrearages after notice by service of citation, answer, if any, and a hearing finding that the defaulting party has failed or refused to carry out the terms of the order. The judgment may be enforced by any means available for the enforcement of judgment for debts.
(c)   It is an affirmative defense to an allegation of contempt of court or the violation of a condition of probation requiring payment of court-ordered maintenance that the obligor:
    (1)   lacked the ability to provide maintenance in the amount ordered;
    (2)   lacked property that could be sold, mortgaged, or otherwise pledged to raise the funds needed;
    (3)   attempted unsuccessfully to borrow the needed funds; and
    (4)   did not know of a source from which the money could have been borrowed or otherwise legally obtained.
(d)   The issue of the existence of an affirmative defense does not arise unless evidence is admitted supporting the defense. If the issue of the existence of an affirmative defense arises, an obligor must prove the affirmative defense by a preponderance of the evidence.
(e)   A court may enforce an order for spousal maintenance under this chapter by ordering garnishment of the obligor's wages or by any other means available under this section.

Sec. 8.060. Putative Spouse
In a suit to declare a marriage void, a putative spouse who did not have knowledge of an existing impediment to a valid marriage may be awarded maintenance if otherwise qualified to receive maintenance under this chapter.

Sec. 8.061. Unmarried Cohabitants
An order for maintenance is not authorized between unmarried cohabitants under any circumstances.

TITLE 1. THE MARRIAGE RELATIONSHIP

SUBTITLE C. DISSOLUTION OF MARRIAGE

CHAPTER 8. MAINTENANCE

SUBCHAPTER C. INCOME WITHHOLDING

Sec. 8.101. Income Withholding; General Rule

(a)   In a proceeding in which periodic payments of spousal maintenance are ordered, modified, or enforced, the court may order that income be withheld from the disposable earnings of the obligor as provided by this chapter.

(b)   This subchapter does not apply to contractual alimony or spousal maintenance, regardless of whether the alimony or maintenance is taxable, unless:

    (1)   the contract specifically permits income withholding; or

    (2)   the alimony or maintenance payments are not timely made under the terms of the contract.

(c)   An order or writ of withholding for spousal maintenance may be combined with an order or writ of withholding for child support only if the obligee has been appointed managing conservator of the child for whom the child support is owed and is the conservator with whom the child primarily resides.

(d)   An order or writ of withholding that combines withholding for spousal maintenance and child support must:

    (1)   require that the withheld amounts be paid to the appropriate place of payment under Section 154.004;

    (2)   be in the form prescribed by the Title IV-D agency under Section 158.106;

    (3)   clearly indicate the amounts withheld that are to be applied to current spousal maintenance and to any maintenance arrearages; and

    (4)   subject to the maximum withholding allowed under Section 8.106, order that withheld income be applied in the following order of priority:

        (A)   current child support;

        (B)   current spousal maintenance;

        (C)   child support arrearages; and

        (D)   spousal maintenance arrearages.

(e)   Garnishment for the purposes of spousal maintenance does not apply to unemployment insurance benefit payments.

Sec. 8.102. Withholding for Arrearages in Addition to Current Spousal Maintenance

(a)   The court may order that, in addition to income withheld for current spousal maintenance, income be withheld from the disposable earnings of the obligor to be applied toward the liquidation of any arrearages.

(b)   The additional amount withheld to be applied toward arrearages must be whichever of the following amounts will discharge the arrearages in the least amount of time:

    (1)   an amount sufficient to discharge the arrearages in not more than two years; or

    (2)   20 percent of the amount withheld for current maintenance.

Sec. 8.103. Withholding for Arrearages When Current Maintenance Is Not Due

A court may order income withholding to be applied toward arrearages in an amount sufficient to discharge those arrearages in not more than two years if current spousal maintenance is no longer owed.

Sec. 8.104. Withholding to Satisfy Judgment for Arrearages

The court, in rendering a cumulative judgment for arrearages, may order that a reasonable amount of income be withheld from the disposable earnings of the obligor to be applied toward the satisfaction of the judgment.

Sec. 8.105. Priority of Withholding

An order or writ of withholding under this chapter has priority over any garnishment, attachment, execution, or other order affecting disposable earnings, except for an order or writ of withholding for child support under Chapter 158.

Sec. 8.106. Maximum Amount Withheld From Earnings

An order or writ of withholding must direct that an obligor's employer withhold from the obligor's disposable earnings the lesser of:

    (1)   the amount specified in the order or writ; or

    (2)   an amount that, when added to the amount of income being withheld by the employer for child support, is equal to 50 percent of the obligor's disposable earnings.

Sec. 8.107. Order Or Writ Binding On Employer Doing Business In This State

An order or writ of withholding issued under this chapter and delivered to an employer doing business in this state is binding on the employer without regard to whether the obligor resides or works outside this state.

Sec. 8.108. Voluntary Writ Of Withholding By Obligor

(a)   An obligor may file with the clerk of the court a notarized or acknowledged request signed by the obligor and the obligee for the issuance and delivery to the obligor's employer of a writ of withholding. The obligor may file the request under this section regardless of whether a writ or order has been served on any party or whether the obligor owes arrearages.

(b)   Receipt of a request under this section, the clerk shall issue and deliver a writ of withholding in the manner provided by this subchapter.

(c)   An employer who receives a writ of withholding issued under this section may request a hearing in the same manner and according to the same terms provided by Section 8.205.

(d)   An obligor whose employer receives a writ of withholding issued under this section may request a hearing in the manner provided by Section 8.258.

(e)   An obligee may contest a writ of income withholding issued under this section by requesting, not later than the 180th day after the date on which the obligee discovers that the writ was issued, a hearing to be conducted in the manner provided by Section 8.258 for a hearing on a motion to stay.

(f)   A writ of withholding under this section may not reduce the total amount of spousal maintenance, including arrearages, owed by the obligor.

TITLE 1. THE MARRIAGE RELATIONSHIP

SUBTITLE C. DISSOLUTION OF MARRIAGE

CHAPTER 8. MAINTENANCE

SUBCHAPTER D. PROCEDURE

Sec. 8.151. Time Limit

The court may issue an order or writ for withholding under this chapter at any time before all spousal maintenance and arrearages are paid.

Sec. 8.152. Contents of Order of Withholding

(a)   An order of withholding must state:
   (1)   the style, cause number, and court having jurisdiction to enforce the order;
   (2)   the name, address, and, if available, the social security number of the obligor;
   (3)   the amount and duration of the spousal maintenance payments, including the amount and duration of withholding for arrearages, if any; and
   (4)   the name, address, and, if available, the social security number of the obligee.

(b)   The order for withholding must require the obligor to notify the court promptly of any material change affecting the order, including a change of employer.

(c)   If requested by an obligee, the court may exclude from an order of withholding the obligee's address and social security number if the obligee or a member of the obligee's family or household is a victim of family violence and is the subject of a protective order to which the obligor is also subject. On granting a request under this subsection, the court shall order the clerk to:
   (1)   strike the address and social security number required by Subsection (a) from the order or writ of withholding; and
   (2)   maintain a confidential record of the obligee's address and social security number to be used only by the court.

Sec. 8.153. Request For Issuance of Order or Writ of Withholding

An obligor or obligee may file with the clerk of the court a request for issuance of an order or writ of withholding.

Sec. 8.154. Issuance And Delivery of Order or Writ of Withholding

(a)   Receipt of a request for issuance of an order or writ of withholding, the clerk of the court shall deliver a certified copy of the order or writ to the obligor's current employer or to any subsequent employer of the obligor. The clerk shall attach a copy of Subchapter E to the order or writ.

(b)   Not later than the fourth working day after the date the order is signed or the request is filed, whichever is later, the clerk shall issue and deliver the certified copy of the order or writ by:
   (1)   certified or registered mail, return receipt requested, to the employer; or
   (2)   service of citation to:
      (A)   the person authorized to receive service of process for the employer in civil cases generally; or
      (B)   a person designated by the employer by written notice to the clerk to receive orders or notices of income withholding.

TITLE 5. THE PARENT-CHILD RELATIONSHIP AND THE SUIT AFFECTING THE PARENT-CHILD RELATIONSHIP

SUBTITLE A. GENERAL PROVISIONS

CHAPTER 101. DEFINITIONS

Sec. 101.015. Health Insurance

"Health insurance" means insurance coverage that provides basic health care services, including usual physician services, office visits, hospitalization, and laboratory, X-ray, and emergency services, that may be provided through a health maintenance organization or other private or public organization, other than medical assistance under Chapter 32, Human Resources Code.

Sec. 101.024. Parent

(a) "Parent" means the mother, a man presumed to be the father, a man legally determined to be the father, a man who has been adjudicated to be the father by a court of competent jurisdiction, a man who has acknowledged his paternity under applicable law, or an adoptive mother or father. Except as provided by Subsection (b), the term does not include a parent as to whom the parent-child relationship has been terminated.

(b) For purposes of establishing, determining the terms of, modifying, or enforcing an order, a reference in this title to a parent includes a person ordered to pay child support under Section 154.001(a-1) or to provide medical support for a child.

TITLE 5. THE PARENT-CHILD RELATIONSHIP AND THE SUIT AFFECTING THE PARENT-CHILD RELATIONSHIP

SUBTITLE A. GENERAL PROVISIONS

CHAPTER 102. FILING SUIT

Sec. 102.003. General Standing to File Suit

(a) An original suit may be filed at any time by:
  (1) a parent of the child;
  (2) the child through a representative authorized by the court;
  (3) a custodian or person having the right of visitation with or access to the child appointed by an order of a court of another state or country;
  (4) a guardian of the person or of the estate of the child;
  (5) a governmental entity;
  (6) an authorized agency;
  (7) a licensed child placing agency;
  (8) a man alleging himself to be the father of a child filing in accordance with Chapter 160, subject to the limitations of that chapter, but not otherwise;
  (9) a person, other than a foster parent, who has had actual care, control, and possession of the child for at least six months ending not more than 90 days preceding the date of the filing of the petition;
  (10) a person designated as the managing conservator in a revoked or unrevoked affidavit of relinquishment under Chapter 161 or to whom consent to adoption has been given in writing under Chapter 162;
  (11) a person with whom the child and the child's guardian, managing conservator, or parent have resided for at least six months ending not more than 90 days preceding the date of the filing of the petition if the child's guardian, managing conservator, or parent is deceased at the time of the filing of the petition;
  (12) a person who is the foster parent of a child placed by the Department of Protective and Regulatory Services in the person's home for at least 12 months ending not more than 90 days preceding the date of the filing of the petition;
  (13) a person who is a relative of the child within the third degree by consanguinity, as determined by Chapter 573, Government Code, if the child's parents are deceased at the time of the filing of the petition; or
  (14) a person who has been named as a prospective adoptive parent of a child by a pregnant woman or the parent of the child, in a verified written statement to confer standing executed under Section 102.0035, regardless of whether the child has been born.

(b) In computing the time necessary for standing under Subsections (a)(9), (11), and (12), the court may not require that the time be continuous and uninterrupted but shall consider the child's principal residence during the relevant time preceding the date of commencement of the suit.

(c) Notwithstanding the time requirements of Subsection (a)(12), a person who is the foster parent of a child may file a suit to adopt a child for whom the person is providing foster care at any time after the person has been approved to adopt the child. The standing to file suit under this subsection applies only to the adoption of a child who is eligible to be adopted.

Sec. 102.004. Standing for Grandparent or Other Person

(a) In addition to the general standing to file suit provided by Section 102.003, a grandparent may file an original suit requesting managing conservatorship if there is satisfactory proof to the court that:
  (1) the order requested is necessary because the child's present circumstances would significantly impair the child's physical health or emotional development; or
  (2) both parents, the surviving parent, or the managing conservator or custodian either filed the petition or consented to the suit.

(b) An original suit requesting possessory conservatorship may not be filed by a grandparent or other person. However, the court may grant a grandparent or other person deemed by the court to have had substantial past contact with the child leave to intervene in a pending suit filed by a person authorized to do so under this subchapter if there is satisfactory proof to the court that appointment of a parent as a sole managing conservator or both parents as joint managing conservators would significantly impair the child's physical health or emotional development.

(c) Possession of or access to a child by a grandparent is governed by the standards established by Chapter 153.

[AUTHOR'S NOTE: *This relates to the situation where there are minor children*]

Sec. 102.008. Contents of Petition

(a) The petition and all other documents in a proceeding filed under this title (except a suit for adoption of an adult) shall be entitled "In the interest of _____, a child."

(b) The petition must include:
   (1) a statement that the court in which the petition is filed has continuing exclusive jurisdiction or that no court has continuing jurisdiction of the suit;
   (2) the name, sex, place and date of birth, and place of residence of the child, except that if adoption of a child is requested, the name of the child may be omitted;
   (3) the full name, age, and place of residence of the petitioner and the petitioner's relationship to the child or the fact that no relationship exists;
   (4) the names, ages, and place of residence of the parents, except in a suit in which adoption is requested;
   (5) the name and place of residence of the managing conservator, if any, or the child's custodian, if any, appointed by an order of the court in another state or country;
   (6) the names and places of residence or the guardians of the person and estate of the child, if any;
   (7) the names and places of residence of possessory conservators or other persons, if any, having possession of or access to the child under an order of the court;
   (8) the name and place of residence of the alleged father of the child or a statement that the identity of the father of the child is unknown;
   (9) a full description and statement of value of all property owned or possessed by the child;
   (10) a statement describing what action the court is requested to make concerning the child and the statutory grounds on which the request is made; and
   (11) any other information required by this title.

TITLE 5. THE PARENT-CHILD RELATIONSHIP AND THE SUIT AFFECTING THE PARENT-CHILD RELATIONSHIP

SUBTITLE A. GENERAL PROVISIONS

CHAPTER 105. SETTINGS, HEARINGS, AND ORDERS

Sec. 105.006.   Contents of Final Order
(a) A final order must contain:
   (1) the social security number and driver's license number of each party to the suit, including the child, except that the child's social security number or driver's license number is not required if the child has not been assigned a social security number or driver's license number; and
   (2) each party's current residence address, mailing address, home telephone number, name of employer, address of employment, and work telephone number, except as provided by Subsection (c).
(b) Except as provided by Subsection (c), the court shall order each party to inform each other party of an intended change in any of the information required by this section as long as any person, as a result of the order, is under an obligation to pay child support or is entitled to possession of or access to a child. The court shall order that notice of the intended change be given at the earlier of:
   (1) the 60th day before the date the party intends to make the change; or
   (2) the fifth day after the date that the party knew of the change, if the party did not know or could not have known of the change in sufficient time to comply with Subdivision (1).
(c) If a court finds after notice and hearing that requiring a party to provide the information required by this section is likely to cause the child or a conservator harassment, abuse, serious harm, or injury, the court may:
   (1) order the information not to be disclosed to another party; or
   (2) render any other order the court considers necessary.
(d) An order in a suit that orders child support or possession of or access to a child must contain the following notice in bold-faced type or in capital letters:

"FAILURE TO OBEY A COURT ORDER FOR CHILD SUPPORT OR FOR POSSESSION OF OR ACCESS TO A CHILD MAY RESULT IN FURTHER LITIGATION TO ENFORCE THE ORDER, INCLUDING CONTEMPT OF COURT. A FINDING OF CONTEMPT MAY BE PUNISHED BY CONFINEMENT IN JAIL FOR UP TO SIX MONTHS, A FINE OF UP TO $500 FOR EACH VIOLATION, AND A MONEY JUDGMENT FOR PAYMENT OF ATTORNEY'S FEES AND COURT COSTS.

"FAILURE OF A PARTY TO MAKE A CHILD SUPPORT PAYMENT TO THE PLACE AND IN THE MANNER REQUIRED BY A COURT ORDER MAY RESULT IN THE PARTY NOT RECEIVING CREDIT FOR MAKING THE PAYMENT.

"FAILURE OF A PARTY TO PAY CHILD SUPPORT DOES NOT JUSTIFY DENYING THAT PARTY COURT-ORDERED POSSESSION OF OR ACCESS TO A CHILD. REFUSAL BY A PARTY TO ALLOW POSSESSION OF OR ACCESS TO A CHILD DOES NOT JUSTIFY FAILURE TO PAY COURT-ORDERED CHILD SUPPORT TO THAT PARTY."

(e) Except as provided by Subsection (c), an order in a suit that orders child support or possession of or access to a child must also contain the following order in bold-faced type or in capital letters:

"EACH PERSON WHO IS A PARTY TO THIS ORDER IS ORDERED TO NOTIFY EACH OTHER PARTY WITHIN 10 DAYS AFTER THE DATE OF ANY CHANGE IN THE PARTY'S CURRENT RESIDENCE ADDRESS, MAILING ADDRESS, HOME TELEPHONE NUMBER, NAME OF EMPLOYER, ADDRESS OF EMPLOYMENT, AND WORK TELEPHONE NUMBER. THE PARTY IS ORDERED TO GIVE NOTICE OF AN INTENDED CHANGE IN ANY OF THE REQUIRED INFORMATION TO EACH OTHER PARTY ON OR BEFORE THE 60TH DAY BEFORE THE INTENDED CHANGE. IF THE PARTY DOES NOT KNOW OR COULD NOT HAVE KNOWN OF THE CHANGE IN SUFFICIENT TIME TO PROVIDE 60-DAY NOTICE, THE PARTY IS ORDERED TO GIVE NOTICE OF THE CHANGE ON OR BEFORE THE FIFTH DAY AFTER THE DATE THAT THE PARTY KNOWS OF THE CHANGE.

"THE DUTY TO FURNISH THIS INFORMATION TO EACH OTHER PARTY CONTINUES AS LONG AS ANY PERSON, BY VIRTUE OF THIS ORDER, IS UNDER AN OBLIGATION TO PAY CHILD SUPPORT OR IS ENTITLED TO POSSESSION OF OR ACCESS TO A CHILD.

"FAILURE BY A PARTY TO OBEY THE ORDER OF THIS COURT TO PROVIDE EACH OTHER PARTY WITH THE CHANGE IN THE REQUIRED INFORMATION MAY RESULT IN FURTHER LITIGATION TO ENFORCE THE ORDER, INCLUDING CONTEMPT OF COURT. A FINDING OF CONTEMPT MAY BE PUNISHED BY CONFINEMENT IN JAIL FOR UP TO SIX MONTHS, A FINE OF UP TO $500 FOR EACH VIOLATION, AND A MONEY JUDGMENT FOR PAYMENT OF ATTORNEY'S FEES AND COURT COSTS."

(e1) An order in a suit that provides for the possession of or access to a child must contain the following prominently displayed statement in boldfaced type, in capital letters, or underlined:

"NOTICE TO ANY PEACE OFFICER OF THE STATE OF TEXAS: YOU MAY USE REASONABLE EFFORTS TO ENFORCE THE TERMS OF CHILD CUSTODY SPECIFIED IN THIS ORDER. A PEACE OFFICER WHO RELIES ON THE TERMS OF A COURT ORDER AND THE OFFICER'S AGENCY ARE ENTITLED TO THE APPLICABLE IMMUNITY AGAINST ANY CLAIM, CIVIL OR OTHERWISE, REGARDING THE OFFICER'S GOOD FAITH ACTS PERFORMED IN THE SCOPE OF THE OFFICER'S DUTIES IN ENFORCING THE TERMS OF THE ORDER THAT RELATE TO CHILD CUSTODY. ANY PERSON WHO KNOWINGLY PRESENTS FOR ENFORCEMENT AN ORDER THAT IS INVALID OR NO LONGER IN EFFECT COMMITS AN OFFENSE THAT MAY BE PUNISHABLE BY CONFINEMENT IN JAIL FOR AS LONG AS TWO YEARS AND A FINE OF AS MUCH AS $ 10,000."

TITLE 5. THE PARENT-CHILD RELATIONSHIP AND THE SUIT AFFECTING THE PARENT-CHILD RELATIONSHIP

SUBTITLE B. SUITS AFFECTING THE PARENT-CHILD RELATIONSHIP

CHAPTER 153. CONSERVATORSHIP, POSSESSION, AND ACCESS

SUBCHAPTER A. GENERAL PROVISIONS

Sec. 153.001. Public Policy
(a) The public policy of this state is to:
  (1) assure that children will have frequent and continuing contact with parents who have shown the ability to act in the best interest of the child;
  (2) provide a safe, stable, and nonviolent environment for the child; and
  (3) encourage parents to share in the rights and duties of raising their child after the parents have separated or dissolved their marriage.
(b) A court may not render an order that conditions the right of a conservator to possession of or access to a child on the payment of child support.

Sec. 153.002. Best Interest of Child
The best interest of the child shall always be the primary consideration of the court in determining the issues of conservatorship and possession of and access to the child.

Sec. 153.002. No Discrimination Based on Sex or Marital Status
The court shall consider the qualifications of the parties without regard to their marital status or to the sex of the party or the child in determining:
  (1) which party to appoint as sole managing conservator;
  (2) whether to appoint a party as joint managing conservator; and
  (3) the terms and conditions of conservatorship and possession of and access to the child.

Sec. 153.004. History of Domestic Violence
(a) In determining whether to appoint a party as a sole or joint managing conservator, the court shall consider evidence of the intentional use of abusive physical force by a party against the party's spouse, a parent of the child, or any person younger than 18 years of age committed within a two-year period preceding the filing of the suit or during the pendency of the suit.
(b) The court may not appoint joint managing conservators if credible evidence is presented of a history or pattern of past or present child neglect, or physical or sexual abuse by one parent directed against the other parent, a spouse, or a child, including a sexual assault in violation of Section 22.011 or 22.021, Penal Code, that results in the other parent becoming pregnant with the child. A history of sexual abuse includes a sexual assault that results in the other parent becoming pregnant with the child, regardless of the prior relationship of the parents. It is a rebuttable presumption that the appointment of a parent as the sole managing conservator of a child or as the conservator who has the exclusive right to determine the primary residence of a child is not in the best interest of the child if credible evidence is presented of a history or pattern of past or present child neglect, or physical or sexual abuse by that parent directed against the other parent, a spouse, or a child.
(c) The court shall consider the commission of family violence in determining whether to deny, restrict, or limit the possession of a child by a parent who is appointed as a possessory conservator.
(d) The court may not allow a parent to have access to a child for whom it is shown by a preponderance of the evidence that there is a history or pattern of committing family violence during the two years preceding the date of the filing of the suit or during the pendency of the suit, unless the court:

(1)   finds that awarding the parent access to the child would not endanger the child's physical health or emotional welfare and would be in the best interest of the child; and

(2)   renders a possession order that is designed to protect the safety and well-being of the child and any other person who has been a victim of family violence committed to the parent and that may include a requirement that:

(A)   the periods of access be continuously supervised by an entity or person chosen by the court;

(B)   the exchange of possession of the child occur in a protective setting;

(C)   the parent abstain from the consumption of alcohol or a controlled substance, as defined by Chapter 481, Health and Safety Code, within 12 hours prior to or during the period of access to the child; or

(D)   the parent attend and complete a battering intervention and prevention program as provided by Article 42.141, Code of Criminal Procedure, or, if such a program is not available, complete a course of treatment under Section 153.010.

(e)   It is a rebuttable presumption that it is not in the best interest of a child for a parent to have unsupervised visitation with the child if credible evidence is presented of a history or pattern of past or present child neglect or physical or sexual abuse by that parent directed against the other parent, a spouse, or a child.

(f)   In determining under this section whether there is credible evidence of a history or pattern of past or present child neglect or physical or sexual abuse by a parent directed against the other parent, a spouse, or a child, the court shall consider whether a protective order was rendered under Chapter 85, Title 4, against the parent during the two-year period preceding the filing of the suit or during the pendency of the suit.

Sec. 153.005.   Appointment of Sole or Joint Managing Conservator

(a)   In a suit, the court may appoint a sole managing conservator or may appoint joint managing conservators. If the parents are or will be separated, the court shall appoint at least one managing conservator.

(b)   A managing conservator must be a parent, a competent adult, an authorized agency, or a licensed child-placing agency.

Sec. 153.007.   Agreed Parenting Plan

(a)   To promote the amicable settlement of disputes between the parties to a suit, the parties may enter into a written agreed parenting plan containing provisions for conservatorship and possession of the child and for modification of the parenting plan, including variations from the standard possession order.

(b)   If the court finds that the agreed parenting plan is in the child's best interest, the court shall render an order in accordance with the parenting plan.

(c)   Terms of the agreed parenting plan contained in the order or incorporated by reference regarding conservatorship or support of or access to a child in an order may be enforced by all remedies available for enforcement of a judgment, including contempt, but are not enforceable as a contract.

(d)   If the court finds the agreed parenting plan is not in the child's best interest, the court may request the parties to submit a revised parenting plan or the court may render an order for the conservatorship and possession of the child.

Sec. 153.0071.   Alternate Dispute Resolution Procedures

(a)   On written agreement of the parties, the court may refer a suit affecting the parent-child relationship to arbitration. The agreement must state whether the arbitration is binding or non-binding.

(b)   If the parties agree to binding arbitration, the court shall render an order reflecting the arbitrator's award unless the court determines at a non-jury hearing that the award is not in the best interest of the child. The burden of proof at a hearing under this subsection is on the party seeking to avoid rendition of an order based on the arbitrator's award.

(c)   On the written agreement of the parties or on the court's own motion, the court may refer a suit affecting the parent-child relationship to mediation.

(d)   A mediated settlement agreement is binding on the parties if the agreement:

(1)   provides, in a prominently displayed statement that is in boldfaced type or capital letters or underlined, that the agreement is not subject to revocation;

(2)   is signed by each party to the agreement; and

(3)   is signed by the party's attorney, if any, who is present at the time the agreement is signed.

(e)   If a mediated settlement agreement meets the requirements of Subsection (d), a party is entitled to judgment on the mediated settlement agreement notwithstanding Rule 11, Texas Rules of Civil Procedure, or another rule of law.

(e-1) Notwithstanding Subsections (d) and (e), a court may decline to enter a judgment on a mediated settlement agreement if the court finds that:

(1)   a party to the agreement was a victim of family violence, and that circumstance impaired the party's ability to make decisions; and

(2)   the agreement is not in the child's best interest.

(f)   A party may at any time prior to the final mediation order file a written objection to the referral of a suit affecting the parent-child relationship to mediation on the basis of family violence having been committed by another party against the objecting party or a child who is the subject of the suit. After an objection is filed, the suit may not be referred to mediation unless, on the request of a party, a hearing is held and the court finds that a preponderance of the evidence does not support the objection. If the suit is referred to mediation, the court shall order appropriate measures be taken to ensure the physical and emotional safety of the party who filed the objection. The order shall provide that the parties not be required to have face-to-face contact and that the parties be placed in separate rooms during mediation. This subsection does not apply to suits filed under Chapter 262.

Sec. 153.0072.   Collaborative Law

(a)   On a written agreement of the parties and their attorneys, a suit affecting the parent-child relationship may be conducted under collaborative law procedures.

(b)   Collaborative law is a procedure in which the parties and their counsel agree in writing to use their best efforts and make a good faith attempt to resolve the suit affecting the parent-child relationship on an agreed basis without resorting to judicial intervention except to have the court approve the settlement agreement, make the legal pronouncements, and sign the orders required by law to effectuate the agreement of the parties as the court determines appropriate. The parties' counsel may not serve as litigation counsel except to ask the court to approve the settlement agreement.

(c)   A collaborative law agreement must include provisions for:
  (1)   full and candid exchange of information between the parties and their attorneys as necessary to make a proper evaluation of the case;
  (2)   suspending court intervention in the dispute while the parties are using collaborative law procedures;
  (3)   hiring experts, as jointly agreed, to be used in the procedure;
  (4)   withdrawal of all counsel involved in the collaborative law procedure if the collaborative law procedure does not result in settlement of the dispute; and
  (5)   other provisions as agreed to by the parties consistent with a good faith effort to collaboratively settle the matter.

(d)   Notwithstanding Rule 11, Texas Rules of Civil Procedure, or another rule or law, a party is entitled to judgment on a collaborative law settlement agreement if the agreement:
  (1)   provides, in a prominently displayed statement that is boldfaced, capitalized, or underlined, that the agreement is not subject to revocation; and
  (2)   is signed by each party to the agreement and the attorney of each party.

(e)   Subject to Subsection (g), a court that is notified 30 days before trial that the parties are using collaborative law procedures to attempt to settle a dispute may not, until a party notifies the court that the collaborative law procedures did not result in a settlement:
  (1)   set a hearing or trial in the case;
  (2)   impose discovery deadlines;
  (3)   require compliance with scheduling orders; or
  (4)   dismiss the case.

(f)   The parties shall notify the court if the collaborative law procedures result in a settlement. If they do not, the parties shall file:
  (1)   a status report with the court not later than the 180th day after the date of the written agreement to use the procedures; and
  (2)   a status report on or before the first anniversary of the date of the written agreement to use the procedures, accompanied by a motion for continuance that the court shall grant if the status report indicates the desire of the parties to continue to use collaborative law procedures.

(g)   If the collaborative law procedures do not result in a settlement on or before the second anniversary of the date that the suit was filed, the court may:
  (1)   set the suit for trial on the regular docket; or
  (2)   dismiss the suit without prejudice.

(h)   The provisions for confidentiality of alternative dispute resolution procedures as provided in Chapter 154, Civil Practice and Remedies Code, apply equally to collaborative law procedures under this section.

Sec. 153.008.   Child's Preference of Person to Designate Residence

A child 12 years of age or older may file with the court in writing the name of the person who is the child's preference to have the exclusive right to designate the primary residence of the child, subject to the approval of the court.

Sec. 153.009.   Interview of Child in Chambers

(a)   In a nonjury trial or at a hearing, on the application of a party, the amicus attorney, or the attorney ad litem for the child, the court shall interview in chambers a child 12 years of age or older and may interview in chambers a child under 12 years of age to determine the child's wishes as to conservatorship or as to the person who shall have the exclusive right to determine the child's primary residence. The court may also interview a child in chambers on the court's own motion for a purpose specified by this subsection.

(b)   In a nonjury trial or at a hearing, on the application of a party, the amicus attorney, or the attorney ad litem for the child or on the court's own motion, the court may interview the child in chambers to determine the child's wishes as to possession, access, or any other issue in the suit affecting the parent-child relationship.

(c)   Interviewing a child does not diminish the discretion of the court in determining the best interests of the child.

(d)   In a jury trial, the court may not interview the child in chambers regarding an issue on which a party is entitled to a jury verdict.

(e)   In any trial or hearing, the court may permit the attorney for a party, the amicus attorney, the guardian ad litem for the child, or the attorney ad litem for the child to be present at the interview.

(f)   On the motion of a party, the amicus attorney, or the attorney ad litem for the child, or on the court's own motion, the court shall cause a record of the interview to be made when the child is 12 years of age or older. A record of the interview shall be part of the record in the case.

Sec. 153.014.   Visitation Centers and Visitation Exchange Facilities

A county may establish a visitation center or a visitation exchange facility for the purpose of facilitating the terms of a court order providing for the possession of or access to a child.

Sec. 153.073.   Rights of Parent at All Times

(a)   Unless limited by court, a parent appointed as a conservator of a child has at all times the right:
  (1)   to receive information from any other conservator of the child concerning the health, education, and welfare of the child;

(2)   to confer with the other parent to the extent possible before making a decision concerning the health, education, and welfare of the child;

(3)   of access to medical, dental, psychological, and educational records of the child;

(4)   to consult with a physician, dentist, or psychologist of the child;

(5)   to consult with school officials concerning the child's welfare and educational status, including school activities;

(6)   to attend school activities;

(7)   to be designated on the child's records as a person to be notified in case of an emergency;

(8)   to consent to medical, dental, and surgical treatment during an emergency involving an immediate danger to the health and safety of the child; and

(9)   to manage the estate of the child to the extent the estate has been created by the parent or the parent's family.

(b)   The court shall specify in the order the rights that a parent retains at all times.

Sec. 153.074.   Rights and Duties During Period of Possession

Unless limited by court order, a parent appointed as a conservator of a child has the following rights and duties during the period that the parent has possession of the child:

(1)   the duty of care, control, protection, and reasonable discipline of the child;

(2)   the duty to support the child, including providing the child with clothing, food, shelter, and medical and dental care not involving an invasive procedure;

(3)   the right to consent for the child to medical and dental care not involving an invasive procedure; and

(4)   the right to direct the moral and religious training of the child.

Sec. 153.076.   Duty to Provide Information

(a)   The court shall order that each conservator of a child has a duty to inform the other conservator of the child in a timely manner of significant information concerning the health, education, and welfare of the child.

(b)   The court shall order that each conservator of a child has the duty to inform the other conservator of the child if the conservator resides with for at least 30 days, marries, or intends to marry a person who the conservator knows:

(1)   is registered as a sex offender under Chapter 62, Code of Criminal Procedure; or

(2)   is currently charged with an offense for which on conviction the person would be required to register under that chapter.

(c)   The notice required to be made under Subsection (b) must be made as soon as practicable but not later than the 40th day after the date the conservator of the child begins to reside with the person or the 10th day after the date the marriage occurs, as appropriate. The notice must include a description of the offense that is the basis of the person's requirement to register as a sex offender or of the offense with which the person is charged.

(d)   A conservator commits an offense if the conservator fails to provide notice in the manner required by Subsections (b) and (c). An offense under this subsection is a Class C misdemeanor.

TITLE 5. THE PARENT-CHILD RELATIONSHIP AND THE SUIT
AFFECTING THE PARENT-CHILD RELATIONSHIP

SUBTITLE B. SUITS AFFECTING THE PARENT-CHILD RELATIONSHIP

CHAPTER 153. CONSERVATORSHIP, POSSESSION, AND ACCESS

SUBCHAPTER C. PARENT APPOINTED AS SOLE
OR JOINT MANAGING CONSERVATOR

Sec. 153.131.   Presumption that Parent to be Appointed Managing Conservator

(a)   Unless the court finds that appointment of the parent or parents would not be in the best interest of the child because the appointment would significantly impair the child's physical health or emotional development, a parent shall be appointed sole managing conservator or both parents shall be appointed as joint managing conservators of the child.

(b)   It is a rebuttable presumption that the appointment of the parents of a child as joint managing conservators is in the best interest of the child.

Sec. 153.132.   Rights and Duties of Parent Appointed Sole Managing Conservator

Unless limited by court order, a parent appointed as sole managing conservator of a child has the rights and duties provided by Subchapter B and the following exclusive rights:

(1)   the right to designate the primary residence of the child;

(2)   the right to consent to medical, dental, and surgical treatment involving invasive procedures;

(3)   the right to consent to psychiatric and psychological treatment;

(4)   the right to receive and give receipt for periodic payments for the support of the child and to hold or disburse these funds for the benefit of the child;

(5)   the right to represent the child in legal action and to make other decisions of substantial legal significance concerning the child;

(6)   the right to consent to marriage and to enlistment in the armed forces of the United States;

(7)   the right to make decisions concerning the child's education;

(8)   the right to the services and earnings of the child; and

(9)   except when a guardian of the child's estate or a guardian or attorney ad litem has been appointed for the child, the right to act as an agent of the child in relation to the child's estate if the child's action is required by a state, the United States, or a foreign government.

Parenting Plan for Joint Managing Conservatorship

(a)　If a written agreed parenting plan is filed with the court, the court shall render an order appointing the parents as joint managing conservators only if the parenting plan:

    (1)　designates the conservator who has the exclusive right to designate the primary residence of the child and:

        (A)　establishes, until modified by further order, the geographic area within which the conservator shall maintain the child's primary residence; or

        (B)　specifies that the conservator may designate the child's primary residence without regard to geographic location;

    (2)　specifies the rights and duties of each parent regarding the child's physical care, support, and education;

    (3)　includes provisions to minimize disruption of the child's education, daily routine, and association with friends;

    (4)　allocates between the parents, independently, jointly, or exclusively, all of the remaining rights and duties of a parent provided by Chapter 151;

    (5)　is voluntarily and knowingly made by each parent and has not been repudiated by either parent at the time the order is rendered; and

    (6)　is in the best interest of the child.

(b)　The agreed parenting plan must contain an alternative dispute resolution procedure that the parties agree to use before requesting enforcement or modification of the terms and conditions of the joint conservatorship through litigation, except in an emergency.

Sec. 153.134.　Court-Ordered Joint Conservatorship

(a)　If a written agreed parenting plan is not filed with the court, the court may render an order appointing the parents joint managing conservators only if the appointment is in the best interest of the child, considering the following factors:

    (1)　whether the physical, psychological, or emotional needs and development of the child will benefit from the appointment of joint managing conservators;

    (2)　the ability of the parents to give first priority to the welfare of the child and reach shared decisions in the child's best interest;

    (3)　whether each parent can encourage and accept a positive relationship between the child and the other parent;

    (4)　whether both parents participated in child rearing before the filing of the suit;

    (5)　the geographical proximity of the parents' residences;

    (6)　if the child is 12 years of age or older, the child's preference, if any, regarding the person to have the exclusive right to designate the primary residence of the child; and

    (7)　any other relevant factor.

(b)　In rendering an order appointing joint managing conservators, the court shall:

    (1)　designate the conservator who has the exclusive right to determine the primary residence of the child and:

        (A)　establish, until modified by further order, a geographic area within which the conservator shall maintain the child's primary residence; or

        (B)　specify that the conservator may determine the child's primary residence without regard to geographic location;

    (2)　specify the rights and duties of each parent regarding the child's physical care, support, and education;

    (3)　include provisions to minimize disruption of the child's education, daily routine, and association with friends;

    (4)　allocate between the parents, independently, jointly, or exclusively, all of the remaining rights and duties of a parent as provided by Chapter 151; and

    (5)　if feasible, recommend that the parties use an alternative dispute resolution method before requesting enforcement or modification of the terms and conditions of the joint conservatorship through litigation, except in an emergency.

Sec. 153.136.　[Repealed]

Sec. 153.137.　Guidelines for the Possession of Child By Parent Named as Joint Managing Conservator

The standard possession order provided by Subchapter F constitutes a presumptive minimum amount of time for possession of a child by a parent named as a joint managing conservator who is not awarded the exclusive right to designate the primary residence of the child in a suit.

TITLE 5.　THE PARENT-CHILD RELATIONSHIP AND THE SUIT AFFECTING THE PARENT-CHILD RELATIONSHIP

SUBTITLE B. SUITS AFFECTING THE PARENT-CHILD RELATIONSHIP

CHAPTER 153.　CONSERVATORSHIP, POSSESSION, AND ACCESS

SUBCHAPTER E.　GUIDELINES FOR THE POSSESSION OF A CHILD BY A PARENT NAMED AS POSSESSORY CONSERVATOR

Sec. 153.254.　Child Less Than Three Years of Age

(a)　The court shall render an order appropriate under the circumstances for possession of a child less than three years of age.

(b)　The court shall render a prospective order to take effect on the child's third birthday, which presumptively will be the standard possession order.

Sec. 153.256.　Factors for Court to Consider

In ordering the terms of possession of a child under an order other than a standard possession order, the court shall be guided by the guidelines established by the standard possession order and may consider:

(1) the age, developmental status, circumstances, needs, and best interest of the child;

(2) the circumstances of the managing conservator and of the parent named as a possessory conservator; and

(3) any other relevant factor.

TITLE 5. THE PARENT-CHILD RELATIONSHIP AND THE SUIT AFFECTING THE PARENT-CHILD RELATIONSHIP

SUBTITLE B. SUITS AFFECTING THE PARENT-CHILD RELATIONSHIP

CHAPTER 153. CONSERVATORSHIP, POSSESSION, AND ACCESS

SUBCHAPTER F. STANDARD POSSESSION ORDER

Sec. 153.311.   Mutual Agreement or Specified Terms for Possession

The court shall specify in a standard possession order that the parties may have possession of the child at times mutually agreed to in advance by the parties and, in the absence of mutual agreement, shall have possession of the child under the specified terms set out in the standard order.

Sec. 153.312.   Parents Who Reside 100 miles or Less Apart

(a) If the possessory conservator resides 100 miles or less from the primary residence of the child, the possessory conservator shall have the right to possession of the child as follows:

    (1) on weekends beginning at 6 p.m. on the first, third, and fifth Friday of each month and ending at 6 p.m. on the following Sunday or, at the possessory conservator's election made before or at the time of the rendition of the original or modification order, and as specified in the original or modification order, beginning at the time the child's school is regularly dismissed and ending at 6 p.m. on the following Sunday; and

    (2) on Thursdays of each week during the regular school term beginning at 6 p.m. and ending at 8 p.m., or, at the possessory conservator's election made before or at the time of the rendition of the original or modification order, and as specified in the original or modification order, beginning at the time the child's school is regularly dismissed and ending at the time the child's school resumes, unless the court finds that visitation under this subdivision is not in the best interest of the child.

(b) The following provisions govern possession of the child for vacations and certain specific holidays and supersede conflicting weekend or Thursday periods of possession. The possessory conservator and the managing conservator shall have rights of possession of the child as follows:

    (1) the possessory conservator shall have possession in even-numbered years, beginning at 6 p.m. on the day the child is dismissed from school for the school's spring vacation and ending at 6 p.m. on the day before school resumes after that vacation, and the managing conservator shall have possession for the same period in odd-numbered years;

    (2) if a possessory conservator:

        (A) gives the managing conservator written notice by April 1 of each year specifying an extended period or periods of summer possession, the possessory conservator shall have possession of the child for 30 days beginning not earlier than the day after the child's school is dismissed for the summer vacation and ending not later than seven days before school resumes at the end of the summer vacation, to be exercised in not more than two separate periods of at least seven consecutive days each; or

        (B) does not give the managing conservator written notice by April 1 of each year specifying an extended period or periods of summer possession, the possessory conservator shall have possession of the child for 30 consecutive days beginning at 6 p.m. on July 1 and ending at 6 p.m. on July 31;

    (3) if the managing conservator gives the possessory conservator written notice by April 15 of each year, the managing conservator shall have possession of the child on any one weekend beginning Friday at 6 p.m. and ending at 6 p.m. on the following Sunday during one period of possession by the possessory conservator under Subdivision (2), provided that the managing conservator picks up the child from the possessory conservator and returns the child to that same place; and

    (4) if the managing conservator gives the possessory conservator written notice by April 15 of each year or gives the possessory conservator 14 days' written notice on or after April 16 of each year, the managing conservator may designate one weekend beginning not earlier than the day after the child's school is dismissed for the summer vacation and ending not later than seven days before school resumes at the end of the summer vacation, during which an otherwise scheduled weekend period of possession by the possessory conservator will not take place, provided that the weekend designated does not interfere with the possessory conservator's period or periods of extended summer possession or with Father's Day if the possessory conservator is the father of the child.

Sec. 153.313.   Parents Who Reside Over 100 Miles Apart

If the possessory conservator resides more than 100 miles from the residence of the child, the possessory conservator shall have the right to possession of the child as follows:

    (1) either regular weekend possession beginning on the first, third, and fifth Friday as provided under the terms applicable to parents who reside 100 miles or less apart or not more than one weekend per month of the possessory conservator's choice beginning at 6 p.m. on the day school recesses for the weekend and ending at 6 p.m. on the day before school resumes after the weekend, provided that the possessory conservator gives the managing conservator 14 days' written or telephonic notice preceding a designated weekend, and provided that the possessory conservator elects an option for this alternative period of possession by written notice given to the managing conservator within 90 days after the parties begin to reside more than 100 miles apart, as applicable;

    (2) each year beginning on the day the child is dismissed from school for the school's spring vacation and ending at 6 p.m. on the day before school resumes after that vacation;

    (3)   if the possessory conservator:

        (A)   gives the managing conservator written notice by April 1 of each year specifying an extended period or periods of summer possession, the possessory conservator shall have possession of the child for 42 days beginning not earlier than the day after the child's school is dismissed for the summer vacation and ending not later than seven days before school resumes at the end of the summer vacation, to be exercised in not more than two separate periods of at least seven consecutive days each; or

        (B)   does not give the managing conservator written notice by April 1 of each year specifying an extended period or periods of summer possession, the possessory conservator shall have possession of the child for 42 consecutive days beginning at 6 p.m. on June 15 and ending at 6 p.m. on July 27;

    (4)   if the managing conservator gives the possessory conservator written notice by April 15 of each year the managing conservator shall have possession of the child on one weekend beginning Friday at 6 p.m. and ending at 6 p.m. on the following Sunday during one period of possession by the possessory conservator under Subdivision (3), provided that if a period of possession by the possessory conservator exceeds 30 days, the managing conservator may have possession of the child under the terms of this subdivision on two nonconsecutive weekends during that time period, and further provided that the managing conservator picks up the child from the possessory conservator and returns the child to that same place; and

    (5)   if the managing conservator gives the possessory conservator written notice by April 15 of each year, the managing conservator may designate 21 days beginning not earlier than the day after the child's school is dismissed for the summer vacation and ending not later than seven days before school resumes at the end of the summer vacation, to be exercised in not more than two separate periods of at least seven consecutive days each, during which the possessory conservator may not have possession of the child, provided that the period or periods so designated do not interfere with the possessory conservator's period or periods of extended summer possession or with Father's Day if the possessory conservator is the father of the child.

Sec. 153.314. Holiday Possession Unaffected by Distance Parents Reside Apart

The following provisions govern possession of the child for certain specific holidays and supersede conflicting weekend or Thursday periods of possession without regard to the distance the parents reside apart. The possessory conservator and the managing conservator shall have rights of possession of the child as follows:

    (1)   the possessory conservator shall have possession of the child in even-numbered years beginning at 6 p.m. on the day the child is dismissed from school for the Christmas school vacation and ending at noon on December 26, and the managing conservator shall have possession for the same period in odd-numbered years;

    (2)   the possessory conservator shall have possession of the child in odd-numbered years beginning at noon on December 26 and ending at 6 p.m. on the day before school resumes after that vacation, and the managing conservator shall have possession for the same period in even-numbered years;

    (3)   the possessory conservator shall have possession of the child in odd-numbered years, beginning at 6 p.m. on the day the child is dismissed from school before Thanksgiving and ending at 6 p.m. on the following Sunday, and the managing conservator shall have possession for the same period in even-numbered years;

    (4)   the parent not otherwise entitled under this standard order to present possession of a child on the child's birthday shall have possession of the child beginning at 6 p.m. and ending at 8 p.m. on that day, provided that the parent picks up the child from the residence of the conservator entitled to possession and returns the child to that same place;

    (5)   if a conservator, the father shall have possession of the child beginning at 6 p.m. on the Friday preceding Father's Day and ending on Father's Day at 6 p.m., provided that, if he is not otherwise entitled under this standard order to present possession of the child, he picks up the child from the residence of the conservator entitled to possession and returns the child to that same place; and

    (6)   if a conservator, the mother shall have possession of the child beginning at 6 p.m. on the Friday preceding Mother's Day and ending on Mother's Day at 6 p.m., provided that, if she is not otherwise entitled under this standard order to present possession of the child, she picks up the child from the residence of the conservator entitled to possession and returns the child to that same place.

Sec. 153.315. Weekend Possession Extended by Holiday

    (a)   If a weekend period of possession of the possessory conservator coincides with a school holiday during regular school term or with a federal, state, or local holiday during the summer months in which school is not in session, the weekend possession shall end at 6 p.m. on a Monday holiday or school holiday or shall begin at 6 p.m. Thursday for a Friday holiday or school holiday, as applicable.

    (b)   At the possessory conservator's election, made before or at the time of the rendition of the original or modification order, and as specified in the original or modification order, periods of possession extended by a holiday may begin at the time the child's school is regularly dismissed.

Sec. 153.316. General Terms and Conditions

The court shall order the following general terms and conditions of possession of a child to apply without regard to the distance between the residence of a parent and the child:

    (1)   the managing conservator shall surrender the child to the possessory conservator at the beginning of each period of the possessory conservator's possession at the residence of the managing conservator;

    (2)   if the possessory conservator elects to begin a period of possession at the time the child's school is regularly dismissed, the managing conservator shall surrender the child to the possessory conservator at the beginning of each period of possession at the school in which the child is enrolled;

    (3)   the possessory conservator shall be ordered to do one of the following:

        (A)   the possessory conservator shall surrender the child to the managing conservator at the end of each period of possession at the residence of the possessory conservator; or

(B)   the possessory conservator shall return the child to the residence of the managing conservator at the end of each period of possession, except that the order shall provide that if the possessory conservator shall surrender the child to the managing conservator at the end of each period of possession at the residence of the possessory conservator if:

(i)   at the time the original order or a modification of an order establishing terms and conditions of possession or access the possessory conservator and the managing conservator lived in the same county, the possessory conservator's county of residence remains the same after the rendition of the order, and the managing conservator's county of residence changes, effective on the date of the change of residence by the managing conservator; or

(ii)   the possessory conservator and managing conservator lived in the same residence at any time during a six-month period preceding the date on which a suit for dissolution of the marriage was filed and the possessory conservator's county of residence remains the same and the managing conservator's county of residence changes after they no longer live in the same residence, effective on the date the order is rendered;

(4)   if the possessory conservator elects to end a period of possession at the time the child's school resumes, the possessory conservator shall surrender the child to the managing conservator at the end of each period of possession at the school in which the child is enrolled;

(5)   each conservator shall return with the child the personal effects that the child brought at the beginning of the period of possession;

(6)   either parent may designate a competent adult to pick up and return the child, as applicable; a parent or a designated competent adult shall be present when the child is picked up or returned;

(7)   a parent shall give notice to the person in possession of the child on each occasion that the parent will be unable to exercise that parent's right of possession for any specified period;

(8)   written notice shall be deemed to have been timely made if received or postmarked before or at the time that notice is due; and

(9)   if a conservator's time of possession of a child ends at the time school resumes and for any reason the child is not or will not be returned to school, the conservator in possession of the child shall immediately notify the school and the other conservator that the child will not be or has not been returned to school.

Sec. 153.3161.   Limited Possession During Military Deployment

(a)   In addition to the general terms and conditions of possession required by Section 153.316, if a possessory conservator or a joint managing conservator of the child without the exclusive right to designate the primary residence of the child is currently a member of the armed forces of the state or the United States or is reasonably expected to join those forces, the court shall:

(1)   permit that conservator to designate a person who may exercise limited possession of the child during any period that the conservator is deployed outside of the United States; and

(2)   if the conservator elects to designate a person under Subdivision (1), provide in the order for limited possession of the child by the designated person under those circumstances, subject to the court's determination that the limited possession is in the best interest of the child.

(b)   If the court determines that the limited possession is in the best interest of the child, the court shall provide in the order that during periods of deployment:

(1)   the designated person has the right to possession of the child on the first weekend of each month beginning at 6 p.m. on Friday and ending at 6 p.m. on Sunday;

(2)   the other parent shall surrender the child to the designated person at the beginning of each period of possession at the other parent's residence;

(3)   the designated person shall return the child to the other parent's residence at the end of each period of possession;

(4)   the child's other parent and the designated person are subject to the requirements of Sections 153.316(5)-(9);

(5   the designated person has the rights and duties of a nonparent possessory conservator under Section 153.376(a) during the period that the person has possession of the child; and

(6)   the designated person is subject to any provision in a court order restricting or prohibiting access to the child by any specified individual.

(c)   After the deployment is concluded, and the deployed parent returns to that parent's usual residence, the designated person's right to limited possession under this section terminates and the rights of all affected parties are governed by the terms of any court order applicable when a parent is not deployed.

Sec. 153.317.   Alternative Possession Times

If a child is enrolled in school and the possessory conservator elects before or at the time of the rendition of the original or modification order, the standard order may expressly provide that the possessory conservator's period of possession shall begin or end, or both, at a different time expressly set in the standard order under and within the range of alternative times provided by one or both of the following subdivisions:

(1)   instead of a period of possession by a possessory conservator beginning at 6 p.m. on the day school recesses, the period of possession may be set in the standard possession order to begin at the time the child's school is regularly dismissed or at any time between the time the child's school is regularly dismissed and 6 p.m.; and

(2)   except for Thursday evening possession, instead of a period of possession by a possessory conservator ending at 6 p.m. on the day before school resumes, the period of possession may be set in the standard order to end at the time school resumes.

TITLE 5. THE PARENT-CHILD RELATIONSHIP AND THE SUIT
AFFECTING THE PARENT-CHILD RELATIONSHIP

SUBTITLE B. SUITS AFFECTING THE PARENT-CHILD RELATIONSHIP

CHAPTER 153. CONSERVATORSHIP, POSSESSION, AND ACCESS

SUBCHAPTER H. RIGHTS OF GRANDPARENT, AUNT, OR UNCLE

Sec. 153.431.   Appointment of Grandparent, Aunt, or Uncle as Managing Conservator
    If both of the parents of a child are deceased, the court may consider appointment of a parent, sister, or brother of a deceased parent as a managing conservator of the child, but that consideration does not alter or diminish the discretionary power of the court.

Sec. 153.432.   Suit for Possession or Access by Grandparent
    (a)   A biological or adoptive grandparent may request possession of or access to a grandchild by filing:
        (1)   an original suit; or
        (2)   a suit for modification as provided by Chapter 156.
    (b)   A grandparent may request possession of or access to a grandchild in a suit filed for the sole purpose of requesting the relief, without regard to whether the appointment of a managing conservator is an issue in the suit.

Sec. 153.433.   Possession of or Access to Grandchild
    The court shall order reasonable possession of or access to a grandchild by a grandparent if:
        (1)   at the time the relief is requested, at least one biological or adoptive parent of the child has not had that parent's parental rights terminated;
        (2)   the grandparent requesting possession of or access to the child overcomes the presumption that a parent acts in the best interest of the parent's child by proving by a preponderance of the evidence that denial of possession of or access to the child would significantly impair the child's physical health or emotional well-being; and
        (3)   the grandparent requesting possession of or access to the child is a parent of a parent of the child and that parent of the child:
            (A)   has been incarcerated in jail or prison during the three-month period preceding the filing of the petition;
            (B)   has been found by a court to be incompetent;
            (C)   is dead; or
            (D)   does not have actual or court-ordered possession of or access to the child

Sec. 153.434.   Limitation on Right to Request Possession or Access
    A biological or adoptive grandparent may not request possession of or access to a grandchild if:
        (1)   each of the biological parents of the grandchild has:
            (A)   died;
            (B)   had the person's parental rights terminated; or
            (C)   executed an affidavit of waiver of interest in child or an affidavit of relinquishment of parental rights under Chapter 161 and the affidavit designates an authorized agency, licensed child-placing agency, or person other than the child's stepparent as the managing conservator of the child; and
        (2)   the grandchild has been adopted, or is the subject of a pending suit for adoption, by a person other than the child's stepparent.

TITLE 5. THE PARENT-CHILD RELATIONSHIP AND THE SUIT
AFFECTING THE PARENT-CHILD RELATIONSHIP

SUBTITLE B. SUITS AFFECTING THE PARENT-CHILD RELATIONSHIP

CHAPTER 153. CONSERVATORSHIP, POSSESSION, AND ACCESS

SUBCHAPTER J. RIGHTS OF SIBLINGS

[**AUTHOR'S NOTE:** *The Texas Legislature enacted another Subchapter J. Both are valid.*]

Sec. 153.551.   Suit for Access
    (a)   The sibling of a child who is separated from the child because of an action taken by the Department of Family and Protective Services may request access to the child by filing:
        (1)   an original suit; or
        (2)   a suit for modification as provided by Chapter 156.
    (b)   The sibling of a child may request access to the child in a suit filed for the sole purpose of requesting the relief, without regard to whether the appointment of a managing conservator is an issue in the suit.

Sec. 153.552.   Access to Sibling
    The court shall order reasonable access to a child by the child's sibling if the court finds that access is in the best interest of the child.

TITLE 5. THE PARENT-CHILD RELATIONSHIP AND THE SUIT AFFECTING THE PARENT-CHILD RELATIONSHIP

SUBTITLE B. SUITS AFFECTING THE PARENT-CHILD RELATIONSHIP

CHAPTER 153. CONSERVATORSHIP, POSSESSION, AND ACCESS

SUBCHAPTER J. PARENTING PLAN AND PARENTING COORDINATOR

Sec. 153.601.   Definitions

In this subchapter:
(1)   "Dispute resolution process" means a process of alternative dispute resolution conducted in accordance with Section 153.0071 of this chapter and Chapter 154, Civil Practice and Remedies Code.
(2)   "High-conflict case" means a suit affecting the parent-child relationship in which the parties demonstrate a pattern of:
    (A)   repetitious litigation;
    (B)   anger and distrust;
    (C)   difficulty in communicating about and cooperating in the care of their children; or
    (D)   other behaviors that in the discretion of the court warrant the appointment of a parenting coordinator.
(3)   "Parenting coordinator" means an impartial third party appointed by the court to assist parties in resolving issues relating to parenting and other family issues arising from an order in a suit affecting the parent-child relationship.
(4)   "Parenting plan" means a temporary or final court order that sets out the rights and duties of parents in a suit affecting the parent-child relationship and includes provisions relating to conservatorship, possession of and access to a child, and child support, and a dispute resolution process to minimize future disputes.

Sec. 153.602.   Requirement for Temporary Parenting Plan
(a)   A temporary order that establishes a conservatorship in a suit affecting the parent-child relationship must incorporate a temporary parenting plan. The temporary parenting plan must comply with the requirements for a final parenting plan under Section 153.603.
(b)   Subject to Subsection (c), if the parties cannot agree to a temporary parenting plan, the court may, on the motion of a party or on the court's own motion, order the parties to participate in a dispute resolution process to establish a temporary parenting plan.
(c)   At any time before the court orders the parties to participate in a dispute resolution process under Subsection (b), a party may file a written objection to the referral of the suit to a dispute resolution process on the basis of family violence having been committed by another party against the objecting party or a child who is the subject of the suit. After an objection is filed, the suit may not be referred to a dispute resolution process unless, on the request of a party, a hearing is held and the court finds that a preponderance of the evidence does not support the objection. If the suit is referred to a dispute resolution process, the court shall order appropriate measures be taken to ensure the physical and emotional safety of the party who filed the objection. The order may provide that the parties not be required to have face-to-face contact and that the parties be placed in separate rooms during the dispute resolution process.
(d)   If a dispute resolution process is not available or is not successful, a party may request and the court may order an expedited hearing to establish a temporary parenting plan.

Sec. 153.603.   Requirement of Final Parenting Plan
(a)   A final order in a suit affecting the parent-child relationship must incorporate a final parenting plan. A final parenting plan must:
(1)   establish the rights and duties of each parent with respect to the child, consistent with the criteria in this chapter;
(2)   minimize the child's exposure to harmful parental conflict;
(3)   provide for the child's changing needs as the child grows and matures, in a way that minimizes the need for further modifications to the final parenting plan; and
(4)   provide for a dispute resolution process or other voluntary dispute resolution procedures, before court action, unless precluded or limited by Section 153.0071.
(b)   In providing for a dispute resolution process, the parenting plan must state that:
(1)   preference shall be given to carrying out the parenting plan; and
(2)   the parties shall use the designated process to resolve disputes.
(c)   If the parties cannot reach agreement on a final parenting plan, the court, on the motion of a party or on the court's own motion, may order appropriate dispute resolution proceedings under Section 153.0071 to determine a final parenting plan.
(d)   If the parties have not reached agreement on a final parenting plan on or before the 30th day before the date set for trial, each party shall file with the court and serve a proposed final parenting plan. Failure by a party to comply with this subsection may result in the court's adoption of the proposed final parenting plan filed by the opposing party if the court finds that plan to be in the best interest of the child.
(e)   Each party filing a proposed final parenting plan must attach:
(1)   a verified statement of income determined in accordance with the child support guidelines and related provisions prescribed by Chapter 154; and
(2)   a verified statement that the plan is proposed in good faith and is in the best interest of the child.

Sec. 153.604.   Modification of Final Parenting Plan
(a)   In a suit for modification, a proposed parenting plan shall be filed with the court and served with the petition for modification and with the response to the petition for modification, unless the modification is sought only with regard to child support. The

obligor party's proposed parenting plan must be accompanied by a verified statement of income determined in accordance with the child support guidelines and related provisions prescribed by Chapter 154.

(b) The procedure for modifying a final parenting plan is governed by Chapter 156.

Sec. 153.605. Appointment of Parenting Coordinator

(a) In a suit affecting the parent-child relationship, the court may, on its own motion or on a motion or agreement of the parties, appoint a parenting coordinator to assist the parties in resolving issues related to parenting or other family issues in the suit.

(b) The court may not appoint a parenting coordinator if any party objects unless the court makes specific findings that:

    (1) the case is or is likely to become a high-conflict case; or

    (2) the appointment of a parenting coordinator is in the best interest of any minor child in the suit.

(c) Notwithstanding any other provision of this subchapter, a party may at any time prior to the appointment of a parenting coordinator file a written objection to the appointment of a parenting coordinator on the basis of family violence having been committed by another party against the objecting party or a child who is the subject of the suit. After an objection is filed, a parenting coordinator may not be appointed unless, on the request of a party, a hearing is held and the court finds that a preponderance of the evidence does not support the objection. If a parenting coordinator is appointed, the court shall order appropriate measures be taken to ensure the physical and emotional safety of the party who filed the objection. The order may provide that the parties not be required to have face-to-face contact and that the parties be placed in separate rooms during the parenting coordination.

Sec. 153.606. Authority of Parenting Coordinator

(a) The authority of a parenting coordinator must be specified in the order appointing the parenting coordinator and limited to matters that will aid the parties in:

    (1) identifying disputed issues;

    (2) reducing misunderstandings;

    (3) clarifying priorities;

    (4) exploring possibilities for problem solving;

    (5) developing methods of collaboration in parenting;

    (6) developing a parenting plan; and

    (7) complying with the court's order regarding conservatorship or possession of and access to the child.

(b) The appointment of a parenting coordinator does not divest the court of:

    (1) its exclusive jurisdiction to determine issues of conservatorship, support, and possession of and access to the child; and

    (2) the authority to exercise management and control of the suit.

(c) The parenting coordinator may not modify any order, judgment, or decree but may urge or suggest that the parties agree to minor temporary departures from a parenting plan if the parenting coordinator is authorized by the court to do so. Any agreement made by the parties and the parenting coordinator may be reduced to writing and presented to the court for approval.

(d) Meetings between the parenting coordinator and the parties may be informal and are not required to follow any specific procedures.

(e) A parenting coordinator may not:

    (1) be compelled to produce work product developed during the appointment as parenting coordinator;

    (2) be required to disclose the source of any information;

    (3) submit a report into evidence, except as required by Section 153.608; or

    (4) testify in court.

(f) Subsection (e) does not affect the duty to report child abuse or neglect under Section 261.101.

Sec. 153.607. Removal of Parenting Coordinator

(a) Except as otherwise provided by this section, the court shall reserve the right to remove the parenting coordinator in the court's discretion.

(b) The court may remove the parenting coordinator:

    (1) on the request and agreement of both parties; or

    (2) on the motion of a party, if good cause is shown.

Sec. 153.608. Report of Parenting Coordinator

A parenting coordinator shall submit a written report to the court and to the parties as often as ordered by the court. In the report, the parenting coordinator may give only an opinion regarding whether the parenting coordination is succeeding and should continue.

Sec. 153.609. Compensation of Parenting Coordinator

(a) A court may not appoint a parenting coordinator, other than an employee described by Subsection (c) or a volunteer appointed under Subsection (d), unless the court finds that the parties have the means to pay the fees of the parenting coordinator.

(b) Any fees of a parenting coordinator appointed under Subsection (a) shall be allocated between the parties as determined by the court.

(c) Public funds may not be used to pay the fees of a parenting coordinator. Notwithstanding this prohibition, a court may appoint an employee of the court, the domestic relations office, or a comparable county agency to act as a parenting coordinator if personnel are available to serve that function.

(d) If due to hardship the parties are unable to pay the fees of a parenting coordinator, and a public employee is not available under Subsection (c), the court, if feasible, may appoint a person to act as a parenting coordinator on a volunteer basis.

Sec. 153.610.   Qualifications of Parenting Coordinator
 (a) The court shall determine the required qualifications of a parenting coordinator, provided that a parenting coordinator must at least:
  (1) hold a bachelor's degree in counseling, education, family studies, psychology, or social work and, unless waived by the court, complete a parenting coordinator course of at least 16 hours; or
  (2) hold a graduate degree in a mental health profession, with an emphasis in family and children's issues.
 (b) In addition to the qualifications prescribed by Subsection (a), a parenting coordinator must complete at least eight hours of family violence dynamics training provided by a family violence service provider.
 (c) The actions of a parenting coordinator who is not an attorney do not constitute the practice of law.

Sec. 153.611.   Exception for Certain Title IV-D Proceedings
 Notwithstanding any other provision of this subchapter, this subchapter does not apply to a proceeding in a Title IV-D case relating to the determination of parentage or establishment, modification, or enforcement of a child support or medical support obligation.

TITLE 5. THE PARENT-CHILD RELATIONSHIP AND THE SUIT AFFECTING THE PARENT-CHILD RELATIONSHIP

SUBTITLE B. SUITS AFFECTING THE PARENT-CHILD RELATIONSHIP

CHAPTER 154. CHILD SUPPORT

SUBCHAPTER A. COURT-ORDERED CHILD SUPPORT

Sec. 154.001.   Support of Child
 (a) The court may order either or both parents to support a child in the manner specified by the order:
  (1) until the child is 18 years of age or until graduation from high school, whichever occurs later;
  (2) until the child is emancipated through marriage, through removal of the disabilities of minority by court order, or by other operation of law;
  (3) until the death of the child; or
  (4) if the child is disabled as defined in this chapter, for an indefinite period.
 (a-1) The court may order each person who is financially able and whose parental rights have been terminated with respect to a child in substitute care for whom the department has been appointed managing conservator to support the child in the manner specified by the order:
  (1) until the earliest of:
   (A) the child's adoption;
   (B) the child's 18th birthday or graduation from high school, whichever occurs later;
   (C) removal of the child's disabilities of minority by court order, marriage, or other operation of law; or
   (D) the child's death; or
  (2) if the child is disabled as defined in this chapter, for an indefinite period.
 (b) The court may order either or both parents to make periodic payments for the support of a child in a proceeding in which the Department of Protective and Regulatory Services is named temporary managing conservator. In a proceeding in which the Department of Protective and Regulatory Services is named permanent managing conservator of a child whose parents' rights have not been terminated, the court shall order each parent that is financially able to make periodic payments for the support of the child.
 (c) In a Title IV-D case, if neither parent has physical possession or conservatorship of the child, the court may render an order providing that a nonparent or agency having physical possession may receive, hold, or disburse child support payments for the benefit of the child.

Sec. 154.012.   Support Paid in Excess of Support Order
 (a) If an obligor is not in arrears and the obligor's child support obligation has terminated, the obligee shall return to the obligor a child support payment made by the obligor that exceeds the amount of support ordered, regardless of whether the payment was made before, on, or after the date the child support obligation terminated.
 (b) An obligor may file a suit to recover a child support payment under Subsection (a). If the court finds that the obligee failed to return a child support payment under Subsection (a), the court shall order the obligee to pay to the obligor attorney's fees and all court costs in addition to the amount of support paid after the date the child support order terminated. For good cause shown, the court may waive the requirement that the obligee pay attorney's fees and costs if the court states the reasons supporting that finding.

Sec. 154.013.   Continuation of Duty To Pay Support after Death of Obligee
 (a) A child support obligation does not terminate on the death of the obligee but continues as an obligation to the child named in the support order, as required by this section.
 (b) Notwithstanding any provision of the Probate Code, a child support payment held by the Title IV-D agency, a local registry, or the state disbursement unit or any uncashed check or warrant representing a child support payment made before, on, or after the date of death of the obligee shall be paid proportionately for the benefit of each surviving child named in the support order and not to the estate of the obligee. The payment is free of any creditor's claim against the deceased obligee's estate and may be disbursed as provided by Subsection (c).
 (c) On the death of the obligee, current child support owed by the obligor for the benefit of the child or any amount described by Subsection (b) shall be paid to:
  (1) a person, other than a parent, who is appointed as managing conservator of the child;

(2)   a person, including the obligor, who has assumed actual care, control, and possession of the child, if a managing conservator or guardian of the child has not been appointed;

(3)   the county clerk, as provided by Section 887, Texas Probate Code, in the name of and for the account of the child for whom the support is owed;

(4)   a guardian of the child appointed under Chapter XIII, Texas Probate Code, as provided by that code; or

(5)   the surviving child, if the child is an adult or has otherwise had the disabilities of minority removed.

(d)   On presentation of the obligee's death certificate, the court shall render an order directing payment of child support paid but not disbursed to be made as provided by Subsection (c). A copy of the order shall be provided to:

    (1)   the obligor;

    (2)   as appropriate:

        (A)   the person having actual care, control, and possession of the child;

        (B)   the county clerk; or

        (C)   the managing conservator or guardian of the child, if one has been appointed;

    (3)   the local registry or state disbursement unit and, if appropriate, the Title IV-D agency; and

    (4)   the child named in the support order, if the child is an adult or has otherwise had the disabilities of minority removed.

(e)   The order under Subsection (d) must contain:

    (1)   a statement that the obligee is deceased and that child support amounts otherwise payable to the obligee shall be paid for the benefit of a surviving child named in the support order as provided by Subsection (c);

    (2)   the name and age of each child named in the support order; and

    (3)   the name and mailing address of, as appropriate:

        (A)   the person having actual care, control, and possession of the child;

        (B)   the county clerk; or

        (C)   the managing conservator or guardian of the child, if one has been appointed.

(f)   On receipt of the order required under this section, the local registry, state disbursement unit, or Title IV-D agency shall disburse payments as required by the order

[**AUTHOR'S NOTE:** *The Texas Legislature enacted two statutes numbered Section 154.013. Both are valid.]*

Sec. 154.014.   Payments in Excess of Court-Ordered Amount

(a)   If a child support agency or local child support registry receives from an obligor who is not in arrears a child support payment in an amount that exceeds the court-ordered amount, the agency or registry, to the extent possible, shall give effect to any expressed intent of the obligor for the application of the amount that exceeds the court-ordered amount.

(b)   If the obligor does not express an intent for the application of the amount paid in excess of the court-ordered amount, the agency or registry shall:

    (1)   credit the excess amount to the obligor's future child support obligation; and

    (2   promptly disperse the excess amount to the obligee.

(c)   This section does not apply to an obligee who is a recipient of public assistance under Chapter 31, Human Resources Code.

TITLE 5. THE PARENT-CHILD RELATIONSHIP AND THE SUIT AFFECTING THE PARENT-CHILD RELATIONSHIP

SUBTITLE B. SUITS AFFECTING THE PARENT-CHILD RELATIONSHIP

CHAPTER 154. CHILD SUPPORT

SUBCHAPTER B. COMPUTING NET RESOURCES AVAILABLE

Sec. 154.061.   Computing Net Monthly Income

OFFICE OF THE ATTORNEY GENERAL
2006 TAX CHARTS

Pursuant to § 154.061(b) of the Texas Family Code, the Office of the Attorney General of Texas, as the Title IV-D agency, has promulgated the following tax charts to assist courts in establishing the amount of a child support order. These tax charts are applicable to employed and self-employed persons in computing net monthly income.

INSTRUCTIONS FOR USE

To use these tables, first compute the obligor's annual gross income. Then recompute to determine the obligor's average monthly gross income. These tables provide a method for calculating "monthly net income" for child support purposes, subtracting from monthly gross income the social security taxes and the federal income tax withholding for a single person claiming one personal exemption and the standard deduction. Thereafter, in many cases the guidelines call for a number of additional steps to complete the necessary calculations. For example, §§ 154.06–1154.070 provide for appropriate additions to "income" as that term is defined for federal income tax purposes, and for certain subtractions from monthly net income, in order to arrive at the net resources of the obligor available for child support purposes. If necessary, one may compute an obligee's net resources using similar steps.

EMPLOYED PERSONS
2006 TAX CHART

Monthly Gross Wages	Social Security Taxes		Federal Income Taxes**	Net Monthly Income
	Old-Age, Survivors and Disability Insurance Taxes (6.2%)*	Hospital (Medicare) Insurance Taxes (1.45%)*		
$100.00	$6.20	$1.45	$0.00	$92.35
$200.00	$12.40	$2.90	$0.00	$184.70
$300.00	$18.60	$4.35	$0.00	$277.05
$400.00	$24.80	$5.80	$0.00	$369.40
$500.00	$31.00	$7.25	$0.00	$461.75
$600.00	$37.20	$8.70	$0.00	$554.10
$700.00	$43.40	$10.15	$0.00	$646.45
$800.00	$49.60	$11.60	$9.58	$729.22
$892.67***	$55.35	$12.94	$18.85	$805.53
$900.00	$55.80	$13.05	$19.58	$811.57
$1,000.00	$62.00	$14.50	$29.58	$893.92
$1,100.00	$68.20	$15.95	$39.58	$976.27
$1,200.00	$74.40	$17.40	$49.58	$1,058.62
$1,300.00	$80.60	$18.85	$59.58	$1,140.97
$1,400.00	$86.80	$20.30	$72.92	$1,219.98
$1,500.00	$93.00	$21.75	$87.92	$1,297.33
$1,600.00	$99.20	$23.20	$102.92	$1,374.68
$1,700.00	$105.40	$24.65	$117.92	$1,452.03
$1,800.00	$111.60	$26.10	$132.92	$1,529.38
$1,900.00	$117.80	$27.55	$147.92	$1,606.73
$2,000.00	$124.00	$29.00	$162.92	$1,684.08
$2,100.00	$130.20	$30.45	$177.92	$1,761.43
$2,200.00	$136.40	$31.90	$192.92	$1,838.78
$2,300.00	$142.60	$33.35	$207.92	$1,916.13
$2,400.00	$148.80	$34.80	$222.92	$1,993.48
$2,500.00	$155.00	$36.25	$237.92	$2,070.83
$2,600.00	$161.20	$37.70	$252.92	$2,148.18
$2,700.00	$167.40	$39.15	$267.92	$2,225.53
$2,800.00	$173.60	$40.60	$282.92	$2,302.88
$2,900.00	$179.80	$42.05	$297.92	$2,380.23
$3,000.00	$186.00	$43.50	$312.92	$2,457.58
$3,100.00	$192.20	$44.95	$327.92	$2,534.93
$3,200.00	$198.40	$46.40	$342.92	$2,612.28
$3,300.00	$204.60	$47.85	$362.08	$2,685.47
$3,400.00	$210.80	$49.30	$387.08	$2,752.82
$3,500.00	$217.00	$50.75	$412.08	$2,820.17
$3,600.00	$223.20	$52.20	$437.08	$2,887.52
$3,700.00	$229.40	$53.65	$462.08	$2,954.87
$3,800.00	$235.60	$55.10	$487.08	$3,022.22
$3,900.00	$241.80	$56.55	$512.08	$3,089.57
$4,000.00	$248.00	$58.00	$537.08	$3,156.92
$4,250.00	$263.50	$61.63	$599.58	$3,325.29
$4,500.00	$279.00	$65.25	$662.08	$3,493.67
$4,750.00	$294.50	$68.88	$724.58	$3,662.04
$5,000.00	$310.00	$72.50	$787.08	$3,830.42
$5,250.00	$325.50	$76.13	$849.58	$3,998.79
$5,500.00	$341.00	$79.75	$912.08	$4,167.17
$5,750.00	$356.50	$83.38	$974.58	$4,335.54
$6,000.00	$372.00	$87.00	$1,037.08	$4,503.92
$6,250.00	$387.50	$90.63	$1,099.58	$4,672.29
$6,500.00	$403.00	$94.25	$1,162.08	$4,840.67
$6,750.00	$418.50	$97.88	$1,224.58	$5,009.04
$7,000.00	$434.00	$101.50	$1,290.46	$5,174.04
$7,500.00	$465.00	$108.75	$1,430.46	$5,495.79
$8,000.00	$486.70****	$116.00	$1,570.46	$5,826.84
$8,245.44*****	$486.70	$119.56	$1,639.18	$6,000.00

$8,500.00	$486.70	$123.25	$1,710.46	$6,179.59
$9,000.00	$486.70	$130.50	$1,850.46	$6,532.34
$9,500.00	$486.70	$137.75	$1,990.46	$6,885.09
$10,000.00	$486.70	$145.00	$2,130.46	$7,237.84
$10,500.00	$486.70	$152.25	$2,270.46	$7,590.59
$11,000.00	$486.70	$159.50	$2,410.46	$7,943.34
$11,500.00	$486.70	$166.75	$2,550.46	$8,296.09
$12,000.00	$486.70	$174.00	$2,690.46	$8,648.84
$12,500.00	$486.70	$181.25	$2,830.46	$9,001.59
$13,000.00	$486.70	$188.50	$2,973.54	$9,351.26
$13,500.00	$486.70	$195.75	$3,115.59	$9,701.96
$14,000.00	$486.70	$203.00	$3,278.72	$10,031.58
$14,500.00	$486.70	$210.25	$3,447.35	$10,355.70
$15,000.00	$486.70	$217.50	$3,614.77	$10,681.03

Footnotes to Employed Persons 2006 Tax Chart:

* An employed person not subject to the Old-Age, Survivors and Disability Insurance/Hospital (Medicare) Insurance taxes will be allowed the reductions reflected in these columns, unless it is shown that such person has no similar contributory plan such as teacher retirement, federal railroad retirement, federal civil service retirement, etc.

** These amounts represent one-twelfth (1/12) of the annual Federal income tax calculated for a single taxpayer claiming one personal exemption ($3,300.00, subject to reduction in certain cases, as described in the next paragraph of this footnote) and taking the standard deduction ($5,150.00).

For a single taxpayer with an adjusted gross income in excess of $150,500.00, the deduction for the personal exemption is reduced by two-thirds (2/3) of two percent (2%) for each $2,500.00 or fraction thereof by which adjusted gross income exceeds $150,500.00. The deduction for the personal exemption is no longer reduced for adjusted gross income in excess of $273,000.00. For example, monthly gross wages of $15,000.00 times 12 months equals $180,000.00. The excess over $150,500.00 is $29,500.00. $29,500.00 divided by $2,500.00 equals 11.80. The 11.80 amount is rounded up to 12. The reduction percentage is 16.00% (2/3 x 2% x 12 = 16.00%). The $3,300.00 deduction for one personal exemption is reduced by $528.00 ($3,300.00 x 16.00% = $528.00) to $2,772.00 ($3,300.00 - $528.00 = $2,772.00). For adjusted gross income in excess of $273,000.00 the deduction for the personal exemption is $1,100.00.

*** The amount represents one-twelfth (1/12) of the gross income of an individual earning the federal minimum wage ($5.15 per hour) for a 40-hour week for a full year. $5.15 per hour x 40 hours per week x 52 weeks per year equals $10,712.00 per year. One-twelfth (1/12) of $10,712.00 equals $892.67.

**** For annual gross wages above $94,200.00, this amount represents a monthly average of the Old-Age, Survivors and Disability Insurance tax based on the 2006 maximum Old-Age, Survivors and Disability Insurance tax of $5,840.40 per person (6.2% of the first $94,200.00 of annual gross wages equals $5,840.40). One-twelfth (1/12) of $5,840.40 equals $486.70.

***** This amount represents the point where the monthly gross wages of an employed individual would result in $6,000.00 of net resources.

* *

References Relating to Employed Persons 2006 Tax Chart:
1. Old-Age, Survivors and Disability Insurance Tax
   (a) Contribution Base
      (1) Social Security Administration's notice dated October 18, 2005, and appearing in 70 Fed. Reg. 61,677 (October 25, 2005)
      (2) Section 3121(a) of the Internal Revenue Code of 1986, as amended (26 U.S.C. § 3121(a))
      (3) Section 230 of the Social Security Act, as amended (42 U.S.C. § 430)
   (b) *Tax Rate*
      (1) Section 3101(a) of the Internal Revenue Code of 1986, as amended (26 U.S.C. § 3101(a))
2. Hospital (Medicare) Insurance Tax
   (a) Contribution Base
      (1) Section 3121(a) of the Internal Revenue Code of 1986, as amended (26 U.S.C. § 3121(a))
      (2) Omnibus Budget Reconciliation Act of 1993, Pub. L. No. 103-66, § 13207, 107 Stat. 312, 467-69 (1993)
   (b) Tax Rate
      (1) Section 3101(b) of the Internal Revenue Code of 1986, as amended (26 U.S.C. § 3101(b))
3. Federal Income Tax
   (a) Tax Rate Schedule for 2006 for Single Taxpayers
      (1) Revenue Procedure 2005-70, Section 3.01, Table 3 which appears in Internal Revenue Bulletin 2005-47, dated November 21, 2005
      (2) Section 1(c), (f) and (i) of the Internal Revenue Code of 1986, as (26 U.S.C. § 1(c), 1(f), 1(i))
   (b) Standard Deduction
      (1) Revenue Procedure 2005-70, Section 3.10(1), which appears in Internal Revenue Bulletin 2005-47, dated November 21, 2005
      (2) Section 63(c) of the Internal Revenue Code of 1986, as amended (26 U.S.C. § 63(c))
   (c) Personal Exemption
      (1) Revenue Procedure 2005-70, Section 3.17, which appears in Internal Revenue Bulletin 2005-47, dated November 21, 2005
      (2) Section 151(d) of the Internal Revenue Code of 1986, as amended (26 U.S.C. § 151(d))

SELF-EMPLOYED PERSONS
2006 TAX CHART

Monthly Net Earnings from Self-Employment*	Social Security Taxes		Federal Income Taxes***	Net Monthly Income
	Old-Age, Survivors and Disability Insurance Taxes (12.4%)**	Hospital (Medicare) Insurance Taxes (2.9%)**		
$100.00	$11.45	$2.68	$0.00	$85.87
$200.00	$22.90	$5.36	$0.00	$171.74
$300.00	$34.35	$8.03	$0.00	$257.62
$400.00	$45.81	$10.71	$0.00	$343.48
$500.00	$57.26	$13.39	$0.00	$429.35
$600.00	$68.71	$16.07	$0.00	$515.22
$700.00	$80.16	$18.75	$0.00	$601.09
$800.00	$91.61	$21.43	$3.93	$683.03
$900.00	$103.06	$24.10	$13.23	$759.61
$1,000.00	$114.51	$26.78	$22.52	$836.19
$1,100.00	$125.97	$29.46	$31.81	$912.76
$1,200.00	$137.42	$32.14	$41.11	$989.33
$1,300.00	$148.87	$34.82	$50.40	$1,065.91
$1,400.00	$160.32	$37.49	$59.69	$1,142.50
$1,500.00	$171.77	$40.17	$72.02	$1,216.04
$1,600.00	$183.22	$42.85	$85.96	$1,287.97
$1,700.00	$194.67	$45.53	$99.90	$1,359.90
$1,800.00	$206.13	$48.21	$113.84	$1,431.82
$1,900.00	$217.58	$50.88	$127.78	$1,503.76
$2,000.00	$229.03	$53.56	$141.72	$1,575.69
$2,100.00	$240.48	$56.24	$155.66	$1,647.62
$2,200.00	$251.93	$58.92	$169.60	$1,719.55
$2,300.00	$263.38	$61.60	$183.54	$1,791.48
$2,400.00	$274.83	$64.28	$197.48	$1,863.41
$2,500.00	$286.29	$66.95	$211.42	$1,935.34
$2,600.00	$297.74	$69.63	$225.36	$2,007.27
$2,700.00	$309.19	$72.31	$239.30	$2,079.20
$2,800.00	$320.64	$74.99	$253.24	$2,151.13
$2,900.00	$332.09	$77.67	$267.18	$2,223.06
$3,000.00	$343.54	$80.34	$281.13	$2,294.99
$3,100.00	$354.99	$83.02	$295.07	$2,366.92
$3,200.00	$366.44	$85.70	$309.01	$2,438.85
$3,300.00	$377.90	$88.38	$322.95	$2,510.77
$3,400.00	$389.35	$91.06	$336.89	$2,582.70
$3,500.00	$400.80	$93.74	$350.83	$2,654.63
$3,600.00	$412.25	$96.41	$373.50	$2,717.84
$3,700.00	$423.70	$99.09	$396.73	$2,780.48
$3,800.00	$435.15	$101.77	$419.97	$2,843.11
$3,900.00	$446.60	$104.45	$443.20	$2,905.75
$4,000.00	$458.06	$107.13	$466.43	$2,968.38
$4,250.00	$486.68	$113.82	$524.52	$3,124.98
$4,500.00	$515.31	$120.52	$582.60	$3,281.57
$4,750.00	$543.94	$127.21	$640.69	$3,438.16
$5,000.00	$572.57	$133.91	$698.77	$3,594.75
$5,250.00	$601.20	$140.60	$756.86	$3,751.34
$5,500.00	$629.83	$147.30	$814.94	$3,907.93
$5,750.00	$658.46	$153.99	$873.03	$4,064.52
$6,000.00	$687.08	$160.69	$931.11	$4,221.12
$6,250.00	$715.71	$167.38	$989.20	$4,377.71
$6,500.00	$744.34	$174.08	$1,047.28	$4,534.30
$6,750.00	$772.97	$180.78	$1,105.36	$4,690.89
$7,000.00	$801.60	$187.47	$1,163.45	$4,847.48
$7,500.00	$858.86	$200.86	$1,282.10	$5,158.18
$8,000.00	$916.11	$214.25	$1,412.21	$5,457.43
$8,500.00	$973.37	$227.64	$1,542.32	$5,756.67
$8,849.16*****	$973.40****	$236.99	$1,638.77	$6,000.00

$9,000.00	$973.40	$241.03	$1,680.44	$6,105.13
$9,500.00	$973.40	$254.42	$1,818.56	$6,453.62
$10,000.00	$973.40	$267.82	$1,956.69	$6,802.09
$10,500.00	$973.40	$281.21	$2,094.81	$7,150.58
$11,000.00	$973.40	$294.60	$2,232.94	$7,499.06
$11,500.00	$973.40	$307.99	$2,371.06	$7,847.55
$12,000.00	$973.40	$321.38	$2,509.19	$8,196.03
$12,500.00	$973.40	$334.77	$2,647.31	$8,544.52
$13,000.00	$973.40	$348.16	$2,785.44	$8,893.00
$13,500.00	$973.40	$361.55	$2,925.62	$9,239.43
$14,000.00	$973.40	$374.94	$3,065.80	$9,585.86
$14,500.00	$973.40	$388.33	$3,219.03	$9,919.24
$15,000.00	$973.40	$401.72	$3,384.25	$10,240.63

Footnotes to Self-Employed Persons 2006 Tax Chart:

*   Determined without regard to Section 1402(a)(12) of the Internal Revenue Code of 1986, as amended (26 U.S.C.) (the "Code").

**   In calculating each of the Old-Age, Survivors and Disability Insurance tax and the Hospital (Medicare) Insurance tax, net earnings from self-employment are reduced by the deduction under Section 1402(a)(12) of the Code. The deduction under Section 1402(a)(12) of the Code is equal to net earnings from self-employment (determined without regard to Section 1402(a)(12) of the Code) multiplied by one-half (½) of the sum of the Old-Age, Survivors and Disability Insurance tax rate (12.4%) and the Hospital (Medicare) Insurance tax rate (2.9%). The sum of these rates is 15.3% (12.4% + 2.9% = 15.3%). One-half (½) of the combined rate is 7.65% (15.3% x ½ = 7.65%). The deduction can be computed by multiplying the net earnings from self-employment (determined without regard to Section 1402(a)(12) of the Code) by 92.35%. This gives the same deduction as multiplying the net earnings from self-employment (determined without regard to Section 1402(a)(12) of the Code) by 7.65% and then subtracting the result.

For example, the Social Security taxes imposed on monthly net earnings from self-employment (determined without regard to Section 1402(a)(12) of the Code) of $2,500.00 are calculated as follows:
   (i) Old-Age, Survivors and Disability Insurance Taxes:
       $2,500.00 x 92.35% x 12.4% = $286.29
   (ii) Hospital (Medicare) Insurance Taxes:
       $2,500.00 x 92.35% x 2.9% = $66.95

***   These amounts represent one-twelfth (¹⁄₁₂) of the annual Federal income tax calculated for a single taxpayer claiming one personal exemption ($3,300.00, subject to reduction in certain cases, as described below in this footnote) and taking the standard deduction ($5,150.00).

In calculating the annual Federal income tax, gross income is reduced by the deduction under Section 164(f) of the Code. The deduction under Section 164(f) of the Code is equal to one-half (½) of the self-employment taxes imposed by Section 1401 of the Code for the taxable year. For example, monthly net earnings from self-employment of $15,000.00 times 12 months equals $180,000.00. The Old-Age, Survivors and Disability Insurance taxes imposed by Section 1401 of the Code for the taxable year equal $11,680.80 ($94,200.00 x 12.4% = $11,680.80). The Hospital (Medicare) Insurance taxes imposed by Section 1401 of the Code for the taxable year equal $4,820.67 ($180,000.00 x .9235 x 2.9% = $4,820.67). The sum of the taxes imposed by Section 1401 of the Code for the taxable year equals $16,501.47 ($11,680.80 + $4,820.67 = $16,501.47). The deduction under Section 164(f) of the Code is equal to one-half (½) of $16,501.47 or $8,250.74.
For a single taxpayer with an adjusted gross income in excess of $150,500.00, the deduction for the personal exemption is reduced by two-thirds (⅔) of two percent (2%) for each $2,500.00 or fraction thereof by which adjusted gross income exceeds $150,500.00. The deduction for the personal exemption is no longer reduced for adjusted gross income in excess of $273,000.00. For example, monthly net earnings from self-employment of $15,000.00 times 12 months equals $180,000.00. The $180,000.00 amount is reduced by $8,250.74 (i.e., the deduction under Section 164(f) of the Code -- see the immediately preceding paragraph of this footnote for the computation) to arrive at adjusted gross income of $171,749.26. The excess over $150,500.00 is $21,249.26. $21,249.26 divided by $2,500.00 equals 8.50. The 8.50 amount is rounded up to 9. The reduction percentage is 12% (2/3 x 2% x 9 = 12%). The $3,300.00 deduction for one personal exemption is reduced by $396.00 ($3,300.00 x 12% = $396.00) to $2,904.00 ($3,300.00 - $396.00 = $2,904.00). For adjusted gross income in excess of $273,000.00 the deduction for the personal exemption is $1,100.00.

****   For annual net earnings from self-employment (determined with regard to Section 1402(a)(12) of the Code) above $94,200.00, this amount represents a monthly average of the Old-Age, Survivors and Disability Insurance tax based on the 2006 maximum Old-Age, Survivors and Disability Insurance tax of $11,680.80 per person (12.4% of the first $94,200.00 of net earnings from self-employment (determined with regard to Section 1402(a)(12) of the Code) equals $11,680.80). One-twelfth (¹⁄₁₂) of $11,680.80 equals $973.40.

*****   This amount represents the point where the monthly net earnings from self-employment of a self-employed individual would result in $6,000.00 of net resources.

* * * * * * * * * * * * * * * * * * * *

References Relating to Self-Employed Persons 2006 Tax Chart:
1. Old-Age, Survivors and Disability Insurance Tax
   (a) Contribution Base
       (1) Social Security Administration's notice dated October 18, 2005, and appearing in 70 Fed. Reg. 61,677 (October 25, 2005)

(2) Section 1402(b) of the Internal Revenue Code of 1986, as amended (26 U.S.C. § 1402(b))

(3) Section 230 of the Social Security Act, as amended (42 U.S.C. § 430)

(b) Tax Rate

(1) Section 1401(a) of the Internal Revenue Code of 1986, as amended (26 U.S.C. § 1401(a))

(c) Deduction Under Section 1402(a)(12)

(1) Section 1402(a)(12) of the Internal Revenue Code of 1986, as amended (26 U.S.C. §1402(a)(12))

2. Hospital (Medicare) Insurance Tax

(a) Contribution Base

(1) Section 1402(b) of the Internal Revenue Code of 1986, as amended (26 U.S.C. § 1402(b))

(2) Omnibus Budget Reconciliation Act of 1993, Pub. L. No. 103-66, § 13207, 107 Stat. 312, 467-69 (1993)

(b) Tax Rate

(1) Section 1401(b) of the Internal Revenue Code of 1986, as amended (26 U.S.C. § 1401(b))

(c) Deduction Under Section 1402(a)(12)

(1) Section 1402(a)(12) of the Internal Revenue Code of 1986, as amended (26 U.S.C. §1402(a)(12))

3. Federal Income Tax

(a) Tax Rate Schedule for 2006 for Single Taxpayers

(1) Revenue Procedure 2005-70, Section 3.01, Table 3 which appears in Internal Revenue Bulletin 2005-47, dated November 21, 2005

(2) Section 1(c), (f) and (i) of the Internal Revenue Code of 1986, as (26 U.S.C. § 1(c), 1(f), 1(i))

(b) Standard Deduction

(1) Revenue Procedure 2005-70, Section 3.10(1), which appears in Internal Revenue Bulletin 2005-47, dated November 21, 2005

(2) Section 63(c) of the Internal Revenue Code of 1986, as amended (26 U.S.C. § 63(c))

(c) Personal Exemption

(1) Revenue Procedure 2005-70, Section 3.17, which appears in Internal Revenue Bulletin 2005-47, dated November 21, 2005

(2) Section 151(d) of the Internal Revenue Code of 1986, as amended (26 U.S.C. § 151(d))

(d) Deduction Under Section 164(f)

(1) Section 164(f) of the Internal Revenue Code of 1986, as amended (26 U.S.C. § 164(f))

Sec. 154.063.   Party to Furnish Information

The court shall require a party to:

(1)   furnish information sufficient to accurately identify that party's net resources and ability to pay child support; and

(2)   produce copies of income tax returns for the past two years, a financial statement, and current pay stubs.

Sec. 154.064.   Medical Support for Child Presumptively Provided By Obligor

The guidelines for support of a child are based on the assumption that the court will order the obligor to provide medical support for the child in addition to the amount of child support calculated in accordance with those guidelines.

Sec. 154.065.   Self-Employment Income

(a)   Income from self-employment, whether positive or negative, includes benefits allocated to an individual from a business or undertaking in the form of a proprietorship, partnership, joint venture, close corporation, agency, or independent contractor, less ordinary and necessary expenses required to produce that income.

(b)   In its discretion, the court may exclude from self-employment income amounts allowable under federal income tax laws as depreciation, tax credits, or any other business expenses shown by the evidence to be inappropriate in making the determination of income available for the purpose of calculating child support.

Sec. 154.066.   Intentional Unemployment or Underemployment

If the actual income of the obligor is significantly less than what the obligor could earn because of intentional unemployment or underemployment, the court may apply the support guidelines to the earning potential of the obligor.

Sec. 154.067.   Deemed Income

(a)   When appropriate, in order to determine the net resources available for child support, the court may assign a reasonable amount of deemed income attributable to assets that do not currently produce income. The court shall also consider whether certain property that is not producing income can be liquidated without an unreasonable financial sacrifice because of cyclical or other market conditions. If there is no effective market for the property, the carrying costs of such an investment, including property taxes and note payments, shall be offset against the income attributed to the property.

(b)   The court may assign a reasonable amount of deemed income to income-producing assets that a party has voluntarily transferred or on which earnings have intentionally been reduced.

Sec. 154.068.   Wage or Salary Presumption

In the absence of evidence of the wages and salary income of a party, the court shall presume that the party has wages or salary equal to the federal minimum wage for a 40-hour week.

Sec. 154.069.   Net Resources of Spouse

(a)   The court may not add any portion of the net resources of a spouse to the net resources of an obligor or obligee in order to calculate the amount of child support to be ordered.

(b)   The court may not subtract the needs of a spouse, or of a dependent of a spouse, from the net resources of the obligor or obligee.

Sec. 154.070.   Child Support Received by Obligor

In a situation involving multiple households due child support, child support received by an obligor shall be added to the obligor's net resources to compute the net resources before determining the child support credit or applying the percentages in the multiple household table in this chapter.

TITLE 5. THE PARENT-CHILD RELATIONSHIP AND THE SUIT AFFECTING THE PARENT-CHILD RELATIONSHIP

SUBTITLE B. SUITS AFFECTING THE PARENT-CHILD RELATIONSHIP

CHAPTER 154. CHILD SUPPORT

SUBCHAPTER C. CHILD SUPPORT GUIDELINES

Sec. 154.121.   Guidelines for the Support of a Child

The child support guidelines in this subchapter are intended to guide the court in determining an equitable amount of child support.

Sec. 154.123.   Additional Factors for Court to Consider

(a)   The court may order periodic child support payments in an amount other than established by the guidelines if the evidence rebuts the presumption that application of the guidelines is in the best interest of the child and justifies a variance from the guidelines.

(b)   In determining whether application of the guidelines would be unjust or inappropriate under the circumstances, the court shall consider evidence of all relevant factors, including:

(1)   the age and needs of the child;

(2)   the ability of the parents to contribute to the support of the child;

(3)   any financial resources available for the support of the child;

(4)   the amount of time of possession of and access to a child;

(5)   the amount of the obligee's net resources, including the earning potential of the obligee if the actual income of the obligee is significantly less than what the obligee could earn because the obligee is intentionally unemployed or underemployed and including an increase or decrease in the income of the obligee or income that may be attributed to the property and assets of the obligee;

(6)   child care expenses incurred by either party in order to maintain gainful employment;

(7)   whether either party has the managing conservatorship or actual physical custody of another child;

(8)   the amount of alimony or spousal maintenance actually and currently being paid or received by a party;

(9)   the expenses for a son or daughter for education beyond secondary school;

(10)   whether the obligor or obligee has an automobile, housing, or other benefits furnished by his or her employer, another person, or a business entity;

(11)   the amount of other deductions from the wage or salary income and from other compensation for personal services of the parties;

(12)   provisions for health care insurance and payment of uninsured medical expenses;

(13)   special or extraordinary educational, health care, or other expenses of the parties or of the child;

(14)   the cost of travel in order to exercise possession of and access to a child;

(15)   positive or negative cash flow from any real and personal property and assets, including a business and investments;

(16)   debts or debt service assumed by either party; and

(17)   any other reason consistent with the best interest of the child, taking into consideration the circumstances of the parents.

Sec. 154.124.   Agreement Concerning Support

(a)   To promote the amicable settlement of disputes between the parties to a suit, the parties may enter into a written agreement containing provisions for support of the child and for modification of the agreement, including variations from the child support guidelines provided by Subchapter C.

(b)   If the court finds that the agreement is in the child's best interest, the court shall render an order in accordance with the agreement.

(c)   Terms of the agreement pertaining to child support in the order may be enforced by all remedies available for enforcement of a judgment, including contempt, but are not enforceable as a contract.

(d)   If the court finds the agreement is not in the child's best interest, the court may request the parties to submit a revised agreement or the court may render an order for the support of the child.

Sec. 154.125.   Application of Guidelines to Net Resources of $6,000 or Less

(a)   The guidelines for the support of a child in this section are specifically designed to apply to situations in which the obligor's monthly net resources are $6,000 or less.

(b)   If the obligor's monthly net resources are $6,000 or less, the court shall presumptively apply the following schedule in rendering the child support order:

CHILD SUPPORT GUIDELINES
BASED ON THE MONTHLY NET RESOURCES OF THE OBLIGOR

1 child	20% of Obligor's Net Resources
2 children	25% of Obligor's Net Resources
3 children	30% of Obligor's Net Resources
4 children	35% of Obligor's Net Resources
5 children	40% of Obligor's Net Resources
6+ children	Not less than the amount for 5 children.

Sec. 154.126.   Application of Guidelines to Net Resources of More Than $6,000 Monthly

(a)   If the obligor's net resources exceed $6,000 per month, the court shall presumptively apply the percentage guidelines to the first $6,000 of the obligor's net resources. Without further reference to the percentage recommended by these guidelines, the court may order additional amounts of child support as appropriate, depending on the income of the parties and the proven needs of the child.

(b)   The proper calculation of a child support order that exceeds the presumptive amount established for the first $6,000 of the obligor's net resources requires that the entire amount of the presumptive award be subtracted from the proven total needs of the child. After the presumptive award is subtracted, the court shall allocate between the parties the responsibility to meet the additional needs of the child according to the circumstances of the parties. However, in no event may the obligor be required to pay more child support than the greater of the presumptive amount or the amount equal to 100 percent of the proven needs of the child.

Sec. 154.128.   Computing Support for Children in More Than One Household

(a)   In applying the child support guidelines for an obligor who has children in more than one household, the court shall apply the percentage guidelines in this subchapter by making the following computation:

(1)   determine the amount of child support that would be ordered if all children whom the obligor has the legal duty to support lived in one household by applying the schedule in this subchapter;

(2)   compute a child support credit for the obligor's children who are not before the court by dividing the amount determined under Subdivision (1) by the total number of children whom the obligor is obligated to support and multiplying that number by the number of the obligor's children who are not before the court;

(3)   determine the adjusted net resources of the obligor by subtracting the child support credit computed under Subdivision (2) from the net resources of the obligor; and

(4)   determine the child support amount for the children before the court by applying the percentage guidelines for one household for the number of children of the obligor before the court to the obligor's adjusted net resources.

(b)   For the purpose of determining a child support credit, the total number of an obligor's children includes the children before the court for the establishment or modification of a support order and any other children, including children residing with the obligor, whom the obligor has the legal duty of support.

(c)   The child support credit with respect to children for whom the obligor is obligated by an order to pay support is computed, regardless of whether the obligor is delinquent in child support payments, without regard to the amount of the order.

Sec. 154.129.   Alternative Method of Computing Support for Children in More Than One Household

In lieu of performing the computation under the preceding section, the court may determine the child support amount for the children before the court by applying the percentages in the table below to the obligor's net resources:

MULTIPLE FAMILY ADJUSTED GUIDELINES
(% OF NET RESOURCES)
Number of children before the court

		1	2	3	4	5	6	7
Number of	0	20.00	25.00	30.00	35.00	40.00	40.00	40.00
other	1	17.50	22.50	27.38	32.20	37.33	27.71	38.00
children for	2	16.00	20.63	25.20	30.33	35.43	36.00	36.44
whom the	3	14.75	19.00	24.00	29.00	34.00	34.67	35.20
obligor	4	13.60	18.33	23.14	28.00	32.89	33.60	34.18
has a	5	13.33	17.86	22.50	27.22	32.00	32.73	33.33
duty of	6	13.14	17.50	22.00	26.60	31.27	32.00	32.62
support	7	13.00	17.22	21.60	26.09	30.67	31.38	32.00

Sec. 154.130.   Findings in Child Support Order

(a)   Without regard to Rules 296 through 299, Texas Rules of Civil Procedure, in rendering an order of child support, the court shall make the findings required by Subsection (b) if:

(1)   a party files a written request with the court not later than 10 days after the date of the hearing;

(2)   a party makes an oral request in open court during the hearing; or

(3)   the amount of child support ordered by the court varies from the amount computed by applying the percentage guidelines.

(b)   If findings are required by this section, the court shall state whether the application of the guidelines would be unjust or inappropriate and shall state the following in the child support order:

(1)   the monthly net resources of the obligor per month are $____;

(2)   the monthly net resources of the obligee per month are $_____;

(3)   the percentage applied to the obligor's net resources for child support by the actual order rendered by the court is _____%;

(4)   the amount of child support if the percentage guidelines are applied to the first $6,000 of the obligor's net resources is $_____;

(5)   if applicable, the specific reasons that the amount of child support per month ordered by the court varies from the amount stated in Subdivision (4) are: _____; and

(6)   if applicable, the obligor is obligated to support children in more than one household; and:

    (A)   the number of children before the court is _____;

    (B)   the number of children not before the court residing in the same household with the obligor is _____; and

    (C)   the number of children not before the court for whom the obligor is obligated by a court order to pay support, without regard to whether the obligor is delinquent in child support payments, and who are not counted under Paragraph (A) or (B) is _____."

(c)   The application of the guidelines under Section 154.129 does not constitute a variance from the child support guidelines requiring specific findings by the court under this section.

Sec. 154.131. Retroactive Child Support

(a)   The child support guidelines are intended to guide the court in determining the amount of retroactive child support, if any, to be ordered.

(b)   In ordering retroactive child support, the court shall consider the net resources of the obligor during the relevant time period and whether:

(1)   the mother of the child had made any previous attempts to notify the obligor of his paternity or probable paternity;

(2)   the obligor had knowledge of his paternity or probable paternity;

(3)   the order of retroactive child support will impose an undue financial hardship on the obligor or the obligor's family; and

(4)   the obligor has provided actual support or other necessaries before the filing of the action.

(c)   It is presumed that a court order limiting the amount of retroactive child support to an amount that does not exceed the total amount of support that would have been due for the four years preceding the date the petition seeking support was filed is reasonable and in the best interest of the child.

(d)   The presumption created under this section may be rebutted by evidence that the obligor:

(1)   knew or should have known that the obligor was the father of the child for whom support is sought; and

(2)   sought to avoid the establishment of a support obligation to the child.

(e)   An order under this section limiting the amount of retroactive support does not constitute a variance from the guidelines requiring the court to make specific findings under Section 154.130.

Sec. 154.133. Application of Guidelines to Children of Obligors Receiving Social Security

In applying the child support guidelines for an obligor who is receiving social security old age benefits and who is required to pay support for a child who receives benefits as a result of the obligor's receipt of social security old age benefits, the court shall apply the guidelines by determining the amount of child support that would be ordered under the child support guidelines and subtracting from that total the amount of benefits or the value of the benefits paid to or for the child as a result of the obligor's receipt of social security old age benefits.

TITLE 5. THE PARENT-CHILD RELATIONSHIP AND THE SUIT AFFECTING THE PARENT-CHILD RELATIONSHIP

SUBTITLE B. SUITS AFFECTING THE PARENT-CHILD RELATIONSHIP

CHAPTER 153. CONSERVATORSHIP, POSSESSION, AND ACCESS

SUBCHAPTER D. MEDICAL SUPPORT FOR CHILD

Sec. 154.181. Medical Support Order

(a)   The court shall render an order for the medical support of the child as provided by this section and section 154.182 in:

(1)   a proceeding in which periodic payments of child support are ordered under this chapter or modified under chapter 156;

(2)   any other suit affecting the parent-child relationship in which the court determines that medical support of the child must be established, modified, or clarified; or

(3)   a proceeding under Chapter 159.

(b)   Before a hearing on temporary orders or a final order, if no hearing on temporary orders is held, the court shall require the parties to the proceedings to disclose in a pleading or other statement:

(1)   if private health insurance is in effect for the child, the identity of the insurance company providing the coverage, the policy number, which parent is responsible for payment of any insurance premium for the coverage, whether the coverage is provided through a parent's employment, and the cost of the premium; or

(2)   if private health insurance is not in effect for the child, whether:

    (A)   the child is receiving medical assistance under Chapter 32, Human Resources Code;

    (B)   the child is receiving health benefits coverage under the state child health plan under Chapter 62, Health and Safety Code, and the cost of any premium; and

    (C)   either parent has access to private health insurance at reasonable cost to that parent.

(c)   In rendering temporary orders, the court shall, except for good cause shown, order that any health insurance coverage in effect for the child continue in effect pending the rendition of a final order, except that the court may not require the continuation of any health insurance that is not available to the parent at reasonable cost. If there is no health insurance coverage in effect for the child or if the insurance in effect is not available at a reasonable cost and the child is not receiving medical assistance under Chapter 32, Human Resources Code, or coverage under the state child health plan under Chapter 62, Health and Safety Code, the court shall, except for good cause shown, order health care coverage for the child as provided under Section 154.182.

(d)   Except for good cause shown, on rendering a final order the court shall require the parent ordered to provide health care coverage for the child as provided under Section 154.182 to produce evidence to the court's satisfaction that the parent has applied for or secured health insurance or has otherwise taken necessary action to provide for health care coverage for the child, as ordered by the court.

(e)   In this section, "reasonable cost" means the cost of a health insurance premium that does not exceed 10 percent of the responsible parent's net income in a month.

Sec. 154.182.   Health Insurance

(a)   The court shall consider the cost and quality of health insurance coverage available to the parties and shall give priority to health insurance coverage available through the employment of one of the parties.

(b)   In determining the manner in which health insurance for the child is to be ordered, the court shall render its order in accordance with the following priorities, unless a party shows good cause why a particular order would not be in the best interest of the child:

    (1)   if health insurance is available for the child through the obligor's employment or membership in a union, trade association, or other organization at reasonable cost to the obligor, the court shall order the obligor to include the child in the obligor's health insurance;

    (2)   if health insurance is not available for the child through the obligor's employment but is available for the child at a reasonable cost through the obligee's employment or membership in a union, trade association, or other organization, the court may order the obligee to provide health insurance for the child, and, in such event, shall order the obligor to pay additional child support to be withheld from earnings under Chapter 158 to the obligee for the actual cost of the health insurance for the child;

    (3)   if health insurance is not available for the child under Subdivision (1) or (2), the court shall order the obligor to provide health insurance for the child if the court finds that health insurance is available to the obligor for the child from another source and at reasonable cost;

    (4)   if neither parent has access to private health insurance at a reasonable cost, the court shall order that the custodial parent or, to the extent permitted by law, the noncustodial parent immediately apply on behalf of the child for participation in a medical assistance program under Chapter 32, Human Resources Code, or the state child health plan under Chapter 62, Health and Safety Code, and that the obligor pay additional child support, to be withheld from income under Chapter 158, to the obligee for the actual cost of participation of the child in the state child health plan; or,

    (5)   if health coverage is not available for the child under Subdivision (1), (2), (3), or (4), the court shall order the obligor to pay the obligee, in addition to any amount ordered under the guidelines for child support, a reasonable amount each month as medical support for the child to be withheld from earnings under Chapter 158.

(c)   In this section, "reasonable cost" has the meaning assigned by Section 154.181(e)

Sec. 154.183.   Health Insurance Additional Support Duty of Obligor

(a)   An amount that an obligor is required to pay for health insurance for the child:

    (1)   is in addition to the amount that the obligor is required to pay for child support under the guidelines for child support;

    (2)   is a child support obligation; and

    (3)   may be enforced as a child support obligation.

(b)   If the court finds and states in the child support order that the obligee will maintain health insurance coverage for the child at the obligee's expense, the court may increase the amount of child support to be paid by the obligor in an amount not exceeding the total expense to the obligee for maintaining health insurance coverage.

(c)   As additional child support, the court shall allocate between the parties, according to their circumstances, the reasonable and necessary health care expenses of a child that are not reimbursed by health insurance.

Sec. 154.184.   Effect of Order

(a)   The court shall render an order for the medical support of the child as provided by this section and Section 154.182 in:

    (1)   a proceeding in which periodic payments of child support are ordered under this chapter or modified under Chapter 156;

    (2)   any other suit affecting the parent-child relationship in which the court determines that medical support of the child must be established, modified, or clarified; or

    (3)   a proceeding under Chapter 159.

(b)   The child shall be automatically enrolled for the first 31 days after the receipt of the order by the employer on the same terms and conditions as apply to any other dependent child.

(c)   The employer shall notify the insurer of the automatic enrollment.

(d)   During the 31-day period, the employer and insurer shall complete all necessary forms and procedures to make the enrollment permanent or shall report in accordance with this subchapter the reasons the coverage cannot be made permanent.

Sec. 154.185.   Parent to Furnish Information

(a)   The court shall order a parent providing health insurance to furnish to either the obligee, obligor, or child support agency the following information not later than the 30th day after the date the notice of rendition of the order is received:

(1)   the social security number of the parent;

(2)   the name and address of the parent's employer;

(3)   whether the employer is self-insured or has health insurance available;

(4)   proof that health insurance has been provided for the child;

(5)   if the employer has health insurance available, the name of the health insurance carrier, the number of the policy, a copy of the policy and schedule of benefits, a health insurance membership card, claim forms, and any other information necessary to submit a claim; and

(6)   if the employer is self-insured, a copy of the schedule of benefits, a membership card, claim forms, and any other information necessary to submit a claim.

(b)   The court shall also order a parent providing health insurance to furnish the obligor, obligee, or child support agency with additional information regarding health insurance coverage not later than the 15th day after the date the information is received by the parent.

Sec. 154.188.   Failure to Provide Required Health Insurance

A parent ordered to provide health insurance or to pay the other parent additional child support for the cost of health insurance who fails to do so is liable for:

(1)   necessary medical expenses of the child, without regard to whether the expenses would have been paid if health insurance had been provided; and

(2)   the cost of health insurance premiums or contributions, if any, paid on behalf of the child.

TITLE 5.   THE PARENT-CHILD RELATIONSHIP AND THE SUIT AFFECTING THE PARENT-CHILD RELATIONSHIP

SUBTITLE B.   SUITS AFFECTING THE PARENT-CHILD RELATIONSHIP

CHAPTER 156.   MODIFICATION

SUBCHAPTER B.   MODIFICATION OF CONSERVATORSHIPS, POSSESSION AND ACCESS, OR DETERMINATION OF RESIDENCE

Sec. 156.105.   Modification of Order Based on Military Deployment

(a)   The military deployment outside this country of a person who is a possessory conservator or a joint managing conservator without the exclusive right to designate the primary residence of the child is a material and substantial change of circumstances sufficient to justify a modification of an existing court order or portion of a decree that sets the terms and conditions for the possession of or access to a child.

(b)   If the court determines that modification is in the best interest of the child, the court may modify the order or decree to provide in a manner consistent with Section 153.3161 for limited possession of the child during the period of the deployment by a person designated by the deployed conservator.

TITLE 5.   THE PARENT-CHILD RELATIONSHIP AND THE SUIT AFFECTING THE PARENT-CHILD RELATIONSHIP

SUBTITLE B.   SUITS AFFECTING THE PARENT-CHILD RELATIONSHIP

CHAPTER 156.   MODIFICATION

SUBCHAPTER E.   MODIFICATION OF CHILD SUPPORT

Sec. 156.401.   Grounds for Modification of Child Support

(a)   Except as provided by Subsection (a-1) or (b), the court may modify an order that provides for the support of a child if:

(1)   the circumstances of the child or a person affected by the order have materially and substantially changed since the earlier of:

(A)   the date of the order's rendition; or

(B)   the date of the signing of a mediated or collaborative law settlement agreement on which the order is based; or

(2)   it has been three years since the order was rendered or last modified and the monthly amount of the child support award under the order differs by either 20 percent or $100 from the amount that would be awarded in accordance with the child support guidelines.

(a-1) If the parties agree to an order under which the amount of child support differs from the amount that would be awarded in accordance with the child support guidelines, the court may modify the order only if the circumstances of the child or a person affected by the order have materially and substantially changed since the date of the order's rendition.

(b)   A support order may be modified only as to obligations accruing after the earlier of:

(1)   the date of service of citation; or

(2)   an appearance in the suit to modify.

(c)   An order of joint conservatorship, in and of itself, does not constitute grounds for modifying a support order.

(d)   Release of a child support obligor from incarceration is a material and substantial change in circumstances for purposes of this section if the obligor's child support obligation was abated, reduced, or suspended during the period of the obligor's incarceration.

Sec. 156.409.   Change in Physical Possession

(a)   If the sole managing conservator of a child or the joint managing conservator who has the exclusive right to determine the primary residence of the child has voluntarily relinquished the primary care and possession of the child to another person for at least six months, the court shall, on the motion of a party or the other person having physical possession of the child, modify an order providing for the support of the child to provide that the other person having physical possession of the child shall have the right to receive and give receipt for payments of support for the child and to hold or disburse money for the benefit of the child.

(b)   Notice of a motion for modification under this section may be served in the manner for serving a notice under Section 157.065.

Sec. 156.410.   Change in Circumstances Resulting from Military Service

(a)   For purposes of Section 156.401, the fact that an obligor has been called into active military service in any branch of the United States armed forces is a material and substantial change in circumstances if that active military service:
(1)   is for at least 30 consecutive days; and
(2)   results in a decrease in the obligor's net resources during the period of service.

(b)   A motion for modification under Subsection (a) must be accompanied by the affidavit of the obligor's commanding officer that states:
(1)   the date on which the obligor's active military service begins and the date on which that service is expected to end; and
(2)   the obligor's anticipated monthly gross income from active military service.

(c)   Return of the obligor from the active military service described by Subsection (a) is a material and substantial change in circumstances for purposes of Section 156.401 for which an obligee may file a motion for modification of a child support order if the court previously modified the order on the grounds described by Subsection (a).

Sec. 156.409.   Change in Physical Possession

(a)   If the sole managing conservator of a child or the joint managing conservator who designates the child's primary residence has voluntarily relinquished the actual care, control, and possession of the child for at least six months, the court may modify an order providing for the support of the child to provide that the person having physical possession of the child shall have the right to receive and give receipt for payments of support for the child and to hold or disburse money for the benefit of the child.

(b)   Notice of a motion for modification under this section may be served in the manner for serving a notice under Section 157.065.

TITLE 5.   THE PARENT-CHILD RELATIONSHIP AND THE SUIT
AFFECTING THE PARENT-CHILD RELATIONSHIP

SUBTITLE B. SUITS AFFECTING THE PARENT-CHILD RELATIONSHIP

CHAPTER 157.   ENFORCEMENT

SUBCHAPTER F.   JUDGMENT AND INTEREST

Sec. 157.265.   Accrual of Interest on Child Support

(a)   Interest accrues on the portion of delinquent child support that is greater than the amount of the monthly periodic support obligation at the rate of six percent simple interest per year from the date the support is delinquent until the date the support is paid or the arrearages are confirmed and reduced to money judgment.

(b)   Interest accrues on child support arrearages that have been confirmed and reduced to money judgment as provided in this subchapter at the rate of six percent simple interest per year from the date the order is rendered until the date the judgment is paid.

(c)   Interest accrues on a money judgment for retroactive or lump-sum child support at the annual rate of six percent simple interest from the date the order is rendered until the judgment is paid.

(d)   Subsection (a) applies to a child support payment that becomes due on or after January 1, 2002.

(e)   Child support arrearages in existence on January 1, 2002, that were not confirmed and reduced to a money judgment on or before that date accrue interest as follows:
(1)   before January 1, 2002, the arrearages are subject to the interest rate that applied to the arrearages before that date; and
(2)   on and after January 1, 2002, the cumulative total of arrearages and interest accumulated on those arrearages described by Subdivision (1) is subject to Subsection (a).

(f)   Subsections (b) and (c) apply to a money judgment for child support rendered on or after January 1, 2002. A money judgment for child support rendered before that date is governed by the law in effect on the date the judgment was rendered, and the former law is continued in effect for that purpose.

Blank Forms

appendix b

The following is a list of the forms found in this appendix. Each form is numbered in the upper outside corner. Be sure you have the correct form number, because several of the forms have the same title and appear to be very similar. The page number where the form begins is also listed below. You can tear the forms out of this book for use, but it would be best to make copies first in case you make a mistake. You can also find these forms on the included CD-ROM. (See "How to Use the CD-ROM, p.vii.)

Where to Find Additional Forms. This book is designed for the most typical divorce situations. In unusual situations, there are numerous other forms that can be filed to obtain various results. To find additional forms, check your nearest law library. Ask the librarian where to find divorce form books. There are specific guides to divorce matters that will contain forms. There are also general form books containing forms on all kinds of legal matters. (Also, see the section on "Legal Research" in Chapter 2.)

Property Inventory

(1) S	(2) Description	(3) ID Number	(4) Value	(5) Balance Owed	(6) Equity	(7) Owner H, W, J	(8) H	(9) W

This page intentionally blank.

Debt Inventory

(1) S	(2) Creditor	(3) Account Number	(4) Notes	(5) Monthly Balance	(6) Balance Owed	(7) Date	(8) Owner H, W, J	(9) H	(10) W

This page intentionally blank.

NO._____

IN THE MATTER OF THE MARRIAGE	§ § §	IN THE DISTRICT COURT
_____	§ §	_____ JUDICIAL DISTRICT
AND	§ §	
_____	§ §	_____ COUNTY, TEXAS

PARENTING PLAN

This Parenting Plan is ☐ Agreed ☐ Proposed
by ☐ Mother ☐ Father ☐ Both Parents
☐ Temporary Order
☐ Final Judgment

The Parents of the minor children are:

Mother's Name: _____
Mother's Address: _____
                             _____
Mother's Telephone Number: _____

Father's Name: _____
Father's Address: _____
                             _____
Father's Telephone Number: _____

The minor children who are subject to this Parenting Plan are:

Child's Name: _____
Child's Residence: _____
                             _____
Child's Birthdate: _____

Child's Name: _____
Child's Residence: _____
                             _____
Child's Birthdate: _____

Child's Name: _____
Child's Residence: _____
                             _____
Child's Birthdate: _____

Child's Name: _____
Child's Residence: _____
                             _____
Child's Birthdate: _____

Both parents recognize the Children's wishes to love and respect each of them, regardless of marital status and place of residence, and that the Children's welfare can best be served by their mutual cooperation as partners in parenting. Neither parent will do anything that may estrange the Children from the other or hamper the natural development of the Children's affection for the other. Neither parent shall speak disparagingly of the other parent or the other's parent's family to the Children or in the presence of the Children.

RESIDENCE OF CHILDREN

☐ Mother
☐ Father
shall designate the primary residence of the Children.

The primary residence of the Children shall be established:
☐ Within the following geographical area: _____
☐ Without regard to geographic location

If _____ desires to change the primary residence of the Children, _____ shall provide _____ with no less than ninety (90) days written notice of the intention to change the primary residence.

CHILD SUPPORT

_____ shall pay to _____ child support in the amount of $_____ per month, for the support of the Children with the first payment being due and payable on _____, 20_____.

Child support shall be paid:
☐ Weekly
☐ Bi-weekly
☐ Semi-monthly
☐ Monthly

Child support shall be paid until the earliest occurrence of one of the following events:
1. A Child reaches the age of 18 years, provided that if the child is fully enrolled in an accredited secondary school program leading toward a high school diploma, the periodic child support payments shall continue to be due and paid until the end of the school year in which the child graduates;
2. A Child marries;
3. A Child dies;
4. A Child's disabilities are removed for general purposes;
5. A Child is emancipated;
6. Until further order of the Court.

Thereafter, the child support shall be reduced to $_____ per month, payable
☐ Weekly
☐ Bi-weekly
☐ Semi-monthly
☐ Monthly

until the occurrence of one of the following events:
☐ The last Child reaches the age of 18 years, provided that if the Child is fully enrolled in an accredited secondary school program leading toward a high school diploma, the periodic child support payments shall continue to be due and paid until the end of the school year in which the Child graduates;
☐ The last Child marries;

☐ The last Child dies;
☐ The last Child's disabilities are removed for general purposes;
☐ The last Child is emancipated;
☐ Until further order of the Court.

ORDER WITHHOLDING FROM EARNINGS FOR CHILD SUPPORT

☐ will be served
☐ will not be served unless _____ is delinquent in child support payments.

FEDERAL INCOME TAX EXEMPTION

The tax exemption for federal, state and local income tax purposes for the Children shall be claimed as follows:
☐ Mother shall claim the following Children: _____
☐ Father shall claim the following Children: _____

OR

The exemptions may be claimed in: ☐ alternate years starting _____
                                       ☐ each year_____

provided, however, if _____ falls behind in child support payments _____
_____ shall be not entitled to the tax exemption for the Children. The parents shall complete the required Internal Revenue Service form to formalize the tax exemption.

HEALTH AND DENTAL INSURANCE

☐ Mother will maintain reasonable health insurance on the Children.
☐ Father will maintain reasonable health insurance on the Children.
☐ Both parents will maintain reasonable health insurance on the Children.

Proof of continuing coverage shall be furnished to the other parent annually or as coverage changes. The parent maintaining coverage shall authorize the other parent to consult with the insurance carrier regarding the coverage in effect and shall provide the other parent with a current health insurance card for the Children.

Uncovered reasonable and necessary medical expenses, which may include but are not limited to, deductibles or copayments, eyeglasses, contact lenses, routine annual physicals, counseling will be paid by:
☐ Mother
☐ Father
☐ Shared equally by parents
After insurance has paid its portion, the parent receiving the bill will send the bill the other parent within ten (10) days. The other parent will pay his or her share within thirty (30) days of receipt of the bill.

If available through his or her employer,
☐ Mother
☐ Father
☐ Both
shall maintain dental, orthodontic, and optical insurance on the Children.

RIGHTS AND DUTIES OF PARENTS

The parents shall have the following rights at all times:
☐ Mother   ☐ Father   the right to receive information from any other conservator of the Children concerning the health, education, and welfare of the Children;

☐ Mother   ☐ Father   the right to confer with the other parent to the extent possible before making a decision concerning the health, education, and welfare of the Children;

☐ Mother   ☐ Father   the right of access to medical, dental, psychological, and educational records of the Children;

☐ Mother   ☐ Father   the right to consult with a physician, dentist, or psychologist of the Children;

☐ Mother   ☐ Father   the right to consult with school officials concerning the Children's welfare and educational status, including school activities;

☐ Mother   ☐ Father   the right to be designated on the Children's records as a person to be notified in case of an emergency;

☐ Mother   ☐ Father   the right to attend school activities;

☐ Mother   ☐ Father   the right to consent to medical, dental, and surgical treatment during an emergency involving an immediate danger to the health and safety of the Children; and,

☐ Mother   ☐ Father   the right to manage the estates of the Children to the extent the estates have been created by the parent or the parent's family.

Each parent shall have the following duties conferred by law:

The duty to inform the other parent of the Children of significant information concerning the health, education, and welfare of the Children in a timely manner; and,

The duty to inform the other parent of the Children if the parent resides with for at least 30 days, marries, or intends to marry a person who the parent knows is registered as a sex offender under Chapter 62 of the Code of Criminal Procedure or is currently charged with an offense for which on conviction the person would be required to register under Chapter 62. This information should be given in the form of a notice made as soon as practicable but not later than 40 days after the date the parent begins to reside with the person or on the 10th day after the marriage occurs. The notice must include a description of the offense that is the basis of the person's requirement to register as a sex offender or of the offense with which the person is charged.

During his/her parenting times, the parents shall have the following rights and duties:

☐ Mother   ☐ Father   the duty of care, control, protection, and reasonable discipline of the Children;

☐ Mother   ☐ Father   the duty to support the Children, including providing the Children with clothing, food, shelter, and medical and dental care not involving an invasive procedure;

☐ Mother   ☐ Father   the right to consent for the Children to medical and dental care not involving an invasive procedure; and

☐ Mother   ☐ Father   the right to direct the moral and religious training of the Children;

OPTION 1

☐ It is in the best interest of the Children that:
☐ The parents consult about making any decision listed below, but all final decisions can be made by:
      ☐ Mother   ☐ Father

OPTION 2

☐ One parent should be designated to make specific decisions. These decision-making areas shall be listed below. The parent designated shall have the sole authority to make the following decisions:

☐ Mother ☐ Father the exclusive right to designate the primary residence of the Children;

☐ Mother ☐ Father the exclusive right to consent to medical, dental, and surgical treatment involving invasive procedures and to consent to psychiatric and psychological treatment of the Children;

☐ Mother ☐ Father the exclusive right to receive and give receipt for periodic payments for the support of the Children and to hold or disburse these funds for the benefit of the Children;

☐ Mother ☐ Father the exclusive right to represent the Children in legal matters and to make other decisions of substantial legal significance concerning the Children;

☐ Mother ☐ Father the exclusive right to consent to marriage and to enlistment in the armed forces of the United States;

☐ Mother ☐ Father the exclusive right to make decisions concerning the Children's education;

☐ Mother ☐ Father the exclusive right to the services and earnings of the Children except as provided by Section 264.0111 of the Texas Family Code;

☐ Mother ☐ Father except when a guardian of the Children's estates of a guardian or attorney ad litem has been appointed for the Children, the exclusive right to act as an agent of the Children in relation to the Children's estates if the Children's action is required by a state, the United States, or a foreign government; and,

☐ Mother ☐ Father the exclusive duty to manage the estate of the Children to the extent the estate has been created by community property or the joint property of the parents.

☐ All other major decisions shall be made jointly.

☐ Each parent shall be responsible for getting records and reports directly from school and medical care providers.

☐ Both parents shall be listed as "emergency contacts" for the Children.

☐ Parents shall always let each other know their current addresses, home, work, and emergency telephone numbers and shall notify each other in writing _____ days before and within _____ days of any changes.

☐ If either parent has any knowledge of any illness, accident, hospitalization, or other circumstance seriously affecting the health of the Children, that parent shall immediately notify the other parent.

☐ Each parent shall determine the Children's nonrecurring organized activities, special training, and social events while residing with that parent.

☐ Unless the parents otherwise agree neither parent shall give permission to the Children to engage in social activities that occur while the Children are with the other parent.

☐ The parents shall agree before enrolling the Children in organized activities such as sports teams, lessons, or special training, which occur even partially during the other parent's time with the Children.

☐ Each parent shall make a good faith effort to give information to the other parent about events and organized activities in the Children's lives including school programs, concerts, award ceremonies, plays, sports events, birthday parties, sleepovers, and other activities in which the Children are participating.

In order for the Children to obtain a driver's license, use a car, purchase a vehicle or use other vehicles such as motorcycles or all terrain vehicles, the parents must ☐ confer ☐ agree.

Before the Children are allowed to view "R" rated movies or have unsupervised access to the Internet the parents must ☐ confer ☐ agree.

Before the Children become employed, the parents must ☐ confer ☐ agree.

Before either parent consents to cosmetic surgery, body piercing, or tattooing, the parents must ☐ confer ☐ agree.

Before the Children may use a firearm, engage in hunting or target practice, the parents must ☐ confer ☐ agree.

PARENTING TIME WITH CHILDREN
(Check boxes for requested periods)

Parents who reside 100 miles or less from the primary residence of the Children

_____, the parent with whom the Children do not have their primary residence, shall have parenting time with the Children as follows:

1. Weekends
Weekends **beginning** on the first, third, and fifth Friday of each month at:
    ☐ 6:00 P.M. - OR -
    ☐ the time the Children's school is regularly dismissed - OR -
    ☐ other time after school dismissal: _____ M.

and **ending** at:
    ☐ 6:00 P.M. on the following Sunday - OR -
    ☐ the time the Children's school resumes after the weekend - OR –
    ☐ other time before school resumes: _____ -OR-
    ☐ other weekend times: _____

If a weekend period of parenting time begins on a Friday that is a school holiday during the regular school term or a federal, state, or local holiday during the summer months when school is not in session, that weekend period of parenting time shall begin on Thursday at:
    ☐ 6:00 P.M. - OR -
    ☐ the time the Children's school is regularly dismissed - OR -
    ☐ other time after school dismissal: _____ M.

If a weekend period of parenting time ends on or is immediately followed by a Monday that is a school holiday during the regular school term or a federal, state or local holiday during the summer months when school is not in session, that weekend period of parenting time shall end at:
    ☐   6:00 P.M. on the Monday holiday or school holiday - OR -
    ☐   6:00 P.M. on the Monday holiday or at the time the Children's school resumes after the school holiday - OR –
    ☐   other time: _____

2. Weekdays - (Choose Option A or B)

OPTION A

On Thursday of each week during the regular school term, beginning at:
☐ 6:00 P.M. - OR -
☐ the time the Children's school is regularly dismissed - OR -
☐ other time after school dismissal: _____ M.

and ending at:
☐ 8:00 P.M. - OR -
☐ the time the Children's school resumes on Friday

OPTION B

On ☐ Tuesday - OR - ☐ Wednesday of each week during the regular school term, beginning at:
☐ 6:00 P.M. - OR -
☐ the time the Children's school is regularly dismissed - OR -
☐ other time after school dismissal: _____ M.

and ending at:
☐ 8:00 P.M.
☐ the time the Children's school resumes the next morning

3. Spring Break
Spring Break in Even-Numbered Years, beginning on the day the Children's school is dismissed at:
☐ 6:00 P.M. - OR -
☐ the time the Children's school is regularly dismissed - OR -
☐ other time after school dismissal: _____ M.

and ending at:
☐ 6:00 P.M. on the day before school resumes after that vacation - OR -
☐ the time the Children's school resumes after that vacation - OR -
☐ other time before school resumes: _____

4. Summers
With written notice to the other parent by April 1:
☐ thirty days during the summer, beginning no earlier than the day after the Children's school is dismissed for the summer vacation and ending no later than seven days before school resumes at the end of the summer vacation in that year, to be exercised in no more than two separate periods of at least seven consecutive days each, as specified in the written notice. If the other parent is the father, the period or periods of extended summer parenting time should not interfere with Father's Day Weekend. These periods of parenting time shall begin and end at 6:00 P.M. - OR -
☐ other periods of summer parenting time: _____

If written notice is not given by April 1 of a year specifying an extended period or periods of summer parenting time for that year, summer parenting time for that year:
☐ shall begin at 6:00 P.M. on July 1 and end at 6:00 P.M. on July 31 - OR -
☐ other thirty-day period during the summer months: _____

_____, the parent with whom the Children primarily reside, shall have a superior right of parenting time with the Children as follows:

1. Spring Break

Spring Break in Odd-Numbered Years, beginning on the day the Children's school is dismissed at:
☐ 6:00 P.M. - OR -
☐ the time the Children's school is regularly dismissed - OR -
☐ other time after school dismissal: _____ M.

and ending at:
☐ 6:00 P.M. on the day before school resumes after that vacation - OR -
☐ the time the Children's school resumes after that vacation - OR -
☐ other time before school resumes: _____

2. Summer Weekend Parenting Time

☐ With written notice to the other parent by April 15, on any one weekend during any one period of the other parent's period of extended summer parenting time, beginning at 6:00 P.M. on Friday and ending at 6:00 P.M. on Sunday, provided that the parent picks up the Children from the other parent and returns the Children to the same place. If the other parent is the father, the weekend selected should not interfere with Father's Day Weekend - OR -
☐ other times: _____

3. Extended Summer Parenting Time

☐ With written notice to the other parent by April 15 or fourteen days' written notice on or after April 16, the parent may designate one weekend beginning no earlier than the day after the child's school is dismissed for the summer vacation and ending no later than seven days before school resumes at the end of the summer vacation, during which an otherwise scheduled weekend period of parenting time of the other parent shall not take place in that year, provided that the weekend so designated does not interfere with the other parent's period or periods of extended summer parenting time. If the other parent is the father, the weekend selected should not interfere with Father's Day Weekend.
- OR -
☐ other times: _____

☐ Other summer arrangements:_____

Parents who reside more than 100 miles
from the primary residence of the Children

_____, the parent with whom the Children do not have their primary residence, shall have parenting time with the Children as follows:

1. Weekends

Select one of the following provisions, depending on the distance between the present residence of Party B and that of the Children
☐ _____ is currently residing 100 miles or less from the primary residence of the Children. If that situation changes, within ninety days after _____ begins to reside more than 100 miles from the primary residence of the Children he/she shall give notice to _____ specifying which option for weekend parenting time he/she will exercise. At that time, _____ may select either Option One or Option Two.

NOTE: COMPLETE OPTION ONE *AND* OPTION 2

OPTION ONE

On weekends beginning on the first, third, and fifth Friday of each month at:
☐ 6:00 P.M. - OR -
☐ the time the Children's school is regularly dismissed - OR -
☐ other time after school dismissal: _____ M.

and ending at:
    ☐ 6:00 P.M. on the following Sunday - OR -
    ☐ the time the Children's school resumes after the weekend - OR -
    ☐ other time before school resumes: _____

OPTION TWO

Not more than one weekend per month of _____'s choice, with fourteen days' notice to _____ preceding each chosen weekend, beginning on the day school recesses for the weekend at:
    ☐ 6:00 P.M. - OR -
    ☐ the time the Children's school is regularly dismissed - OR -
    ☐ other time after school dismissal: _____ M.

and ending at:
    ☐ 6:00 P.M. on the day before school resumes after the weekend - OR -
    ☐ the time the Children's school resumes after the weekend - OR -
    ☐ other time before school resumes: _____

The weekend chosen should not conflict with provisions regarding Christmas, Thanksgiving, a child's birthday, or Mother's/Father's Day Weekend.

Under either Option One or Two, if a weekend period of parenting time begins on a Friday that is a school holiday during the regular school term or a federal, state, or local holiday during the summer months when school is not in session, that weekend period of parenting time shall begin on Thursday at:
    ☐ 6:00 P.M. - OR -
    ☐ the time the Children's school is regularly dismissed - OR -
    ☐ other time after school dismissal: _____ M.

Under either Option One or Two, if a weekend period of parenting time ends on or is immediately followed by a Monday that is a school holiday during the regular school term or a federal, state or local holiday during the summer months when school is not in session, that weekend period of time shall end at:
    ☐ 6:00 P.M. on the Monday holiday or school holiday - OR -
    ☐ 6:00 P.M. on the Monday holiday or at the time the children's school resumes after the school holiday - OR -
    ☐ other time before school resumes: _____

- OR -

☐ _____ is currently residing more than 100 miles from the primary residence of the Children. _____ shall have weekend parenting time with the Children as follows:

SELECT AND COMPLETE OPTION ONE *OR* OPTION TWO

☐ Option One:
On weekends beginning on the first, third, and fifth Friday of each month at:
    ☐ 6:00 P.M. - OR -
    ☐ the time the Children's school is regularly dismissed - OR -
    ☐ other time after school dismissal: _____ M.

and ending at:
    ☐ 6:00 P.M. on the following Sunday - OR -
    ☐ the time the Children's school resumes after the weekend - OR -
    ☐ other time before school resumes: _____

- OR –

☐ **Option Two:**
Not more than one weekend per month of _____'s choice, with fourteen days' notice to _____ preceding each chosen weekend, beginning on the day school recesses for the weekend at:

    ☐ 6:00 P.M. - OR -
    ☐ the time the Children's school is regularly dismissed - OR -
    ☐ other time after school dismissal: _____ M.

and ending at:

    ☐ 6:00 P.M. on the day before school resumes after the weekend - OR -
    ☐ the time the Children's school resumes after the weekend - OR -
    ☐ other time before school resumes: _____

The weekend chosen should not conflict with provisions regarding Christmas, Thanksgiving, a child's birthday, or Mother's/Father's Day Weekend.

Under either Option One or Two, if a weekend period of parenting time begins on a Friday that is a school holiday during the regular school term or a federal, state, or local holiday during the summer months when school is not in session, that weekend period of parenting time shall begin on Thursday at:

    ☐ 6:00 P.M. - OR -
    ☐ the time the Children's school is regularly dismissed - OR -
    ☐ other time after school dismissal: _____ M.

Under either Option One or Two, if a weekend period of parenting time ends on or is immediately followed by a Monday that is a school holiday during the regular school term or a federal, state, or local holiday during the summer months when school is not in session, that weekend period of time shall end at:

    ☐ 6:00 P.M. on the Monday holiday or school holiday - OR –
    ☐ 6:00 P.M. on the Monday holiday or at the time the Children's school resumes after the school holiday - OR –
    ☐ other time: _____

1. Spring Break

Spring Break every year, beginning on the day the Children's school is dismissed for the school's spring vacation at:

    ☐ 6:00 P.M. - OR -
    ☐ the time the Children's school is regularly dismissed - OR -
    ☐ other time after school dismissal: _____ M.

and ending at:

    ☐ 6:00 P.M. on the day before school resumes after that vacation - OR -
    ☐ the time the Children's school resumes after that vacation - OR -
    ☐ other time before school resumes: _____

2. Summers

With written notice to the other parent by April 1:

    ☐ forty-two days during the summer, beginning no earlier than the day after the Child's school is dismissed for the summer vacation and ending no later than seven days before school resumes at the end of the summer vacation in that year, to be exercised in no more than two separate periods of at least seven consecutive days each, as specified in the written notice. If the other parent is the Father, the period or periods of extended summer parenting time should not interfere with Father's Day Weekend. These periods of parenting time shall begin and end at 6:00 p.m. - OR -
    ☐ other periods of summer parenting time: _____

If written notice is not given by April 1 of a year specifying an extended period or periods of summer parenting time for that year, summer parenting time for that year:

☐ shall begin at 6:00 P.M. on June 15 and end at 6:00 P.M. on July 27 - OR-

☐ other forty-two-day period during the summer months: _____

When _____ resides more than 100 miles from the primary residence of the Children, _____ (the parent with primary possession) shall have a superior right of parenting time with the Children as follows:

3. Summer Weekend Parenting Time

☐ With written notice to the other parent by April 15, on any one weekend during any one period of the other parent's period of extended summer parenting time, beginning at 6:00 P.M. on Friday and ending at 6:00 P.M. on the following Sunday, provided that if a period of parenting time by the other parent in that year exceeds thirty days, the parent may have parenting time with the Children under the terms of this provision on any two nonconsecutive weekends during that period, and provided that the parent picks up the Children from the other parent and returns the Children to the same place. If the other parent is the Father, the weekends selected should not interfere with Father's Day Weekend. - OR -

☐ other times: _____

4. Extended Summer Parenting Time

☐ With written notice to the other parent by April 15, the parent may designate twenty-one days beginning no earlier than the day after the child's school is dismissed for the summer vacation and ending no later than seven days before school resumes at the end of the summer vacation in that year, to be exercised in no more than two separate periods of at least seven consecutive days each, during which the other parent shall not have parenting time with the Children, provided that the period or periods so designated do not interfere with the other parent's period or periods of extended summer parenting time. If the other parent is the Father, the periods selected should not interfere with Father's Day Weekend. - OR -

☐ other times: _____

☐ Other summer arrangements: _____

HOLIDAYS UNAFFECTED BY DISTANCE

1. Christmas Holidays in Even-Numbered Years

_____ (parent without primary possession) shall have parenting time with the Children beginning on the day the Children are dismissed from school for the Christmas school vacation at:

☐ 6:00 P.M. - OR -

☐ the time the Children's school is regularly dismissed - OR -

☐ other time after school dismissal: _____ M.

and ending at:

☐ noon on December 26 - OR -

☐ _____ M. on December _____.

_____ (parent with primary possession) shall have parenting time with the Children beginning at:

☐ noon on December 26 - OR -

☐ _____ M. on December _____.

and ending at:

☐ 6:00 P.M. on the day before school resumes after that Christmas school vacation - OR -

☐ _____ M. on _____.

2. Christmas Holidays in Odd-Numbered Years
_____ (parent with primary possession) shall have parenting time with the Children beginning on the day the Children are dismissed from school for the Christmas school vacation at:
    ☐ 6:00 P.M. - OR -
    ☐ the time the Children's school is regularly dismissed - OR -
    ☐ other time after school dismissal: _____ M.

and ending at:
    ☐ noon on December 26 - OR -
    ☐ _____ M. on December _____.

_____ (parent without primary possession) shall have parenting time with the Children beginning at:
    ☐ noon on December 26 - OR -
    ☐ _____ M. on December _____.

and ending at:
    ☐ 6:00 P.M. on the day before school resumes after that Christmas school vacation - OR
    ☐ the time the Children's school resumes after that Christmas school vacation –OR-
    ☐ _____ M. on _____.

3. Thanksgiving in Odd-Numbered Years
_____ (parenting without primary possession) shall have parenting time with the Children in odd-numbered years beginning on the day the Children's school is dismissed for the Thanksgiving holiday at:
    ☐ 6:00 P.M. - OR -
    ☐ the time the Children's school is regularly dismissed - OR -
    ☐other time after school dismissal: _____ M.

and ending at:
    ☐ 6:00 P.M. on the Sunday following Thanksgiving - OR -
    ☐ the time the Children's school resumes after that Thanksgiving holiday - OR -
    ☐ other time before school resumes: _____

4. Thanksgiving in Even-Numbered Years
_____ (parent with primary possession) shall have parenting time with the Children in even-numbered years beginning on the day the Children's school is dismissed for the Thanksgiving holiday at:
    ☐ 6:00 P.M. - OR -
    ☐ the time the Children's school is regularly dismissed - OR -
    ☐ other time after school dismissal: _____ M.

and ending at:
    ☐ 6:00 P.M. on the Sunday following Thanksgiving - OR -
    ☐ the time the Children's school resumes after that Thanksgiving holiday - OR -
    ☐ other time before school resumes: _____

5. Child's Birthday
If a parent is not otherwise entitled to present parenting time with a child on the child's birthday, that parent shall have parenting time with the child
    ☐ [check if desired] and the child's minor sibling[s]

on the child's birthday beginning at 6:00 P.M. and ending at 8:00 P.M. on that day, provided that the parent picks up the Children from the other parent's residence and returns the Children to that same place.

6. Father's Day Weekend

Father shall have parenting time with the children each year beginning on the Friday preceding Father's Day at:

    ☐ 6:00 P.M. - OR –
    ☐ other time: _____ M.

and ending on Father's Day at:

    ☐ 6:00 P.M. - OR -
    ☐ other time: _____ M.

- OR -

    ☐ Father shall have parenting time with the Children on Father's Day from _____ A.M. until _____ P.M.

If Father is not otherwise entitled to present parenting time, he shall pick up the Children from Mother's residence and return the Children to that same place.

7. Mother's Day Weekend

Mother shall have parenting time with the Children each year beginning on the Friday preceding Mother's Day at:

    ☐ 6:00 P.M. - OR -
    ☐ other time: _____ M

and ending on Mother's Day at:

    ☐ 6:00 P.M. - OR -
    ☐ other time: _____ M

- OR –

    ☐ Mother shall have parenting time with the Children on Mother's Day from _____ A.M. until _____ P.M.

If Mother is not otherwise entitled to present parenting time, she shall pick up the Children from Father's residence and return the Children to that same place.

8. Other Periods

_____ shall have parenting time with the Children: _____
_____

_____ shall have parenting time with the Children: _____
_____

_____ shall have parenting time with the Children at all times not assigned to _____
_____

If _____ is deployed in military service outside the United States, the following person is designated as the person who may exercise possession of the Children on the first weekend of each month beginning at 6:00 P.M. on the first Friday of each month and ending at 6:00 P.M. on the Sunday immediately following each such Friday: _____
_____
(name, address, and telephone number of designated person).

PARENTING TIMES - GENERAL RULES

1. Surrender of Child at Times of Visitation
At the beginning of parenting time, _____ shall pick up the Children:
      at the residence of the parent with primary possession   -OR -
      at the following location: _____
      and _____ shall surrender the Children to _____ at that time.

If a parenting time begins at the end of the Children's school day, _____ shall pick up the Children:
      ☐ at the Children's school - OR -
      ☐ the location where the school bus takes the child - OR -
      ☐ the following after-school care location: _____

or if school is not in session on that day, at the following location: _____ and _____ shall surrender the Children to _____.

If the Children will not be in school on the day the parenting time begins, _____ (parent with primary possession) shall notify _____ in advance.

At the end of his/her parenting time, _____ shall
      ☐ surrender the Children to _____ at his/her own residence -OR -
      ☐ return the Children to _____'s residence, except that if both parents live in the same county at the time an order is rendered and _____ (parent without primary possession) remains in the county but _____ (parent with primary possession) moves out of the county, then, beginning on the date _____ moves, _____ shall surrender the Children to _____ at the residence of _____.

If _____ 's parenting time ends at the time the Children's school resumes, _____ shall deliver the Children:
      ☐ to school in time for the beginning of the Children's school day - OR -
      ☐ to _____'s residence at _____ M.

or, if school is not in session on that day, to the following location: _____ at _____ M.

If _____ parenting time ends at the time the Children's school resumes and for any reason the Children is not or will not be returned to school, _____ should immediately notify
      ☐ the school
      ☐ _____
      ☐ the following person: _____

that the Children will not be or have not been returned to school.

2. Children's Personal Effects
If the Children bring personal effects from their home for parenting time with the other parent, the Children shall return home with such personal effects.

3. Authorized Persons
Each parent may designate a competent adult to pick up and return the Children at the beginning or end of periods of parenting time.

4. Missed Parenting Times

Each parent shall notify the other parent on each occasion that such parent will be unable to exercise a period of parenting time. The parent who is unable to exercise a period of parenting time shall notify the other parent no less than twenty-four hours prior to the scheduled parenting time.

DISAGREEMENTS OR MODIFICATION OF PLAN

Should the parents disagree about this Parenting Plan or wish to modify it, they must make a good faith effort to resolve the issue by the process selected below before returning to Court:

☐ Collaborative law
☐ Mediation
☐ Nonbinding arbitration
☐ Binding arbitration
☐ Parenting coordinator
☐ Other:_____

[Use this provision if both of the parents have agreed to the Parenting Plan.]

AGREEMENT OF THE PARTIES

We have agreed to the foregoing Parenting Plan and request that the Court adopt the Parenting Plan as an Order of the Court.

_____   _____

Mother   Father

[Use this provision if both parents have not agreed to the Parenting Plan.]

This Parenting Plan is submitted by _____, the **Petitioner/Respondent.**

_____
Petitioner/Respondent

CERTIFICATE OF SERVICE

I certify that a copy of this Parenting Plan has been delivered to **Petitioner/Respondent** by certified mail, return receipt, and regular mail in accordance with Rule 21a of the Texas Rules of Civil Procedure.

_____
Petitioner/Respondent

VERIFICATION OF INCOME AND PARENTING PLAN

_____ appeared in person before me today and stated under oath:

"My name is _____. I am competent to make this Affidavit. The facts stated in this Affidavit are within my personal knowledge and are true and correct.

I am the **Petitioner/Respondent** in this case.

My net monthly resources are $_____.

This Parenting Plan to which this Affidavit is attached is proposed in good faith and in the best interest of the Children."

_____
Petitioner/Respondent

STATE OF TEXAS   §
                             §
COUNTY OF _____ §

SIGNED under oath before me, a notary public, by _____, the **Petitioner/Respondent.**

_____
Notary Public, State of Texas

Child Support Guidelines Worksheet

		Father	Mother
Step 1:	Determine monthly gross income: (Schedule A)	$	$
Step 2:	Determine monthly deductions: (Schedule B)	$	$
Step 3:	Determine Monthly Net Resources (Subtract Step 2 from Step 1):	$	$
Step 4:	Determine child support guideline amount (Schedule C):	$	$

SCHEDULE A

AVERAGE GROSS MONTHLY income shall include the following.

		FATHER per month	MOTHER per month
a.	Gross Salary or Wages (AFDC excluded)		
b.	Bonuses, Commissions, Allowance, Overtime, Tips, etc.		
c.	Business Income from sources such as self-employment, partnership, close corporations, joint ventures, and/or independent contractors (gross receipts minus ordinary and necessary expenses required to produce income)		
d.	Disability Benefits		
e.	Workers' Compensation		
f.	Unemployment Compensation		
g.	Pension, Retirement, or Annuity payments		
h.	Social Security Benefits		
i.	Spousal Support received from prior marriage		
j.	Interest, Dividends, Royalty Income		
k.	Income from trusts and estates		

l.   Rental Income (gross receipts minus
     ordinary and necessary expenses
     required to produce income)

_____

m.   Gains derived from dealing in property (not
     including nonrecurring gains)

_____

n.   Itemize any other income of a recurring
     nature or factor considered

_____

TOTAL MONTHLY GROSS INCOME: $ $

_____

SCHEDULE B

THE JUDGE SHALL DEDUCT THE FOLLOWING FROM GROSS INCOME

		FATHER per month	MOTHER per month
a.	Federal income taxes (based on withholding for a single person claiming one personal exemption and the standard deduction)		
b.	FICA or self-employment taxes		
c.	Mandatory union dues		
d.	Health insurance payments for the child		
	TOTAL ALLOWABLE MONTHLY DEDUCTIONS	$	$

SCHEDULE C

Child Support Based On
Monthly Net Resources Of The Obligor

1 child	20% of Obligor's Net Resources
2 children	25% of Obligor's Net Resources
3 children	30% of Obligor's Net Resources
4 children	35% of Obligor's Net Resources
5 children	40% of Obligor's Net Resources
6+ children	Not less than the amount for 5 children

Note: If the Obligor's net resources exceed $6,000 per month, the percentages set forth above are applied to the first $6,000. The court may order additional support depending upon the needs of the child.

SCHEDULE D

Other Factors To Be Considered
In Determining Child Support

The court may take into account the following factors when determining child support and may adjust the amount determined under the guidelines accordingly:

1. The amount of net resources the obligor could have if he or she is intentionally unemployed or underemployed to avoid payment of child support.

2. Age and needs of the child.

3. Child-care expenses incurred by either parent to maintain employment.

4. Whether the parent has physical custody of another child.

5. The amount of child support being paid or received by either parent under another child support order.

6. Education expenses for a child beyond high school.

7. Other resources provided by an employer, business, or other person (automobile, housing, etc.).

8. Alimony or spousal support being paid or received.

9. Amount of other deductions from wages.

10. Provision for health care insurance and payment of uninsured medical expenses.

11. Spousal or extraordinary educational, health care, or other expenses of the parents or child.

12. Cost of travel to visit the child.

13. Positive or negative cash flow from any real and personal property and assets.

14. Debts assumed by either parent.

15. Any other reason consistent with the best interests of the child taking into consideration the circumstances of the parents.

NO. _____

IN THE MATTER OF THE MARRIAGE OF	§ § §	IN THE DISTRICT COURT
_____	§ §	_____ JUDICIAL DISTRICT
AND	§ §	
_____	§ §	_____ COUNTY, TEXAS

ORIGINAL PETITION FOR DIVORCE

TO THE HONORABLE JUDGE OF SAID COURT:

This suit is brought by _____, Petitioner, Social Security Number _____, who is ____ years of age and resides in _____ County, Texas. Respondent, _____, Social Security Number _____, is _____ years of age and resides at _____.

I.

Petitioner has been a domiciliary of the State of Texas for the preceding six-month period and a resident of _____ County for the preceding ninety-day period.

II.

No process is necessary at this time.

III.

The parties were married on or about _____, _____, in _____, [and ceased to live together as husband and wife on or about _____, _____].

The marriage has become insupportable because of discord or conflict of personalities between Petitioner and Respondent that destroys the legitimate ends of the marriage relationship and prevents any reasonable expectation of reconciliation.

IV.

There are no minor or dependent children born or adopted of this marriage and none is expected.

V.

Petitioner requests the Court to order a division of the estate of the Parties in a manner that the Court deems just and right, as provided by law.

VI.

Petitioner requests a change of name to _____.

VII.

A protective order under Chapter 71 or Section 3.581 of the Texas Family Code is/is not in effect with regard to the parties of this suit.

(The protective order was issued by the _____ Court in Cause No. _____ and was entered on the following date: _____. A copy of the protective order is attached to this petition.)

WHEREFORE Petitioner prays that citation and notice issue as required by law and that the Court grant a divorce and decree such other relief as more specifically requested in this Petition.

Petitioner prays that Petitioner's name be changed as requested above.

Petitioner prays that Respondent be ordered to pay the fees and costs of this suit.

Petitioner prays for general relief.

Respectfully submitted,

_____

Name: _____

Address: _____

_____

Telephone: _____

NO. _____

IN THE MATTER OF	§	IN THE DISTRICT COURT
THE MARRIAGE OF	§	
	§	
_____	§	_____ JUDICIAL DISTRICT
	§	
AND	§	
	§	
_____	§	_____ COUNTY, TEXAS

ORIGINAL PETITION FOR DIVORCE

TO THE HONORABLE JUDGE OF SAID COURT:

This suit is brought by _____, Petitioner, Social Security Number _____, who is _____ years of age and resides in _____ County, Texas. Respondent, _____, Social Security Number _____, is _____ years of age and resides at _____.

I.

Petitioner has been a domiciliary of the State of Texas for the preceding six-month period and a resident of _____ County for the preceding ninety-day period.

II.

Process should be served on Respondent at _____ _____.

III.

The parties were married on or about _____, _____, in _____, [and ceased to live together as husband and wife on or about _____, _____].

The marriage has become insupportable because of discord or conflict of personalities between Petitioner and Respondent that destroys the legitimate ends of the marriage relationship and prevents any reasonable expectation of reconciliation.

IV.

There are no minor or dependent children born or adopted of this marriage and none is expected.

V.

Petitioner requests the Court to order a division of the estate of the Parties in a manner that the Court deems just and right, as provided by law.

VI.

Petitioner requests a change of name to _____.

VII.

A protective order under Chapter 71 or Section 3.581 of the Texas Family Code is/is not in effect with regard to the parties of this suit.

(The protective order was issued by the _____ Court in Cause No. _____ and was entered on the following date: _____. A copy of the protective order is attached to this petition.)

WHEREFORE Petitioner prays that citation and notice issue as required by law and that the Court grant a divorce and decree such other relief as more specifically requested in this Petition.

Petitioner prays that Petitioner's name be changed as requested above.

Petitioner prays that Respondent be ordered to pay the fees and costs of this suit.

Petitioner prays for general relief.

Respectfully submitted,

_____
Name: _____
Address: _____
_____
Telephone: _____

NO. _____

IN THE MATTER OF	§	IN THE DISTRICT COURT
THE MARRIAGE OF	§	
	§	
_____	§	_____ JUDICIAL DISTRICT
	§	
AND	§	
	§	
_____	§	_____ COUNTY, TEXAS

ORIGINAL PETITION FOR DIVORCE

TO THE HONORABLE JUDGE OF SAID COURT:

This suit is brought by _____, Petitioner, Social Security Number _____, who is _____ years of age and resides in _____ County, Texas. Respondent, _____, Social Security Number _____, is _____ years of age. Respondent's place of residence is unknown.

I.

Petitioner has been a domiciliary of the State of Texas for the preceding six-month period and a resident of _____ County for the preceding ninety-day period.

II.

Citation by publication or other substituted service is necessary for the reasons set forth in the attached affidavit.

III.

The parties were married on or about _____, _____, in _____, [and ceased to live together as husband and wife on or about _____, _____].

The marriage has become insupportable because of discord or conflict of personalities between Petitioner and Respondent that destroys the legitimate ends of the marriage relationship and prevents any reasonable expectation of reconciliation.

IV.

There are no minor or dependent children born or adopted of this marriage and none is expected.

V.

Petitioner requests the Court to order a division of the estate of the Parties in a manner that the Court deems just and right, as provided by law.

VI.

Petitioner requests a change of name to _____.

VII.

A protective order under Chapter 71 or Section 3.581 of the Texas Family Code is/is not in effect with regard to the parties of this suit.

(The protective order was issued by the _____ Court in Cause No. _____ and was entered on the following date: _____. A copy of the protective order is attached to this petition.)

WHEREFORE Petitioner prays that citation and notice issue as required by law and that the Court grant a divorce and decree such other relief as more specifically requested in this Petition.

Petitioner prays that Petitioner's name be changed as requested above.

Petitioner prays that Respondent be ordered to pay the fees and costs of this suit.

Petitioner prays for general relief.

Respectfully submitted,

_____
Name: _____
Address: _____
_____
Telephone: _____

NO. _____

IN THE MATTER OF THE MARRIAGE OF	§	IN THE DISTRICT COURT

_____ §

_____ JUDICIAL DISTRICT

AND §

_____ §

_____ COUNTY, TEXAS

ORIGINAL PETITION FOR DIVORCE
AND APPLICATION FOR TEMPORARY ORDERS

TO THE HONORABLE JUDGE OF SAID COURT:

This suit is brought by _____, Petitioner, Social Security Number _____, who is _____ years of age and resides in _____ County, Texas. Respondent, _____, Social Security Number _____, is _____ years of age and resides at _____.

I.

Petitioner has been a domiciliary of the State of Texas for the preceding six-month period and a resident of _____ County for the preceding ninety-day period.

II.

Process should be served on Respondent at _____
_____.

III.

The parties were married on or about _____, _____, in _____, [and ceased to live together as husband and wife on or about _____, _____].

The marriage has become insupportable because of discord or conflict of personalities between Petitioner and Respondent that destroys the legitimate ends of the marriage relationship and prevents any reasonable expectation of reconciliation.

IV.

There are no minor or dependent children born or adopted of this marriage and none is expected.

V.

Petitioner requests the Court to order a division of the estate of the Parties in a manner that the Court deems just and right, as provided by law.

VI.

Petitioner requests a change of name to _____.

VII.

A protective order under Chapter 71 or Section 3.581 of the Texas Family Code is/is not in effect with regard to the parties of this suit.

(The protective order was issued by the _____ Court in Cause No. _____ and was entered on the following date: _____. A copy of the protective order is attached to this petition.)

VIII.

APPLICATION FOR TEMPORARY ORDERS

Petitioner requests the Court, after notice and hearing, for the protection of the parties, to make temporary orders, including but not limited to the following:

Petitioner has insufficient income for support, and Petitioner requests the Court to order Respondent to make payments for the support of Petitioner during the pendency of this suit.

WHEREFORE Petitioner prays that citation and notice issue as required by law and that the Court grant a divorce and decree such other relief as more specifically requested in this Petition.

Petitioner prays that Petitioner's name be changed as requested above.

Petitioner prays that Respondent be ordered to pay the fees and costs of this suit.

Petitioner prays for general relief.

Respectfully submitted,

_____

Name: _____

Address: _____

_____

Telephone: _____

NO. _____

IN THE MATTER OF THE MARRIAGE OF	§	IN THE DISTRICT COURT

_____ §

AND §

_____ §   _____ JUDICIAL DISTRICT

AND IN THE INTERESTS OF §

_____ §

_____, and §

_____ §

MINOR CHILDREN §   _____ COUNTY, TEXAS

ORIGINAL PETITION FOR DIVORCE
AND APPLICATION FOR TEMPORARY ORDERS

TO THE HONORABLE JUDGE OF SAID COURT:

This suit is brought by _____, Petitioner, Social Security Number _____, who is _____ years of age and resides in _____ County, Texas. Respondent, _____, Social Security Number _____, is _____ years of age and resides at _____.

I.

Petitioner has been a domiciliary of the State of Texas for the preceding six-month period and a resident of _____ County for the preceding ninety-day period.

II.

Process should be served on Respondent at _____ _____.

III.

The parties were married on or about _____, _____, in _____, [and ceased to live together as husband and wife on or about _____, _____].

The marriage has become insupportable because of discord or conflict of personalities between Petitioner and Respondent that destroys the legitimate ends of the marriage relationship and prevents any reasonable expectation of reconciliation.

IV.

Petitioner and Respondent are the parents of the following children of this marriage under 18 years of age, who are not under the continuing jurisdiction of any other court:

Name and Sex: _____
Birthplace and Date: _____

Present Residence: _____
Social Security No.: _____

Name and Sex: _____
Birthplace and Date: _____
Present Residence: _____
Social Security No.: _____

Name and Sex: _____
Birthplace and Date: _____
Present Residence: _____
Social Security No.: _____

Name and Sex: _____
Birthplace and Date: _____
Present Residence: _____
Social Security No.: _____

There are no court-ordered conservatorships, court-ordered guardianships, or other court-ordered relationships affecting the children.

No property is owned or possessed by the children.

Petitioner and Respondent, on final hearing, should be appointed joint managing conservator, with all the rights and duties of joint managing conservators, except that Petitioner should be granted the right to establish the primary residence of the child(ren) and make decisions concerning the child(ren)'s education. Respondent should be ordered to make payments for the support of the child(ren) in the manner specified by the Court. Petitioner requests that such payments for the support of the child(ren) survive the death of Respondent and become obligations of Respondent's estate.

V.

Petitioner requests the Court upon final hearing to order a division of the estate of the Parties in a manner that the Court deems just and right, as provided by law.

VI.

Petitioner requests a change of name to _____.

VII.

APPLICATION FOR TEMPORARY ORDERS

Petitioner requests the Court to make the following temporary orders:

1. The Petitioner should be appointed temporary managing conservator, and child support and visitation should be set as set forth in the Parenting Plan attached hereto and incorporated herein for all purposes;

2. Petitioner has insufficient income for support, and requests temporary alimony;

3. Petitioner should be awarded the temporary exclusive use and possession of the home, furnishings, fixtures, and automobile.

Petitioner has incomplete knowledge of the estate of the parties, and, for the preservation of Petitioner's property and rights, Respondent should be ordered to file with the Court a sworn Inventory and Appraisement of all the separate and community property owned and of all obligations, debts and liabilities owed by the parties or either of them. It is further requested that Respondent, in regard to all personal and real property, and insurance policies, set forth the following:

       a. the date and amount of the purchase price;
       b. the total obligation outstanding thereon;
       c. the fair market value.

In regard to any benefit plans incident to employment, Respondent should specify in detail:

       a. the type of plan(s) currently in effect;
       b. the employee/employer contributions thereto during the existence of the plan;
       c. the current cash value;
       d. the date of inception and vesting period;
       e. the amount and dates of funds withdrawn therefrom during the existence of the plan.

Respondent should be ordered to produce copies of the parties' income tax returns, together with any and all supporting schedules and information used in connection with their original income tax returns, for the last four years, and of Respondent's bank records, including canceled checks and statements, for the last four years;

VIII.

A protective order under Chapter 71 or Section 3.581 of the Texas Family Code is/is not in effect with regard to the parties of this suit.

(The protective order was issued by the _____ Court in Cause No. _____ and was entered on the following date: _____. A copy of the protective order is attached to this petition.)

PRAYER

Petitioner prays:

    1. that citation and notice issue as required by law and that the Court grant a divorce and decree such other relief as more specifically requested in this pleading;

    2. that upon notice and hearing the temporary relief requested herein be ordered;

    3. that upon final hearing, the Court make orders regarding conservatorship, support of, and access to the child(ren), according to the best interests of the child(ren).

Petitioner requests all other fair and equitable relief.

               Respectfully submitted,

               _____
               Name: _____
               Address: _____
               _____
               Telephone: _____

This page intentionally blank.

NO. _____

IN THE MATTER OF THE MARRIAGE OF	§ § §	IN THE DISTRICT COURT

_____

AND

_____   §   _____ JUDICIAL DISTRICT

AND IN THE INTERESTS OF

_____

_____, and

_____

MINOR CHILDREN   §   _____ COUNTY, TEXAS

ORIGINAL PETITION FOR DIVORCE
AND APPLICATION FOR TEMPORARY ORDERS

TO THE HONORABLE JUDGE OF SAID COURT:

This suit is brought by _____, Petitioner, Social Security Number _____, who is _____ years of age and resides in _____ County, Texas. Respondent, _____, Social Security Number _____, is _____ years of age and resides at _____.

I.

Petitioner has been a domiciliary of the State of Texas for the preceding six-month period and a resident of _____ County for the preceding ninety-day period.

II.

Citation by publication or other substituted service is necessary for the reasons set forth in the attached affidavit.

III.

The parties were married on or about _____, _____, in _____, [and ceased to live together as husband and wife on or about _____, _____].

The marriage has become insupportable because of discord or conflict of personalities between Petitioner and Respondent that destroys the legitimate ends of the marriage relationship and prevents any reasonable expectation of reconciliation.

IV.

Petitioner and Respondent are the parents of the following children of this marriage under 18 years of age, who are not under the continuing jurisdiction of any other court:

Name and Sex: _____
Birthplace and Date: _____
Present Residence: _____
Social Security No.: _____

Name and Sex: _____

Birthplace and Date: _____

Present Residence: _____

Social Security No.: _____

Name and Sex: _____

Birthplace and Date: _____

Present Residence: _____

Social Security No.: _____

Name and Sex: _____

Birthplace and Date: _____

Present Residence: _____

Social Security No.: _____

There are no court-ordered conservatorships, court-ordered guardianships, or other court-ordered relationships affecting the children.

No property is owned or possessed by the children.

Petitioner and Respondent, on final hearing, should be appointed joint managing conservator, with all the rights and duties of joint managing conservators, except that Petitioner should be granted the right to establish the primary residence of the child(ren) and make decisions concerning the child(ren)'s education. Respondent should be ordered to make payments for the support of the child(ren) in the manner specified by the Court. Petitioner requests that such payments for the support of the child(ren) survive the death of Respondent and become obligations of Respondent's estate.

V.

Petitioner requests the Court upon final hearing to order a division of the estate of the Parties in a manner that the Court deems just and right, as provided by law.

VI.

Petitioner requests a change of name to _____.

VII.

APPLICATION FOR TEMPORARY ORDERS

Petitioner requests the Court to make the following temporary orders:

1. The Petitioner should be appointed temporary managing conservator, and child support and visitation should be set as set forth in the Parenting Plan attached hereto and incorporated herein for all purposes;

2. Petitioner has insufficient income for support, and requests temporary alimony;

3. Petitioner should be awarded the temporary exclusive use and possession of the home, furnishings, fixtures, and automobile.

Petitioner has incomplete knowledge of the estate of the parties, and, for the preservation of Petitioner's property and rights, Respondent should be ordered to file with the Court a sworn Inventory and Appraisement of all the separate and community property owned and of all obligations, debts and liabilities owed by the parties or either of them. It is further requested that

Respondent, in regard to all personal and real property, and insurance policies, set forth the following:

  a. the date and amount of the purchase price;
  b. the total obligation outstanding thereon;
  c. the fair market value.

In regard to any benefit plans incident to employment, Respondent should specify in detail:

  a. the type of plan(s) currently in effect;
  b. the employee/employer contributions thereto during the existence of the plan;
  c. the current cash value;
  d. the date of inception and vesting period;
  e. the amount and dates of funds withdrawn therefrom during the existence of the plan.

Respondent should be ordered to produce copies of the parties' income tax returns, together with any and all supporting schedules and information used in connection with their original income tax returns, for the last four years, and of Respondent's bank records, including canceled checks and statements, for the last four years;

VIII.

A protective order under Chapter 71 or Section 3.581 of the Texas Family Code is/is not in effect with regard to the parties of this suit.

(The protective order was issued by the _____ Court in Cause No. _____ and was entered on the following date: _____. A copy of the protective order is attached to this petition.)

PRAYER

Petitioner prays:

  1. that citation and notice issue as required by law and that the Court grant a divorce and decree such other relief as more specifically requested in this pleading;

  2. that upon notice and hearing the temporary relief requested herein be ordered;

  3. that upon final hearing, the Court make orders regarding conservatorship, support of, and access to the child(ren), according to the best interests of the child(ren).

Petitioner requests all other fair and equitable relief.

Respectfully submitted,

_____
Name: _____
Address: _____
_____
Telephone: _____

This page intentionally blank.

NO. _____

IN THE MATTER OF THE MARRIAGE OF	§ § §	IN THE DISTRICT COURT
_____	§ § §	
AND	§ §	
_____	§ §	_____ JUDICIAL DISTRICT
AND IN THE INTERESTS OF	§ § §	
_____	§ §	
_____, and	§ § §	
_____	§ §	
MINOR CHILDREN	§	_____ COUNTY, TEXAS

WAIVER OF CITATION

STATE OF TEXAS	)
	)
COUNTY OF _____	)

BEFORE ME, the undersigned authority, personally appeared _____, who, by me duly sworn, on oath stated:

I, _____, am the Respondent in the above-entitled and numbered cause. My mailing address is _____ _____. I have been given a copy of the Original Petition for Divorce that has been filed in this cause, and I have read it and understand it. I hereby enter my appearance in this cause and for all purposes and waive the issuance and service of process. I agree that the cause may be taken up and considered by the Court without further notice to me. I further waive the making of a record of testimony in this cause.

I hereby waive all rights, privileges and exemptions existing or which may hereafter exist pursuant to the Soldiers and Sailors Civil Relief Act of 1940, including but not limited to, the appointment of counsel to represent me in this case.

I further agree that the cause may be heard by the presiding Judge of the Court or by a duly appointed master or referee of the Court.

SIGNED on _____, _____.

_____
Respondent

SUBSCRIBED AND SWORN TO before me on this _____ day of _____, _____.

_____
Notary Public, State of Texas
My Commission Expires:

_____

This page intentionally blank.

NO. _____

IN THE MATTER OF THE MARRIAGE OF	§	IN THE DISTRICT COURT
_____	§ § §	_____ JUDICIAL DISTRICT
AND	§ § §	
_____	§	_____ COUNTY, TEXAS

AFFIDAVIT FOR CITATION BY PUBLICATION

STATE OF TEXAS   )
)
COUNTY OF _____   )

BEFORE ME, the undersigned authority, personally appeared _____, who, by me duly sworn, on oath stated:

My name is _____. I am of sound mind and capable of making this affidavit. I am personally acquainted with the facts herein stated.

I am the Petitioner in the above-entitled and numbered cause.

The residence of _____, a party to such cause, is unknown to me. I have exercised due diligence to locate the whereabouts of this party, and have been unable to do so. Thus it is impractical to serve this party personally.

There are no children who are now under the age of eighteen years born or adopted of the marriage of Petitioner and Respondent.

SIGNED on _____, _____

                         Signed: _____

SIGNED under oath before me on

_____, _____

_____
Notary Public, State of Texas

My commission expires:

_____

This page intentionally blank.

NO. _____

IN THE MATTER OF THE MARRIAGE OF	§ § § § § §	IN THE DISTRICT COURT

_____

AND

_____   § _____ JUDICIAL DISTRICT

AND IN THE INTERESTS OF

_____

_____, and

_____

MINOR CHILDREN   § _____ COUNTY, TEXAS

RESPONDENT'S ORIGINAL ANSWER

TO THE HONORABLE JUDGE OF SAID COURT;

_____, Respondent in the above-styled cause, files Respondent's Original Answer to the Original Petition for Divorce, and for such would respectfully show the Court as follows:

Respondent denies all of the allegations contained in the Original Petition and demands strict proof thereof.

WHEREFORE, Respondent prays that all relief requested by Petitioner be denied and for such other relief to which Respondent may be entitled.

Respectfully submitted,

_____

Name: _____

Address: _____

_____

Telephone: _____

CERTIFICATE OF SERVICE

I certify that a true copy of the foregoing document was served on Petitioner, _____ _____, in accordance with the Texas Rules of Civil Procedure on _____, _____.

_____

Respondent

This page intentionally blank.

NO. _____

IN THE MATTER OF THE MARRIAGE OF	§ § § § §	IN THE DISTRICT COURT

_____

AND

_____

§ § § § § § § § _____ JUDICIAL DISTRICT

AND IN THE INTERESTS OF

_____

_____, and

_____

MINOR CHILDREN   § § § _____ COUNTY, TEXAS

AFFIDAVIT OF INABILITY TO PAY COURT COSTS

BEFORE ME, the undersigned authority, on this day personally appeared _____
_____, who, after being by me duly sworn stated under oath as follows:

1.   My total monthly income is $_____.

2.   I receive employment income of $_____.
        My employer's name is: _____.
        My employer's address is: _____
        _____.

3.   I receive additional monthly income of $_____.
        The source of this income is _____
        _____.

4.   The following people are dependent upon me for support:

        <u>Name</u>   <u>Age</u>

        <u>Self</u>_____   _____
        _____   _____
        _____   _____

5.   I DO/DO NOT have a checking account.
        Checking account balance $_____

6.   I DO/DO NOT have a savings account.
        Savings account balance $_____

7.   I own the following property (e.g. real estate, stocks, bonds, notes, automobiles) excluding ordinary household furnishings and clothing:

Property	Value	Encumbrance
_____	_____	_____
_____	_____	_____
_____	_____	_____
_____	_____	_____

8.   I have the following monthly expenses:

Amount

a. Rent/Mortgage   _____
b. Food   _____
c. Clothing   _____
d. Transportation   _____
e. Utilities   _____
f. Child Care   _____
g. _____   _____
h. _____   _____

I am unable to pay the court costs.

I verify that the statements made in this affidavit are true and correct.

_____
AFFIANT

SUBSCRIBED AND SWORN to before me on this _____ day of_____, _____.

_____
Notary Public, State of Texas
My Commission Expires:

_____ NO. _____

NO. _____

IN THE MATTER OF THE MARRIAGE OF	§	IN THE DISTRICT COURT

§
§
§
§

_____

§

AND

§
§

_____   §   _____ JUDICIAL DISTRICT

§

AND IN THE INTERESTS OF   §

§
§

_____   §

§

_____, and   §

§
§

_____   §

§

MINOR CHILDREN   §   _____ COUNTY, TEXAS

TEMPORARY ORDERS

On the _____ day of _____, _____, came on to be heard the application of _____ for temporary orders.

Petitioner, _____, appeared in person.

Respondent, _____, appeared in person.

[Respondent, _____, although duly and properly notified, did not appear.]

The Court, having considered the pleadings and heard the evidence, finds that all necessary prerequisites of the law have been legally satisfied and that this Court has jurisdiction over the parties and subject matter of this cause.

The Court finds that the following orders for the safety and welfare of the children are in the best interest of the children.

IT IS ORDERED that _____ be and is hereby appointed Temporary Managing Conservator of the following children: _____ _____ _____.

IT IS ORDERED that _____ be and is hereby appointed Temporary Possessory Conservator of the following children: _____ _____ _____.

IT IS ORDERED that the Parenting Plan attached hereto and incorporated for all purposes shall govern the rights and duties of the Temporary Possessory Conservator and Temporary Managing Conservator and the visitation rights of the Temporary Possessory Conservator.

IT IS ORDERED that _____ pay to _____ for the support of _____ $_____ per _____, with the first installment being due and payable on _____, _____, and a like installment being due and payable on each _____ and _____ day of each and every _____ thereafter until further order of this Court.

IT IS ORDERED that _____ make all said payments through the _____ County Child Support Office, _____, Texas.

IT IS ORDERED that _____ pay to _____ _____ as temporary support $_____ per _____, with the first installment being due and payable on _____, _____, and a like installment being due and payable on each _____ and _____ day of each and every _____ thereafter until further order of this Court.

IT IS ORDERED that _____ make all said payments through the _____ County Child Support Office, _____, Texas.

The Court finds that the following orders respecting the property and parties are necessary and equitable.

IT IS ORDERED that _____ have the exclusive use and possession of the following property during the pendency of this suit:

    1.   All furniture, furnishings and fixtures currently in _____ _____'s possession.

    2.   The _____ motor vehicle.

    3.   All clothing, jewelry and personal effects currently in _____ _____'s possession.

    4.   The residence located at _____.

    5.   _____.

IT IS ORDERED that _____ have the exclusive use and possession of the following property during the pendency of this suit:

    1.   All furniture, furnishings and fixtures currently in _____ _____'s possession.

    2.   The _____ motor vehicle.

    3.   All clothing, jewelry and personal effects currently in _____ _____'s possession.

    4.   The residence located at _____.

    5.   _____.

IT IS ORDERED that _____ shall pay the following debts, liabilities and obligations during the pendency of this case:

      1.   All ordinary and necessary living expenses incurred by _____ _____ or the parties' minor children except as may be specifically set forth hereinabove.

      2.   The monthly mortgage payment together with all utilities and maintenance for the residence located at _____ _____.

      3.   The monthly debts due and payable on the _____ _____ motor vehicle.

      4.   _____.

      5.   _____.

IT IS ORDERED that _____ shall pay the following debts, liabilities and obligations during the pendency of this case:

      1.   All ordinary and necessary living expenses incurred by _____ _____.

      2.   The monthly debts due and payable on the _____ _____ motor vehicle.

      3.   _____.

      4.   _____.

IT IS ORDERED that _____ shall maintain in full force and effect the medical and health insurance coverage on the children and Petitioner and Respondent shall each be responsible for one-half (1/2) of all medical expenses of the children not covered by insurance.

IT IS ORDERED that both parties file with each other and the Clerk of this Court a sworn inventory and appraisement of all the separate and community property owned by the parties and of all debts owed by the parties, said inventory to be filed forty-five (45) days after the entry by the Court of these Agreed Temporary Orders.

IT IS ORDERED that this case is set for trial on the merits on the _____ day of _____, _____, at _____ o'clock ___.m.

All said temporary orders are without prejudice to either party to petition the Court for new or additional orders.

All said temporary orders shall continue in full force and effect until further order of this Court.

SIGNED this _____ day of _____, _____.

_____
Judge Presiding

This page intentionally blank.

NO. _____

IN THE MATTER OF	§	IN THE DISTRICT COURT
THE MARRIAGE OF	§	
	§	
_____	§	_____ JUDICIAL DISTRICT
	§	
AND	§	
	§	
_____	§	_____ COUNTY, TEXAS

TEMPORARY ORDERS

On the _____ day of _____, _____, came on to be heard the application of _____ for temporary orders.

Petitioner, _____, appeared in person and announced ready.

Respondent, _____, appeared in person and announced ready.

[Respondent, _____, although duly and properly notified, did not appear.]

The Court, having considered the pleadings and heard the evidence and argument of the parties or their counsel, finds that all necessary prerequisites of the law have been legally satisfied and that this Court has jurisdiction over the parties and subject matter of this cause.

The Court finds that there are no children of this marriage under 18 years of age or otherwise entitled to support.

The Court finds that the following orders respecting the property and parties are necessary and equitable.

IT IS ORDERED that _____ pay to _____ as temporary support $_____ per _____, with the first installment being due and payable on _____, _____, and a like installment being due and payable on each _____ and _____ day of each and every month thereafter until further order of this Court.

IT IS ORDERED that _____ make all said payments through the _____ County Child Support Office, _____, Texas.

IT IS ORDERED that _____ have the exclusive use and possession of the following property during the pendency of this suit:

1.   All furniture, furnishings and fixtures currently in _____
_____'s possession.

2.   The _____ motor vehicle.

3.   All clothing, jewelry and personal effects currently in _____
_____'s possession.

4.   The residence located at _____.

5.   _____.

IT IS ORDERED that _____ have the exclusive use and possession of the following property during the pendency of this suit:

    1.   All furniture, furnishings and fixtures currently in _____ _____'s possession.

    2.   The _____ motor vehicle.

    3.   All clothing, jewelry and personal effects currently in _____ _____'s possession.

    4.   The residence located at _____.

    5.   _____.

IT IS ORDERED that _____ shall pay the following debts, liabilities and obligations during the pendency of this case:

    1.   All ordinary and necessary living expenses incurred by _____ _____.

    2.   The monthly mortgage payment together with all utilities and maintenance for the residence located at _____ _____.

    3.   The monthly debts due and payable on the _____ motor vehicle.

    4.   _____.

    5.   _____.

IT IS ORDERED that _____ shall pay the following debts, liabilities and obligations during the pendency of this case:

    1.   All ordinary and necessary living expenses incurred by _____ _____.

    2.   The monthly debts due and payable on the _____ motor vehicle.

    3.   _____.

    4.   _____.

IT IS ORDERED that both parties file with each other or their respective counsel and the Clerk of this Court a sworn inventory and appraisement of all the separate and community property owned by the parties and of all debts owed by the parties, said inventory to be filed forty-five (45) days after the entry by the Court of these Agreed Temporary Orders.

IT IS ORDERED that the Petitioner is hereby specifically authorized to:

    1.   Make expenditures and incur indebtedness for reasonable attorney's fees and costs in connection with this suit.

    2.   Make expenditures and incur indebtedness for necessary and customary living expenses for food, clothing, shelter, transportation, and medical care.

IT IS ORDERED that the Respondent is hereby specifically authorized to:

      1.   Make expenditures and incur indebtedness for reasonable attorney's fees and costs in connection with this suit.

      2.   Make expenditures and incur indebtedness for necessary and customary living expenses for food, clothing, shelter, transportation, and medical care.

IT IS ORDERED that this case is set for trial on the merits on the _____ day of _____, _____, at _____ o'clock ____.m.

All said temporary orders are without prejudice to either party to petition the Court for new or additional orders.

All said temporary orders shall continue in full force and effect until further order of this Court.

SIGNED this _____ day of _____, _____.

_____
Judge Presiding

This page intentionally blank.

NO. _____

IN THE MATTER OF THE MARRIAGE OF	§ § §	IN THE DISTRICT COURT
_____	§ §	_____ JUDICIAL DISTRICT
AND	§ §	
_____	§	_____ COUNTY, TEXAS

DECREE OF DIVORCE

On the _____ day of _____, _____, this case came on for hearing.

Petitioner _____, Social Security Number _____ and Texas Driver's License Number _____, appeared in person.

Respondent _____, Social Security Number _____ and Texas Driver's License Number _____, appeared in person.

[Respondent, _____, Social Security Number _____ and Texas Driver's License Number _____, although duly and properly cited, did not appear and wholly made default.]

[Respondent, _____, Social Security Number _____ and Texas Driver's License Number _____, waived issuance and service of citation by waiver duly filed and did not otherwise appear.]

The record of testimony was waived with the consent of the Court.

The Court, having examined the pleadings, finds that all necessary residence qualifications and prerequisites of law have been legally satisfied and that this Court has jurisdiction of all parties and subject matter of this cause. A jury was waived, and all matters in controversy, including questions of fact and law, were submitted to the Court. All persons entitled to citation were properly cited.

IT IS ORDERED AND DECREED that _____, Petitioner, and _____, Respondent, are divorced and that the marriage between them is dissolved.

The Court finds that there are no children of the marriage and that none is expected.

IT IS ORDERED AND DECREED that the estate of the parties is divided as follows:

Petitioner _____ is awarded the following as Petitioner's sole and separate property, and Respondent is divested of all right, title, interest, and claim in and to such property:
-        the personal property currently in her/his possession;
-        _____;
-        _____.

Respondent _____ is awarded the following as Respondent's sole and separate property, and Petitioner is divested of all right, title, interest, and claim in and to such property:

- the personal property currently in her/his possession;
- _____;
- _____.

IT IS ORDERED AND DECREED that Petitioner shall pay, as a part of the division of the estate of the parties, the following debts, charges, liabilities, and other obligations and shall indemnify and hold Respondent and Respondent's property harmless from any failure to so discharge these debts and obligations:

- _____;
- _____.

IT IS ORDERED AND DECREED that Respondent shall pay, as a part of the division of the estate of the parties, the following debts, charges, liabilities, and other obligations and shall indemnify and hold Petitioner and Petitioner's property harmless from any failure to so discharge these debts and obligations:

- _____;
- _____.

IT IS ORDERED AND DECREED that Petitioner shall pay, as a part of the division of the estate of the parties, the following debts and obligations and shall indemnify and hold Respondent and Respondent's property harmless from any failure to so discharge these debts and obligations:

Any and all debts, charges, liabilities, and other obligations incurred solely by Petitioner from and after their date of separation, _____, _____, unless express provision is made in this decree to the contrary.

IT IS ORDERED AND DECREED that Respondent shall pay, as a part of the division of the estate of the parties, the following debts and obligations, and shall indemnify and hold Petitioner and Petitioner's property harmless from any failure to so discharge these debts and obligations:

Any and all debts, charges, liabilities, and other obligations incurred solely by Respondent from and after their date of separation, _____, _____, unless express provision is made in this decree to the contrary.

IT IS ORDERED AND DECREED that Petitioner's name is hereby changed to _____ _____.

IT IS ORDERED AND DECREED that all costs of court expended in this cause are taxed against the party incurring same.

IT IS ORDERED AND DECREED that, without affecting the finality of this Decree of Divorce, this Court expressly reserves the right to make orders necessary to clarify and enforce this decree.

IT IS ORDERED AND DECREED that all relief requested in this cause and not expressly granted herein is denied.

SIGNED ON _____, _____.

_____
Judge Presiding

NO. _____

IN THE MATTER OF § IN THE DISTRICT COURT
THE MARRIAGE OF §
  §
_____ § _____ JUDICIAL DISTRICT
  §
AND §
  §
_____ § _____ COUNTY, TEXAS

DECREE OF DIVORCE

On the _____ day of _____, _____, this case came on for hearing.

Petitioner _____, Social Security Number
_____ and Texas Driver's License Number _____,
appeared in person.

Respondent _____, Social Security Number
_____ and Texas Driver's License Number _____,
appeared in person.

[Respondent, _____, Social Security Number
_____ and Texas Driver's License Number _____,
waived issuance and service of citation by waiver duly filed and did not otherwise appear.]

The record of testimony was waived with the consent of the Court.

The Court, having examined the pleadings, finds that all necessary residence qualifications and prerequisites of law have been legally satisfied and that this Court has jurisdiction of all parties and subject matter of this cause. A jury was waived, and all matters in controversy, including questions of fact and law, were submitted to the Court. All persons entitled to citation were properly cited.

IT IS ORDERED AND DECREED that _____, Petitioner, and _____, Respondent, are divorced and that the marriage between them is dissolved.

The Court finds that the agreement of the Petitioner and Respondent for the division of their estate is hereby approved and incorporated into this decree by reference as if it were recited herein verbatim.

IT IS ORDERED AND DECREED that Petitioner's name is hereby changed to _____
_____.

IT IS ORDERED AND DECREED that all costs of court expended in this cause are taxed against the party incurring same.

IT IS ORDERED AND DECREED that, without affecting the finality of this Decree of Divorce, this Court expressly reserves the right to make orders necessary to clarify and enforce this decree.

IT IS ORDERED AND DECREED that all relief requested in this cause and not expressly granted herein is denied.

SIGNED ON _____, _____.

_____
Judge Presiding

This page intentionally blank.

NO. _____

IN THE MATTER OF THE MARRIAGE OF	§	IN THE DISTRICT COURT

_____

AND

_____

AND IN THE INTERESTS OF

_____ JUDICIAL DISTRICT

_____

_____, and

_____

MINOR CHILDREN   § _____ COUNTY, TEXAS

DECREE OF DIVORCE

On the _____ day of _____, _____, this cause came on for hearing.

Petitioner _____, Social Security Number _____ and Texas Driver's License Number _____, appeared in person.

Respondent _____, Social Security Number _____ and Texas Driver's License Number _____, appeared in person.

[Respondent _____, Social Security Number _____ and Texas Driver's License Number _____, although duly and properly cited, did not appear and wholly made default.]

[Respondent, _____, Social Security Number _____ and Texas Driver's License Number _____, waived issuance and service of citation by waiver duly filed and did not otherwise appear.]

The record of testimony was waived with the consent of the Court.

The Court finds that the pleadings of Petitioner are in due form and contain all the allegations, information and prerequisites required by law. The Court, after receiving evidence, finds that it has jurisdiction of this cause of action and the parties and that at least 60 days have elapsed since the date the suit was filed. The Court finds Petitioner has been a domiciliary of this state for at least the six-month period preceding the filing of this action and a resident of the county in which this suit is filed for at least a 90-day period preceding the filing of this action. All parties entitled to citation were properly cited.

A jury was waived, and all matters in controversy, including questions of fact and law, were submitted to the Court.

IT IS ORDERED AND DECREED that _____, Petitioner, and _____, Respondent, are divorced and that the marriage between them is dissolved.

The Court finds that the parties are not now expecting another child of the marriage and that Petitioner and Respondent are the parents of the following children under the age of eighteen:

Name and Sex: _____
Birthplace and Date: _____
Present Residence: _____
Social Security No.: _____

Name and Sex: _____
Birthplace and Date: _____
Present Residence: _____
Social Security No.: _____

The Court, having considered the circumstances of the parents and of the children, finds that the orders are in the best interests of the children.

IT IS ORDERED AND DECREED that _____ is appointed sole managing conservator of the children.

IT IS ORDERED AND DECREED that _____ is appointed possessory conservator of the children.

IT IS ORDERED AND DECREED the Parenting Plan attached hereto and incorporated herein for all purposes shall govern the rights, duties, and obligations of Petitioner and Respondent as to the children and the terms and conditions of visitation shall bind the Petitioner and Respondent.

IT IS FURTHER ORDERED that _____ shall notify this Court and the obligee by U.S. certified mail, return receipt requested, of any change of address and of any termination of employment no later than seven (7) days after the change of address or the termination of employment. This notice or a subsequent notice also shall provide the obligor's current address, and the name and address of his current employer, whenever that information becomes available.

IT IS ORDERED that, upon the request of a prosecuting attorney, the Attorney General, the obligee, or the obligor, the Clerk of this Court shall cause a certified copy of the "Order Withholding from Earnings for Child Support" to be delivered to any employer. IT IS FURTHER ORDERED that the Clerk of this Court shall attach a copy of Section 14.43 of the Texas Family Code for the information of any employer.

IT IS ORDERED AND DECREED that all payments shall be made through the _____ County Child Support Office, _____, Texas and then promptly remitted by that agency to Petitioner for the support of the children.

IT IS ORDERED AND DECREED that Respondent, _____, shall pay a $36.00 collection fee, payable to the _____ County Child Support Office on or before _____, _____, and $36.00 on the same day each year thereafter until the last child with regard to whom payment is made reaches 18 years of age, marries, or is otherwise emancipated.

The Court finds that the following is a just and right division of the parties' marital estate, having due regard for the rights of each party and the children of this marriage.

IT IS ORDERED AND DECREED that the estate of the parties is divided as follows:

Petitioner _____ is awarded the following as Petitioner's sole and separate property, and Respondent is divested of all right, title, interest, and claim in and to such property:

☐   the personal property currently in her/his possession;

☐   _____;

_____.

Respondent _____ is awarded the following as Respondent's sole and separate property, and Petitioner is divested of all right, title, interest, and claim in and to such property:

☐   the personal property currently in her/his possession;

☐   _____;

_____.

IT IS ORDERED AND DECREED that Petitioner shall pay, as a part of the division of the estate of the parties, the following debts, charges, liabilities, and other obligations and shall indemnify and hold Respondent and Respondent's property harmless from any failure to so discharge these debts and obligations:

☐   _____;

_____.

IT IS ORDERED AND DECREED that Respondent shall pay, as a part of the division of the estate of the parties, the following debts, charges, liabilities, and other obligations and shall indemnify and hold Petitioner and Petitioner's property harmless from any failure to so discharge these debts and obligations:

☐   _____;

_____.

As additional child support, IT IS ORDERED AND DECREED that Respondent, _____ _____, shall, as long as child support is payable under the terms of this decree, maintain in full force and effect, at Respondent's sole cost and expense, medical and health insurance providing coverage for the children of the parties.

IT IS FURTHER ORDERED AND DECREED that the provisions for child support in this Decree shall be an obligation of the estate of Respondent, _____, and shall not terminate on the death of Respondent.

IT IS ORDERED AND DECREED that Petitioner, _____, shall have the tax exemption for the minor children for the tax year _____ and all subsequent years.

IT IS ORDERED AND DECREED that all costs of court expended in this cause are taxed against the party incurring same.

IT IS ORDERED AND DECREED that without affecting the finality of this decree, this Court expressly reserves the right to make orders necessary to clarify and enforce this decree.

IT IS ORDERED AND DECREED that all relief requested in this cause and not expressly granted is denied.

SIGNED on _____ day of _____, _____.

_____
Judge Presiding

NOTICE

FAILURE TO OBEY A COURT ORDER FOR CHILD SUPPORT OR FOR POSSESSION OF OR ACCESS TO A CHILD MAY RESULT IN FURTHER LITIGATION TO ENFORCE THE ORDER, INCLUDING CONTEMPT OF COURT. A FINDING OF CONTEMPT MAY BE PUNISHED BY CONFINEMENT IN JAIL FOR UP TO SIX MONTHS, A FINE OF UP TO $500 FOR EACH VIOLATION, AND A MONEY JUDGMENT FOR PAYMENT OF ATTORNEY'S FEES AND COURT COSTS.

FAILURE OF A PARTY TO MAKE A CHILD SUPPORT PAYMENT TO THE PLACE AND IN THE MANNER REQUIRED BY A COURT ORDER MAY RESULT IN THE PARTY NOT RECEIVING CREDIT FOR MAKING THE PAYMENT.

FAILURE OF A PARTY TO PAY CHILD SUPPORT DOES NOT JUSTIFY DENYING THAT PARTY COURT-ORDERED POSSESSION OF OR ACCESS TO A CHILD. REFUSAL BY A PARTY TO ALLOW POSSESSION OF OR ACCESS TO A CHILD DOES NOT JUSTIFY FAILURE TO PAY COURT-ORDERED CHILD SUPPORT TO THAT PARTY.

EACH PERSON WHO IS A PARTY TO THIS ORDER OR DECREE IS ORDERED TO NOTIFY EACH OTHER PARTY WITHIN 10 DAYS AFTER THE DATE OF ANY CHANGE IN THE PARTY'S CURRENT RESIDENCE ADDRESS, MAILING ADDRESS, HOME TELEPHONE NUMBER, NAME OF EMPLOYER, ADDRESS OF EMPLOYMENT, AND WORK TELEPHONE NUMBER. THE PARTY IS ORDERED TO GIVE NOTICE OF AN INTENDED CHANGE IN ANY OF THE REQUIRED INFORMATION TO EACH OTHER PARTY ON OR BEFORE THE 60TH DAY BEFORE THE INTENDED CHANGE. IF THE PARTY DOES NOT KNOW OR COULD NOT HAVE KNOWN OF THE CHANGE IN SUFFICIENT TIME TO PROVIDE 60-DAY NOTICE, THE PARTY IS ORDERED TO GIVE NOTICE OF THE CHANGE ON OR BEFORE THE FIFTH DAY AFTER THE DATE THAT THE PARTY KNOWS OF THE CHANGE.

THE DUTY TO FURNISH THIS INFORMATION TO EACH OTHER PARTY CONTINUES AS LONG AS ANY PERSON, BY VIRTUE OF THIS ORDER OR DECREE, IS UNDER AN OBLIGATION TO PAY CHILD SUPPORT OR IS ENTITLED TO POSSESSION OF OR ACCESS TO A CHILD.

FAILURE BY A PARTY TO OBEY THE ORDER OF THIS COURT TO PROVIDE EACH OTHER WITH THE CHANGE IN THE REQUIRED INFORMATION MAY RESULT IN FURTHER LITIGATION TO ENFORCE THE ORDER, INCLUDING CONTEMPT OF COURT. A FINDING OF CONTEMPT MAY BE PUNISHED BY CONFINEMENT IN JAIL FOR UP TO SIX MONTHS, A FINE OF UP TO $500 FOR EACH VIOLATION, AND A MONEY JUDGMENT FOR A PAYMENT OF ATTORNEY'S FEES AND COURT COSTS.

NOTICE TO ANY PEACE OFFICER OF THE STATE OF TEXAS: YOU MAY USE REASONABLE EFFORTS TO ENFORCE THE TERMS OF CHILD CUSTODY SPECIFIED IN THIS ORDER. A PEACE OFFICER WHO RELIES ON THE TERMS OF A COURT ORDER AND THE OFFICER'S AGENCY ARE ENTITLED TO THE APPLICABLE IMMUNITY AGAINST ANY CLAIM, CIVIL OR OTHERWISE, REGARDING THIS OFFICER'S GOOD FAITH ACTS PERFORMED IN THE SCOPE OF THE OFFICER'S DUTIES IN ENFORCING THE TERMS OF THE ORDER THAT RELATE TO CHILD CUSTODY. ANY PERSON WHO KNOWINGLY PRESENTS FOR ENFORCEMENT AN ORDER THAT IS INVALID OR NO LONGER IN EFFECT COMMITS AN OFFENSE THAT MAY BE PUNISHABLE BY CONFINEMENT IN JAIL FOR AS LONG AS TWO YEARS AND A FINE OF AS MUCH AS $10,000.

NO. _____

IN THE MATTER OF THE MARRIAGE OF	§	IN THE DISTRICT COURT
	§	
	§	
_____	§	
	§	
AND	§	
	§	
_____	§	_____ JUDICIAL DISTRICT
	§	
AND IN THE INTERESTS OF	§	
	§	
_____	§	
	§	
_____, and	§	
	§	
_____	§	
MINOR CHILDREN	§	_____ COUNTY, TEXAS

ORDER WITHHOLDING FROM EARNINGS FOR CHILD SUPPORT

The Court ORDERS you, the employer of the Obligor, to withhold income from the Obligor's disposable earnings from this employment as follows:

OBLIGOR:
Name: _____
Address: _____
Social Security Number: _____
Driver's License Number: _____

OBLIGEE:
Name: _____
Address: _____
Social Security Number: _____
Driver's License Number: _____

CHILD:
Name: _____
Address: _____
Social Security Number: _____
Driver's License Number: _____
Birthdate: _____ Birthplace: _____

CHILD:
Name: _____
Address: _____
Social Security Number: _____
Driver's License Number: _____
Birthdate: _____ Birthplace: _____

CHILD:
Name: _____
Address: _____
Social Security Number: _____
Driver's License Number: _____
Birthdate: _____ Birthplace: _____

Withholding Earnings For Current Child Support:
The Court ORDERS that any employer of the Obligor shall begin withholding from Obligor's disposable earnings no later than the first pay period which occurs 14 days following the date this Order is served on the employer.

The amount of earnings to be withheld is:
(1) $_____ if the Obligor is paid monthly
(2) $_____ if the Obligor is paid twice monthly
(3) $_____ if the Obligor is paid every other week
(4) $_____ if the Obligor is paid every week

The employer shall withhold earnings in the above amount for so long as the Obligor is employed or until all children for whom support is due reach the age of eighteen years, marry, die, have had their disabilities of minority removed for general purposes, or until further order of the Court; provided, however, so long as any child who has not married, had disabilities of minority removed, or been otherwise emancipated is fully enrolled on his/her eighteenth birthday in an accredited secondary school in a program leading to a high school diploma, then the employer shall continue to withhold earnings in the above amount for each month of enrollment (and all summer months and vacation breaks occurring between any two scheduled periods of enrollment) until the end of the school year in which the last child graduates. For the purposes of this Order a child is deemed to be "fully enrolled on his/her eighteenth birthday" if such birthday occurs during a summer month following a spring semester and preceding a fall semester of full enrollment.

Maximum Amount Withheld:
The maximum amount to be withheld shall not exceed 50 percent of the Obligor's disposable earnings.

Method of Payment:
The Court ORDERS the employer to pay all amounts withheld on each regular pay day through:
Agency: _____ County Child Support Office
Address: _____, Texas
Agency Account Number: _____

All payments shall be made payable to _____, and shall identify the Obligor, Obligee, and the Agency Account Number.

Calculating Disposable Earnings:
The employer shall calculate the Obligor's disposable earnings which are subject to withholding for child support, as follows:
1.   Determine the "earnings" of the Obligor, which means compensation paid or payable for personal services, whether denominated as wages, salary, commission, bonus, or otherwise, including periodic payments pursuant to a pension, disability and retirement program, and unemployment benefits.
2.   Subtract the following sums to calculate the Obligor's "disposable earnings":
(a)   any amounts required by law to be withheld, i.e., Federal Income Tax and Federal FICA or OASI tax (Social Security), Railroad Retirement Act contributions;
(b)   union dues;
(c)   nondiscretionary retirement contributions by the Obligor; and
(d)   medical, hospitalization, and disability insurance coverage for the Obligor and his or her children.

More Than One Withholding Order:
If this Order contains provisions for withholding from earnings for a child support arrearage, or if the employer is served with another Writ of Withholding or Order Withholding from Earnings for Child Support relating to this Obligor, in this case or another case, the court ORDERS the employer to withhold equal amounts on all orders for current support until each writ or order is individually complied with or until the maximum amount to be withheld from the Obligor's

disposable earnings is reached, whichever occurs first. Thereafter, if the employer is served with a Writ of Withholding or Order Withholding from Earnings for Child Support pertaining to a child support arrearage of this Obligor, the court ORDERS the employer to withhold equal amounts on all orders or writs for child support arrearages until each order or writ is complied with or until the maximum total amount to be withheld from the Obligor's disposable earnings is reached, whichever occurs first.

Notice of Change of Employment:
The Court ORDERS an employer to notify this Court and the Obligee in writing within seven days of the date that the Obligor terminates employment. The employer is ORDERED to provide the Obligor's last known address and the name and address of the Obligor's new employer, if known.

Reference to Income Withholding Law:
Attached to this Order is a copy of Texas Family Code §14.43, which sets forth rights, duties, and potential liabilities of employers, in addition to the provisions of this Order.

SIGNED on _____, _____.

_____
Judge Presiding

This page intentionally blank.

NO. _____

IN THE MATTER OF THE MARRIAGE OF	§ § §	IN THE DISTRICT COURT
_____	§ §	_____ JUDICIAL DISTRICT
AND	§ §	
_____	§ §	_____ COUNTY, TEXAS

STATEMENT OF EVIDENCE

On _____, _____, trial on the merits was held in this cause.

[Petitioner appeared in person. Respondent, _____, was cited by publication. The parties announced ready for trial, and the cause proceeded with the following evidence being introduced and being made a part of the record and filed herein:]

[Petitioner, _____, Social Security Number _____, appeared in person.]

[Respondent, _____, Social Security Number _____, although duly and properly cited, did not appear and wholly made default.]

There being no children, no real estate, and no appreciable amount of property involved, no attorney ad litem was appointed for Respondent.

Testimony was given that Respondent had been properly cited by publication pursuant to the Texas Rules of Civil Procedure.

The pleadings of Petitioner are in due form and contain all the allegations, information, and prerequisites required by law. The Court, after receiving evidence, finds that it has jurisdiction over this cause of action and the parties and that at least 60 days have elapsed since the date the suit was filed. The Court finds Petitioner has been a domiciliary of this state for at least a six-month period preceding the filing of this action and a resident of the county in which this suit is filed for at least a 90-day period preceding the filing of this action. All persons entitled to citation were properly cited.

A jury was waived, and all questions of fact and of law were submitted to the Court.

The Court found that there are no children born or adopted of the marriage of Petitioner and Respondent who are now under 18 years of age or otherwise entitled to support, and none is expected.

Testimony was also given by Petitioner that Petitioner has no idea of Respondent's residence and that Petitioner has exercised due diligence to locate the whereabouts of Respondent and has been unable to do so.

APPROVED on _____, _____.

_____
Judge Presiding

I have read the foregoing and agree that it accurately represents the evidence introduced at the hearing described above.

Name: _____

This page intentionally blank.

NO. _____

IN THE MATTER OF THE MARRIAGE OF	§	IN THE DISTRICT COURT
	§	
_____	§	
	§	
AND	§	
	§	
_____	§	_____ JUDICIAL DISTRICT
	§	
AND IN THE INTERESTS OF	§	
	§	
_____	§	
	§	
_____, and	§	
	§	
_____	§	
MINOR CHILDREN	§	_____ COUNTY, TEXAS

STATEMENT OF EVIDENCE

On _____, _____, trial on the merits was held in this cause.

Petitioner appeared in person. Respondent, _____, was cited by publication. The undersigned attorney ad litem, a licensed attorney, was appointed by the Court to represent the interest of said Respondent and entered a general denial. The parties announced ready for trial, and the cause proceeded with the following evidence being introduced and being made a part of the record and filed herein:

[Petitioner, _____, Social Security Number _____, appeared in person.]

[Respondent, _____, Social Security Number _____, although duly and properly cited, did not appear and wholly made default.]

[_____ was appointed attorney ad litem and appeared in person. Testimony was given by attorney ad litem that Respondent had been properly cited by publication pursuant to the Texas Rules of Civil Procedure.]

The pleadings of Petitioner are in due form and contain all the allegations, information, and prerequisites required by law. The Court, after receiving evidence, finds that it has jurisdiction over this cause of action and the parties and that at least 60 days have elapsed since the date the suit was filed. The Court finds Petitioner has been a domiciliary of this state for at least a six-month period preceding the filing of this action and a resident of the county in which this suit is filed for at least a 90-day period preceding the filing of this action. All persons entitled to citation were properly cited.

A jury was waived, and all questions of fact and of law were submitted to the Court.

The Court finds that Petitioner and Respondent are the parents of the following children now under 18 years of age:

Name and Sex: _____
Birthplace and Date: _____
Present Residence: _____
Social Security Number: _____

Name and Sex: _____
Birthplace and Date: _____
Present Residence: _____
Social Security Number: _____

Name and Sex: _____
Birthplace and Date: _____
Present Residence: _____
Social Security Number: _____

Testimony was given by Petitioner that all children reside with Petitioner.

Testimony was also given by Petitioner that Petitioner has no idea of Respondent's residence and that Petitioner has exercised due diligence to locate the whereabouts of Respondent and has been unable to do so.

APPROVED on _____, _____.

_____
Judge Presiding

I have read the foregoing and agree that it accurately represents the evidence introduced at the hearing described above.

_____   _____

Name: _____   Petitioner: _____

State Bar No. _____   Address: _____

Address: _____   _____

_____   Phone: _____

Phone: _____

ATTORNEY AD LITEM

STANDARD POSSESSION ORDER

IT IS FURTHER ORDERED, ADJUDGED AND DECREED that the managing conservator and the possessory conservator shall be bound by the following terms and provisions, and the possessory conservator shall have possession of the children as follows:

(a)   *Definitions.* In this Order:

   (1)   "School" means the primary or secondary school in which the child is enrolled, or, if the child is not enrolled in a primary or secondary school, the public school district in which the child primarily resides.

   (2)   "Child" applies to all children the subjects of this cause of action under the age of 18 and not otherwise emancipated.

(b)   *Mutual agreement or specified terms for possession.* It is ORDERED that the parties may have possession of the child at any and all times mutually agreed to in advance by the parties and, failing mutual agreement, shall have possession of the child under the specified terms herein set out in this standard order.

(c)   *Parents who reside 100 miles or less apart.* Except as otherwise explicitly provided, if the possessory conservator resides 100 miles or less from the primary residence of the child, the possessory conservator shall have the right to possession of the child as follows, according to the election made as indicated by an "X" or check mark:

   (1)   on weekends beginning at 6 p.m. on the first, third, and fifth Friday of each month and ending at 6 p.m. on the following Sunday or, at the possessory conservator's election made before or at the time of the rendition of the original or modification order, and as specified in the original or modification order, beginning at the time the child's school is regularly dismissed and ending at 6 p.m. on the following Sunday; and

   (2)   on Thursdays of each week during the regular school term beginning at 6 p.m. and ending at 8 p.m., or, at the possessory conservator's election made before or at the time of the rendition of the original or modification order, and as specified in the original or modification order, beginning at the time the child's school is regularly dismissed and ending at the time the child's school resumes, unless the court finds that visitation under this subdivision is not in the best interests of the child.

(d)   *Weekend possession extended by holiday.* Except as otherwise explicitly provided, if a weekend period of possession of the possessory conservator coincides with a school holiday during the regular school term, or with a federal, state or local holiday during the summer months in which school is not in session, the weekend possession shall extend until 6 p.m. on a Monday holiday or school holiday or shall begin at 6 p.m. Thursday for a Friday holiday or school holiday, as applicable.

(e)   *Vacations and holidays.* The following provisions govern possession of the child for vacations and for certain specific holidays, and supersede any conflicting weekend or Thursday periods of possession provided by part (c) and (d) of this Order. The possessory conservator and managing conservator shall have rights of possession of the child as follows:

(1)   The possessory conservator shall have possession of the child in even-numbered years from 6 p.m. on the day the child is dismissed from school for the Christmas vacation until noon on December 26th, and the managing conservator shall have rights of possession for the same period in odd-numbered years;

(2)   The possessory conservator shall have possession of the child in odd- numbered years from noon on December 26th until 6 p.m. on the day before school resumes, and the managing conservator shall have rights of possession for the same period in even-numbered years;

(3)   The possessory conservator shall have possession of the child in odd- numbered years from 6 p.m. on the day the child is dismissed from school before Thanksgiving until 6 p.m. on the following Sunday, and the managing conservator shall have rights of possession for the same period in even-numbered years;

(4)   The possessory conservator shall have possession of the child in even numbered years from 6 p.m. on the day the child is dismissed from school for the school's spring vacation until 6 p.m. on the day before school resumes, and the managing conservator shall have rights of possession for the same period in odd-numbered years;

(5)   If the possessory conservator:

(A)   gives the managing conservator written notice by May 1st of each year specifying an extended period or periods of summer possession, the possessory conservator shall have possession of the child for 30 days beginning no earlier than the day after the child's school is dismissed for the summer vacation and ending no later than seven days prior to school resuming at the end of the summer vacation, to be exercised in no more than two separate periods of at least seven consecutive days each; or

(B)   does not give the managing conservator written notice by May 1st of each year specifying an extended period or periods of summer possession, the possessory conservator shall have possession of the child for 30 consecutive days beginning at 6 p.m. on July 1st and ending at 6 p.m. on July 31st.

(6)   If the managing conservator gives the possessory conservator written notice by June 1st of each year, the managing conservator shall have possession of the child on any one weekend from Friday at 6 p.m. to 6 p.m. on the following Sunday during any one period of possession by the possessory conservator under subdivision (5) above, provided that the managing conservator picks up the child from the possessory conservator and returns the child to that same place;

(7)   If the managing conservator gives the possessory conservator written notice by May 15th of each year or gives the possessory conservator 14 days' written notice on or after May 16th of each year, the managing conservator may designate one weekend beginning no earlier than the day after the child's school is dismissed for the summer vacation and ending no later than seven days prior to school resuming at the end of the summer vacation, during which an otherwise scheduled weekend period of possession by the possessory conservator will not take place, provided that the weekend so designated does not interfere with the possessory conservator's period or periods of extended summer possession or with Father's Day if the possessory conservator is the father of the child;

(8)   The parent not otherwise entitled under this standard order to present possession of a child on the child's birthday shall have possession of the child from 6 p.m. to 8 p.m. on that day, provided that the parent not in possession picks up the child from the child's residence and returns the child to that same place.

(9)   If a conservator, the father shall have possession of the child beginning at 6 p.m. on the Friday preceding Father's Day to 6 p.m. on Father's Day, provided that, if he is not otherwise entitled to present possession of the child, he picks up the child from the child's residence and returns the child to that same place; and

(10)   If a conservator, the mother shall have possession of the child beginning at 6 p.m. on the Friday preceding Mother's Day to 6 p.m. on Mother's Day, provided that, if she is not otherwise entitled to present possession of the child, she picks up the child from the child's residence and returns the child to that same place.

(f)   *Parents who reside over 100 miles apart.* Except as otherwise explicitly provided, if the possessory conservator resides more than 100 miles from the primary residence of the child, the possessory conservator shall have the right to possession of the child as follows:

(1)   Either regular weekend possession beginning on the first, third and fifth Friday as provided under the terms of part (c)(1) of this Order, or not more than one weekend per month of the possessory conservator's choice beginning at 6 p.m. on the day school recesses for the weekend and ending at 6 p.m. on the day before school resumes after the weekend, provided that the possessory conservator gives the managing conservator fourteen days' written or telephonic notice preceding a designated weekend, and provided that the possessory conservator elects an option for this alternative period of possession by written notice given to the managing conservator within 90 days after the parties begin to reside more than 100 miles apart, as applicable, and provided that such weekend possessions do not conflict with parts (e)(1) through (3) and (e)(8) through (10) of this Order;

(2)   The terms of parts (e)(1) through (3) and (e)(8) through (10) of this Order are applicable when the possessory conservator resides more than 100 miles from the residence of the child;

(3)   Each spring school vacation from 6 p.m. on the day school recesses until 6 p.m. on the day before school resumes after that vacation;

(4)   If the possessory conservator:

(A)   gives the managing conservator written notice by May 1st of each year specifying an extended period or periods of summer possession, the possessory conservator shall have possession of the child for 42 days beginning no earlier than the day after the child's school is dismissed for the summer vacation and ending no later than seven days prior to school resuming at the end of summer vacation, to be exercised in no more than two separate periods of at least seven consecutive days each; or

(B)   does not give the managing conservator written notice by May 1st of each year specifying an extended period or periods of summer possession, the possessory conservator shall have possession of the child for 42 consecutive days beginning at 6 p.m. on June 15th and ending at 6 p.m. on July 27th.

(5)   If the managing conservator gives the possessory conservator written notice by June 1st of each year, the managing conservator shall have possession of the child on any one weekend from Friday at 6 p.m. to 6 p.m. on the following Sunday during any one period of possession by the possessory conservator under subdivision (4) of this part, provided that if a period of possession by the possessory conservator exceeds 30 days, the managing conservator may have possession of the child under the terms of this subdivision on any two nonconsecutive weekends during that time period, and further provided that the managing conservator picks up the child from the possessory conservator and returns the child to that same place; and

(6)   If the managing conservator gives the possessory conservator written notice by June 1st of each year, the managing conservator may designate 21 days beginning no earlier than the day after the child's school is dismissed for the summer vacation and ending no later than seven days prior to school resuming at the end of the summer vacation, to be exercised in no more than two separate periods of at least seven consecutive days each, during which the possessory conservator shall not have possession of the child, provided that the period or periods so designated do not interfere with the possessory conservator's period or periods of extended summer possession or with Father's Day if the possessory conservator is the father of the child.

(g)   *General terms and conditions.* Except as otherwise explicitly provided, terms and conditions of possession of a child that apply irrespective of the distance between the residence of a parent and the child are as follows:

(1)   The managing conservator shall surrender the child to the possessory conservator at the beginning of each period of the possessory conservator's possession at the residence of the managing conservator;

(2)   If the possessory conservator elects to begin the period of possession at the time the child's school is regularly dismissed, the managing conservator shall surrender the child to the possessory conservator at the beginning of each period of possession at the school in which the child is enrolled;

(3)   The possessory conservator shall be ordered to do one of the following:

(A)   the possessory conservator shall surrender the child to the managing conservator at the end of each period of possession at the residence of the possessory conservator; or

(B)   the possessory conservator shall return the child to the residence of the managing conservator at the end of each period of possession, except that the order shall provide that the possessory conservator shall surrender the child to the managing conservator at the end of each period of possession at the residence of the possessory conservator if:

(i)   at the time the original order or a modification of an order establishing terms and conditions of possession or access the possessory conservator and the managing conservator lived in the same county, the possessory conservator's county of residence remains the same after the rendition of the order and the managing conservator's county of resident changes, effective on the date of the change of residence by the managing conservator; or

(ii)   the possessory conservator and managing conservator lived in the same residence at any time during the six-month period preceding the date on which a suit for dissolution of the marriage was filed and the possessory conservator's county of residence remains the same and the managing conservator's county of residence changes after they no longer live in the same residence, effective on the date the order is rendered;

(4)   Each conservator shall return with the child the personal effects that the child brought at the beginning of the period of possession;

(5)   Either parent may designate any competent adult to pick up and return the child; a parent or a designated competent adult shall be present when the child is picked up or returned;

(6)   A parent shall give notice to the person in possession of the child on each occasion that the parent will be unable to exercise that parent's right of possession for any specified period; repeated failure of a parent to give notice of an inability to exercise possessory rights may be considered as a factor in a modification of those possessory rights;

(7)   Written notice shall be deemed to have been timely made if received or postmarked before or at the time that notice is due; and

(8)   If a conservator's time of possession ends at the time school resumes, and for any reason the child is not or will not be returned to school, the conservator in possession of the child shall immediately notify the school and the other conservator that the child will not be or has not been returned to school.

This page intentionally blank.

NO. _____

IN THE MATTER OF THE MARRIAGE OF	§	IN THE DISTRICT COURT
	§	
_____	§	
	§	
AND	§	
	§	
_____	§	_____ JUDICIAL DISTRICT
	§	
AND IN THE INTERESTS OF	§	
	§	
_____	§	
	§	
_____, and	§	
	§	
_____	§	
MINOR CHILDREN	§	_____ COUNTY, TEXAS

NOTICE OF HEARING FOR TEMPORARY ORDERS

Notice is given to Respondent, _____, to appear before this Court in its courtroom located at _____, _____, Texas, on the _____ day of _____, _____, at _____ o'clock ___.m. The purpose of the hearing is to determine whether the Court should make temporary orders regarding (1) payments for the support of Petitioner during the pendency of this case; (2) such other and further orders respecting the property and the parties as pled for or as may be deemed necessary and equitable.

SIGNED this _____ day of _____ , _____.

_____
Judge Presiding

This page intentionally blank.

NO. _____

IN THE MATTER OF THE MARRIAGE OF	§	IN THE DISTRICT COURT
_____	§	
AND	§	
_____	§	_____ JUDICIAL DISTRICT
AND IN THE INTERESTS OF	§	
_____	§	
_____, and	§	
_____	§	
MINOR CHILDREN	§	_____ COUNTY, TEXAS

CERTIFICATE OF SERVICE

I certify that a true copy of the foregoing _____ was served on _____ by [first-class mail or hand delivery] on _____, _____, in accordance with the Texas Rules of Civil Procedure.

_____
Name

This page intentionally blank.

NO. _____

IN THE MATTER OF THE MARRIAGE OF	§ § §	IN THE DISTRICT COURT
_____	§ §	_____ JUDICIAL DISTRICT
AND	§ §	
_____	§ §	_____ COUNTY, TEXAS

MARITAL SETTLEMENT AGREEMENT

This suit is brought by _____, Petitioner, Social Security Number _____, who is _____ years of age and resides in _____ County, Texas. Respondent, _____ _____, Social Security Number _____, is _____ years of age and resides in _____ County, Texas.

I.

Petitioner has been a domiciliary of the State of Texas for the preceding six-month period and a resident of _____ County for the preceding ninety-day period.

II.

The parties were married on or about _____, _____, in _____, [and ceased to live together as husband and wife on or about _____, _____].

The marriage has become insupportable because of discord or conflict of personalities between Petitioner and Respondent that destroys the legitimate ends of the marriage relationship and prevents any reasonable expectation of reconciliation.

III.

There are no children born or adopted of this marriage and none is expected.

IV.

Petitioner and Respondent have divided and by this Agreement do hereby divide their estate, including assets, debts, and obligations in a manner that is just and right, with due regard for the rights of the Parties of the marriage. The Parties believe that in order to accomplish such a division, it is best met by a nontaxable transfer of the property in existence as of the date of this Agreement.

V.

Petitioner shall receive the following property:

_____
_____
_____
_____.

VI.

Respondent shall receive the following property:

_____
_____
_____
_____.

VII.

Petitioner shall assume the following debts:

_____
_____
_____
_____.

VIII.

Respondent shall assume the following debts:

_____
_____
_____
_____.

WHEREFORE Petitioner and Respondent have executed this Agreement on the date of the acknowledgments shown below.

_____   _____

Name: _____   Name: _____

Address: _____   Address: _____

_____   _____

Telephone: _____   Telephone: _____

STATE OF TEXAS   )
COUNTY OF _____   )

This instrument was acknowledged before me on _____, _____, by Petitioner, _____.

_____
Notary Public, State of Texas
My Commission Expires:

_____

STATE OF TEXAS   )
COUNTY OF _____   )

This instrument was acknowledged before me on _____, _____, by Respondent, _____.

_____
Notary Public, State of Texas
My Commission Expires:

_____

NO. _____

IN THE MATTER OF THE MARRIAGE OF	§	IN THE DISTRICT COURT
	§	
_____	§	
	§	
AND	§	
	§	
_____	§	_____ JUDICIAL DISTRICT
	§	
AND IN THE INTERESTS OF	§	
	§	
_____	§	
	§	
_____, and	§	
	§	
_____	§	
MINOR CHILDREN	§	_____ COUNTY, TEXAS

DEFAULT CERTIFICATE

PURSUANT TO RULE 239A, TEXAS RULES OF CIVIL PROCEDURE, I HEREBY CERTIFY THAT THE LAST KNOWN MAILING ADDRESS OF THE RESPONDENT IN THIS PROCEEDING IS AS FOLLOWS:

_____
_____
_____

Respectfully submitted,

Signed: _____

Printed name: _____

Address: _____

_____

This page intentionally blank.

ATTACHMENT A

to Subpoena

<u>Witnesses to be produced</u>

_____ , located at _____

_____ , shall designate one or more of its officers or agents who is knowledgeable about the matters subpoenaed to testify on its behalf.

<u>Subject of testimony</u>
Compensation and employee benefits of _____
(hereafter "Respondent"), whose Social Security Number is _____.

<u>Documents to be produced</u>
The originals or copies of the following books, papers or records pertaining to Respondent during the period from January 1, _____ to the date of production of records in response to this subpoena.

1.   W-2 form showing compensation paid to Respondent last year.

2.   Documents showing for each pay period all payments to Respondent this year.

3.   Respondent's current rate of pay and a copy of the voucher accompanying Respondent's most recent pay check showing payroll deductions.

4.   Respondent's payment schedule, that is whether paid weekly, monthly, etc., and the dates each month on which paid.

5.   The persons presently covered by Respondent's medical insurance.

6.   The monthly cost of medical coverage, if any, for Respondent alone.

7.   The monthly additional cost of including Respondent's children in the medical coverage.

8.   Summary plan brochure for any retirement, pension, 401(k) or savings plan in which Respondent is enrolled.

9.   Records revealing the dollar value which is attributed to Respondent's interest in each of such plans.

10. The most recent annual statements to Respondent with regard to the dollar value of Respondent's interest in such plans.

This page intentionally blank.

NO. _____

<table>
<tr><td>IN THE MATTER OF
THE MARRIAGE OF

_____

AND

_____

AND IN THE INTERESTS OF

_____

_____, and

_____
MINOR CHILDREN</td><td>§
§
§
§
§
§
§
§
§
§
§
§
§
§
§
§
§</td><td>IN THE DISTRICT COURT

_____ JUDICIAL DISTRICT

_____ COUNTY, TEXAS</td></tr>
</table>

AFFIDAVIT FOR BUSINESS RECORDS

STATE OF TEXAS   )

COUNTY OF _____   )

Before me, the undersigned authority, personally appeared the undersigned affiant, who being by me duly sworn deposed as follows:

I, _____, am of sound mind and capable of making this affidavit, and am personally acquainted with the facts herein stated. I am the custodian of the attached records of _____, consisting of _____ pages. These records are kept in the regular course of business, and it was in the regular course of business for an employee or representative of this organization, with knowledge of the information therein recorded, to make such records. The records were made at or near the time indicated on them or reasonably soon thereafter. The attached records are originals or exact copies of originals.

_____
Affiant

Subscribed and Sworn to Before me

on _____, _____

_____
Notary Public, State of Texas

My Commission Expires:

_____

This page intentionally blank.

NO. _____

IN THE MATTER OF THE MARRIAGE OF	§	IN THE DISTRICT COURT
	§	
_____	§	
	§	
AND	§	
	§	
_____	§	_____ JUDICIAL DISTRICT
	§	
AND IN THE INTERESTS OF	§	
	§	
_____	§	
	§	
_____, and	§	
	§	
_____	§	
MINOR CHILDREN	§	_____ COUNTY, TEXAS

NOTICE OF HEARING

Notice is given to Respondent, _____, to appear before this Court in its courtroom located at _____, _____, Texas, on the _____ day of _____, _____, at _____ o'clock ____.m. The purpose of the hearing is _____ _____ _____.

SIGNED this _____ day of _____, _____.

_____
Judge Presiding

This page intentionally blank.

NO. _____

IN THE MATTER OF THE MARRIAGE OF	§	IN THE DISTRICT COURT

§
§
§
§
§

IN THE MATTER OF
THE MARRIAGE OF   §   IN THE DISTRICT COURT
                         §
_____   §
                         §
AND   §
                         §
_____   §   _____ JUDICIAL DISTRICT
                         §
AND IN THE INTERESTS OF §
                         §
_____   §
                         §
_____, and   §
                         §
_____   §
MINOR CHILDREN   §   _____ COUNTY, TEXAS

STATEMENT OF HEALTH CARE FOR CHILDREN

TO THE HONORABLE JUDGE OF SAID COURT:

The following minor children are the children of Petitioner and Respondent whose interests are affected by this case:

_____
_____.

The following private health insurance coverage is in effect for each of the children:

     Name of Insurance Company: _____
     Policy Number: _____
     Parent Responsible for Payment of Premium: _____
     Cost of Premium: _____

     Insurance Provided Through Parent's Employer: Yes _____   No _____

There is no private health insurance coverage in effect for the children. However, the following applies:

_____ The children are receiving medical assistance under Chapter 32, Human Resources Code.

_____ The children are receiving health benefits coverage under the state health plan under Chapter 62, Health and Safety Code, and the cost of the premium is _____.

_____ Petitioner has access to private health insurance at a reasonable cost to Petitioner.

_____ Respondent has access to private health insurance at a reasonable cost to Respondent.

SIGNED ON THIS _____ day of _____, 20_____.

                                          Name: _____

This page intentionally blank.

Reporting Form

For

Suits Affecting the Parent-Child Relationship and Divorce

GENERAL REQUIREMENT:

All divorces/annulments (with or without children) and all suits affecting the parent-child relationship must be reported through the clerk of the court to the Bureau of Vital Statistics (BVS). The Office of the Attorney General (OAG), in cooperation with BVS is also using this existing reporting system for the state case registry for child support enforcement.

Consolidated reporting by petitioners, attorneys, and the courts is designed to make mandatory reporting more efficient, timely, and improve the quality of reporting. However, this reporting system is only as good or timely as you make it; therefore, your attention in completing and filing this report is critical.

Legal basis for this reporting is contained in:

Health & Safety Code	Sec. 192.0051
	Sec. 194.002
Family Code	Sec. 108.001
	Sec. 108.002
	Sec. 108.004
	Sec. 108.008

For information concerning reporting or questions about this form, contact BVS at (512) 458-7368 or by e-mail (BVSWEB@TDH.STATE.TX.US).

For information on the court of continuing jurisdiction of a child, contact BVS at (512) 458-7372. Inquiries should be addressed to BVS, 1100 West 49th Street, Austin, Texas, 78756-3191; inquiries may also be faxed to (512) 458-7783.

TDH
TEXAS DEPARTMENT OF HEALTH

This section must be completed for each report filed.

1a - e   Enter the required information to identify the court proceeding.

2   Check <u>only</u> if the court found evidence of domestic violence or child abuse.

3   Check the type of suit being reported; this also which sections of the form <u>must</u> be completed. If more than one type of order applies, check all that apply. Check "other" and specify the type of suit if none of the types listed apply. Transfers from one jurisdiction to another must be reported in this section (if court number is unknown, specify "unknown").

4a - e   Complete the attorney information to assist in questions or follow back; 4b only applies to OAG cases.

All divorces/annulments must be reported, even if there were no minor children. All information is required.

5 - 10   Report the husband's information.

11 - 16   Report the wife's information, including her maiden name.

17   Report the number of minor children affected by this divorce; if none, record "0." This number must correspond to the listing of children in Section 3.

18 - 19   Report the date and place of the marriage being dissolved.

20.   Check the appropriate box for the petitioner.

Every child affected by the suit being reported must be listed, and <u>all</u> items concerning that child must be completed. If more than four children are affected, attach an additional form, mark it "continuation" at the top, and continue to list the additional children. Attach the continuation form to the original form.

21 - 24(a)   Enter the legal name of the child at the time this suit was initiated.

21 - 24(f)   Report any prior names or A.K.A. names used for this child; if no prior or A.K.A. names, leave this item blank.

21 - 24(g)   Enter the new legal name if this suit legally changes the name of the child; if no legal name change, leave this item blank.

This section <u>must</u> be completed if the suit being reported includes a child support order. All information is required. The information reported in this section is vital to the state case registry system.

25   Report the relationship of the obligee to the child(ren) listed in Section 3.

26 - 32   Report the obligee's information.

33   Report the relationship of the first obligor to the child(ren) listed in Section 3.

34 - 43   Report the first obligor's information.

44   If the suit involves a second obligor, report that person's relationship to the child(ren) listed in Section 3.

45 - 54   If the suit involves a second obligor, report that person's information.

This section should be completed <u>only</u> if the order being reported involves a paternity establishment or a non-paternity establishment. If the order determines that a man is not the father of the child and should be removed from the birth certificate, check "Yes" in item 59. If no biological father has been established, leave items 55–58 blank.

55 - 58   Report the biological father's information.

59   Check the appropriate box to answer the following question: "Does this order remove information pertaining to a father from a child's Certificate of Birth?"

This section should only be completed if the order being reported terminates the parental rights of one or more individuals.

60 - 62   Report the name and relationship to the child(ren) listed in Section 3 for each person whose parental rights are terminated in this suit.

THIS FORM MUST BE SIGNED BY THE CLERK OF THE COURT AND MAILED TO THE BUREAU OF VITAL STATISTICS.

INFORMATION ON SUIT AFFECTING THE FAMILY RELATIONSHIP
(EXCLUDING ADOPTIONS)

SECTION 1 GENERAL INFORMATION (REQUIRED)	STATE FILE NUMBER

1a. COUNTY _____ 1b. COURT NO. _____

1d. CAUSE NO. _____ 1e. DATE OF ORDER (mm/dd/yyyy) _____

2. HAS THERE BEEN A FINDING BY THE COURT OF: ☐ DOMESTIC VIOLENCE ? ☐ CHILD ABUSE ?

3. TYPE OF ORDER (CHECK ALL THAT APPLY):

☐ DIVORCE/ ANNULMENT **WITH** CHILDREN(Sec 1, 2, 3, 4)   ☐ DIVORCE/ ANNULMENT **WITHOUT** CHILDREN(Sec 1, 2)

☐ PATERNITY **WITH** CHILD SUPPORT (Sec 1, 3, 4, 5)   ☐ PATERNITY **WITHOUT** CHILD SUPPORT (Sec 1, 3, 5)

☐ CHILD SUPPORT OBLIGATION/MODIFICATION (Sec 1, 3, 4)   ☐ TERMINATION OF RIGHTS (Sec 1, 3, 6)

☐ CONSERVATORSHIP (Sec 1, 3)   ☐ OTHER (Specify)_____

☐ TRANSFER TO (Sec 1, 3) COUNTY_____ COURT NO. _____ STATE COURT ID# _____

4a. NAME OF ATTORNEY FOR PETITIONER	4b. ATTORNEY GENERAL ACCT/CASE #
4c. CURRENT MAILING ADDRESS: STREET & NO. CITY STATE ZIP	4d. TELEPHONE NUMBER ( )

SECTION 2 (IF APPLICABLE) REPORT OF DIVORCE OR ANNULMENT OF MARRIAGE

HUSBAND

5. FIRST NAME MIDDLE LAST SUFFIX	6. DATE OF BIRTH (mm/dd/yyyy)
7. PLACE OF BIRTH CITY STATE OR FOREIGN COUNTRY	8. RACE	9. SOCIAL SECURITY NUMBER
10. USUAL RESIDENCE   STREET NAME & NUMBER   CITY   STATE   ZIP

WIFE

11. FIRST NAME MIDDLE LAST	MAIDEN	12. DATE OF BIRTH (mm/dd/yyyy)
13. PLACE OF BIRTH CITY STATE OR FOREIGN COUNTRY	14. RACE	15. SOCIAL SECURITY NUMBER
16. USUAL RESIDENCE   STREET NAME & NUMBER   CITY   STATE   ZIP

17. NUMBER OF MINOR CHILDREN	18. DATE OF MARRIAGE (mmddyyyy)	19. PLACE OF MARRIAGE CITY STATE	20. PETITIONER IS ☐ HUSBAND ☐ WIFE

SECTION 3 (IF APPLICABLE) CHILDREN AFFECTED BY THIS SUIT

CHILD 1

21a. FIRST NAME MIDDLE LAST SUFFIX	21b. DATE OF BIRTH (mm/dd/yyyy)
21c. SOCIAL SECURITY NUMBER	21d. SEX	21e. BIRTHPLACE CITY COUNTY STATE
21f. PRIOR NAME OF CHILD FIRST MIDDLE LAST SUFFIX	21g. NEW NAME OF CHILD FIRST MIDDLE LAST SUFFIX

CHILD 2

22a. FIRST NAME MIDDLE LAST SUFFIX	22b. DATE OF BIRTH (mm/dd/yyyy)
22c. SOCIAL SECURITY NUMBER	22d. SEX	22e. BIRTHPLACE CITY COUNTY STATE
22f. PRIOR NAME OF CHILD FIRST MIDDLE LAST SUFFIX	22g. NEW NAME OF CHILD FIRST MIDDLE LAST SUFFIX

CHILD 3

23a. FIRST NAME MIDDLE LAST SUFFIX	23b. DATE OF BIRTH (mm/dd/yyyy)
23c. SOCIAL SECURITY NUMBER	23d. SEX	23e. BIRTHPLACE CITY COUNTY STATE
23f. PRIOR NAME OF CHILD FIRST MIDDLE LAST SUFFIX	23g. NEW NAME OF CHILD FIRST MIDDLE LAST SUFFIX

CHILD 4

24a. FIRST NAME MIDDLE LAST SUFFIX	24b. DATE OF BIRTH (mm/dd/yyyy)
24c. SOCIAL SECURITY NUMBER	24d. SEX	24e. BIRTHPLACE CITY COUNTY STATE
24f. PRIOR NAME OF CHILD FIRST MIDDLE LAST SUFFIX	24g. NEW NAME OF CHILD FIRST MIDDLE LAST SUFFIX

TDH
TEXAS DEPARTMENT OF HEALTH

SECTION 4 (IF APPLICABLE) OBLIGEE/OBLIGOR INFORMATION

OBLIGEE

THIS PARTY TO THE SUIT IS (CHECK ONE): ☐ 25a. TDPRS ☐ 25b. NON-PARENT CONSERVATOR - COMPLETE 26 - 32

☐ 25c. HUSBAND AS SHOWN ON FRONT OF THIS FORM - COMPLETE 31 - 32 ONLY ☐ 25d. WIFE AS SHOWN ON FRONT OF THIS FORM - COMPLETE 31 - 32 ONLY

☐ 25e. BIOLOGICAL FATHER - COMPLETE 26 - 32 ☐ 25f. BIOLOGICAL MOTHER - COMPLETE 26 - 32

26. FIRST NAME	MIDDLE	LAST	SUFFIX	MAIDEN

27. DATE OF BIRTH (mm/dd/yyyy)	28. PLACE OF BIRTH CITY	STATE OR FOREIGN COUNTRY

29. USUAL RESIDENCE STREET NAME & NUMBER	CITY	COUNTY	STATE	ZIP

30. SOCIAL SECURITY NUMBER	31. DRIVER LICENSE NO & STATE	32. TELEPHONE NUMBER ( )

OBLIGOR #1

THIS PARTY TO THE SUIT IS (CHECK ONE): ☐ 33a. NON-PARENT CONSERVATOR - COMPLETE 34 - 43

☐ 33b. HUSBAND AS SHOWN ON FRONT OF THIS FORM - COMPLETE 39 - 43 ONLY ☐ 33c. WIFE AS SHOWN ON FRONT OF THIS FORM - COMPLETE 39 - 43 ONLY

☐ 33d. BIOLOGICAL FATHER - COMPLETE 34 - 43 ☐ 33e. BIOLOGICAL MOTHER - COMPLETE 34 - 43

34. FIRST NAME	MIDDLE	LAST	SUFFIX	MAIDEN

35. DATE OF BIRTH (mm/dd/yyyy)	36. PLACE OF BIRTH CITY	STATE OR FOREIGN COUNTRY

37. USUAL RESIDENCE STREET NAME & NUMBER	CITY	COUNTY	STATE	ZIP

38. SOCIAL SECURITY NUMBER	39. DRIVER LICENSE NO & STATE	40. TELEPHONE NUMBER ( )

41. EMPLOYER NAME	42. EMPLOYER TELEPHONE NUMBER ( )

43. EMPLOYER PAYROLL ADDRESS STREET NAME & NUMBER	CITY	STATE	ZIP

OBLIGOR #2

THIS PARTY TO THE SUIT IS (CHECK ONE): ☐ 44a. NON-PARENT CONSERVATOR - COMPLETE 45 - 54

☐ 44b. HUSBAND AS SHOWN ON FRONT OF THIS FORM - COMPLETE 50 - 54 ONLY ☐ 44c. WIFE AS SHOWN ON FRONT OF THIS FORM - COMPLETE 50 - 54 ONLY

☐ 44d. BIOLOGICAL FATHER - COMPLETE 45 - 54 ☐ 44e. BIOLOGICAL MOTHER - COMPLETE 45 - 54

45. FIRST NAME	MIDDLE	LAST	SUFFIX	MAIDEN

46. DATE OF BIRTH (mm/dd/yyyy)	47. PLACE OF BIRTH CITY	STATE OR FOREIGN COUNTRY

48. USUAL RESIDENCE STREET NAME & NUMBER	CITY	COUNTY	STATE	ZIP

49. SOCIAL SECURITY NUMBER	50. DRIVER LICENSE NO & STATE	51. TELEPHONE NUMBER ( )

52. EMPLOYER NAME	53. EMPLOYER TELEPHONE NUMBER ( )

54. EMPLOYER PAYROLL ADDRESS STREET NAME & NUMBER	CITY	STATE	ZIP

SECTION 5 (IF APPLICABLE) FOR ORDERS CONCERNING PATERNITY ESTABLISHMENT OF BIOLOGICAL FATHER

55. BIOLOGICAL FATHER'S NAME FIRST MIDDLE LAST SUFFIX	56. DATE OF BIRTH (mm/dd/yyyy)

57. SOCIAL SECURITY NUMBER	58. CURRENT MAILING ADDRESS STREET NAME & NUMBER CITY STATE ZIP

59. DOES THIS ORDER REMOVE INFORMATION PERTAINING TO A FATHER FROM A CHILD'S CERTIFICATE OF BIRTH? ☐ NO ☐ YES

SECTION 6 TERMINATION OF RIGHTS Information related to the individual(s) whose rights are being terminated in this suit

60a. FIRST NAME	MIDDLE NAME	LAST NAME	SUFFIX	60b. RELATIONSHIP
61a. FIRST NAME	MIDDLE NAME	LAST NAME	SUFFIX	61b. RELATIONSHIP
62a. FIRST NAME	MIDDLE NAME	LAST NAME	SUFFIX	62b. RELATIONSHIP

Comments: _____

_____

_____

I certify that the above order was granted on the date and place as stated.

SIGNATURE OF THE CLERK OF THE COURT

Form **8332**

(Rev. December 2000)

Department of the Treasury
Internal Revenue Service

Release of Claim to Exemption
for Child of Divorced or Separated Parents

▶ **Attach** to noncustodial parent's return **each year** exemption is claimed.
Caution: *Do not use this form if you were never married.*

OMB No. 1545-0915

Attachment
Sequence No. **115**

Name of noncustodial parent claiming exemption

Noncustodial parent's
social security number (SSN) ▶

Part I	**Release of Claim to Exemption for Current Year**

I agree not to claim an exemption for _____

Name(s) of child (or children)

for the tax year 20_____ .

_____
Signature of custodial parent releasing claim to exemption

Custodial parent's SSN

Date

Note: *If you choose not to claim an exemption for this child (or children) for future tax years, also complete Part II.*

Part II	**Release of Claim to Exemption for Future Years** (If completed, see **Noncustodial parent** below.)

I agree not to claim an exemption for _____

Name(s) of child (or children)

for the tax year(s) _____ .

(Specify. See instructions.)

_____
Signature of custodial parent releasing claim to exemption

Custodial parent's SSN

Date

General Instructions

Purpose of form. If you are a **custodial parent** and you were ever married to the child's **noncustodial parent,** you may use this form to release your claim to your child's exemption. To do so, complete this form (or a similar statement containing the same information required by this form) and give it to the noncustodial parent who will claim the child's exemption. The noncustodial parent must attach this form or similar statement to his or her tax return **each year** the exemption is claimed.

You are the **custodial parent** if you had custody of the child for most of the year. You are the **noncustodial parent** if you had custody for a shorter period of time or did not have custody at all. For the definition of custody, see **Pub. 501,** Exemptions, Standard Deduction, and Filing Information.

Support test for children of divorced or separated parents. Generally, the custodial parent is treated as having provided over half of the child's support if:

● The child received over half of his or her total support for the year from one or both of the parents **and**

● The child was in the custody of one or both of the parents for more than half of the year.

Note: *Public assistance payments, such as Temporary Assistance for Needy Families (TANF), are not support provided by the parents.*

For this support test to apply, the parents must be one of the following:

● Divorced or legally separated under a decree of divorce or separate maintenance,

● Separated under a written separation agreement, **or**

● Living apart at all times during the last 6 months of the year.

Caution: *This support test does not apply to parents who never married each other.*

If the support test applies, and the other four dependency tests in your tax return instruction booklet are also met, the custodial parent can claim the child's exemption.

Exception. The custodial parent will not be treated as having provided over half of the child's support if **any** of the following apply.

● The custodial parent agrees not to claim the child's exemption by signing this form or similar statement.

● The child is treated as having received over half of his or her total support from a person under a multiple support agreement (**Form 2120,** Multiple Support Declaration).

● A pre-1985 divorce decree or written separation agreement states that the noncustodial parent can claim the child as a dependent. But the noncustodial parent must provide at least $600 for the child's support during the year. This rule does not apply if the decree or agreement was changed after 1984 to say that the noncustodial parent cannot claim the child as a dependent.

Additional information. For more details, see **Pub. 504,** Divorced or Separated Individuals.

Specific Instructions

Custodial parent. You may agree to release your claim to the child's exemption for the current tax year or for future years, or both.

● Complete **Part I** if you agree to release your claim to the child's exemption for the current tax year.

● Complete **Part II** if you agree to release your claim to the child's exemption for any or all future years. If you do, write the specific future year(s) or "all future years" in the space provided in Part II.

 To help ensure future support, you may not want to release your claim to the child's exemption for future years.

Noncustodial parent. Attach this form or similar statement to your tax return for **each year** you claim the child's exemption. You may claim the exemption **only** if the other four dependency tests in your tax return instruction booklet are met.

Note: *If the custodial parent released his or her claim to the child's exemption for any future year, you **must** attach a copy of this form or similar statement to your tax return for each future year that you claim the exemption. **Keep a copy for your records.***

Paperwork Reduction Act Notice. We ask for the information on this form to carry out the Internal Revenue laws of the United States. You are required to give us the information. We need it to ensure that you are complying with these laws and to allow us to figure and collect the right amount of tax.

You are not required to provide the information requested on a form that is subject to the Paperwork Reduction Act unless the form displays a valid OMB control number. Books or records relating to a form or its instructions must be retained as long as their contents may become material in the administration of any Internal Revenue law. Generally, tax returns and return information are confidential, as required by Internal Revenue Code section 6103.

The time needed to complete and file this form will vary depending on individual circumstances. The estimated average time is:

Recordkeeping . . . . 7 min.

Learning about the law or the form . . . . 5 min.

Preparing the form . . . . . . 7 min.

Copying, assembling, and sending the form to the IRS . . 14 min.

If you have comments concerning the accuracy of these time estimates or suggestions for making this form simpler, we would be happy to hear from you. You can write to the Tax Forms Committee, Western Area Distribution Center, Rancho Cordova, CA 95743-0001. **Do not** send the form to this address. Instead, see the Instructions for Form 1040 or Form 1040A.

Cat. No. 13910F

Form **8332** (Rev. 12-2000)